The author, Alison Stewart-Reed, grew up in the UK in the county of Berkshire within a close-knit family as one of six children. She keeps in regular contact with all her siblings but now lives with her husband in Devon, where she enjoys spending time with their grown son, who lives nearby. Alison has always enjoyed creative writing, something she shared with her mother, who was a prolific writer in her own right. It was Mary's passing that moved Alison to produce her memoir, based on the secret diaries that her mother faithfully kept as a young girl. Written by her own hand, Mary wrote a factual and honest account of her daily life as an adolescent growing up in the 1950s. Alison hopes to evoke a strong sense of empathy in the reader as she opens a very private window into her mother's young adult life, wanting to portray the wonderful person Mary was and, in doing so, preserving her memory in a rare and unique way for all the family.

To my amazing mum, without whom this work would never exist. I know you'd be embarrassed but so excited at the same time. In any case, I'm too old to be sent to my room.

To my amazing dad, I'm sure you knew most of this but sorry if anything shocks.

To my siblings: Samantha, Adam, Bradley, Ashley, and Barnaby, how lucky were we to have had them as our parents.

To my wonderful husband, Paul, and son, Benjamin, for their love and support.

Alison Stewart-Reed

# MUM'S SECRET DIARIES

AUSTIN MACAULEY PUBLISHERS™

LONDON * CAMBRIDGE * NEW YORK * SHARJAH

A CIP catalogue record for this title is available from the British Library.

ISBN 9781035833245 (Paperback)
ISBN 9781035833252 (Hardback)
ISBN 9781035833269 (ePub e-book)
ISBN 9781528989800 (Audiobook)

www.austinmacauley.com

First Published 2024
Austin Macauley Publishers Ltd®
1 Canada Square
Canary Wharf
London
E14 5AA

I have to start by thanking my awesome siblings for allowing these very private and intimate diaries of our mothers to be made public and for seeing the potential enjoyment that reading about her daily antics might bring to others. Also, for letting me create a fitting memoir to such a wonderful lady. I deeply thank you.

My immense gratitude goes to Graham Stewart-Reed who spent hours reading early drafts, making concise notes when proof reading and sitting with me many times picking up on spelling, grammar and my need to put commas everywhere! I really appreciated your professional help and advice.

I would like to thank everyone on the Austin Macauley team who helped create this publication and without whom this book would not exist. You have given me the opportunity to produce a moving memoir and amazing tribute to a much-loved Mother who is sorely missed. For making it all come together, you have my complete thanks.

And lastly for my husband Paul, who supported me financially whilst I took the time editing and gave me the peace and quiet I needed to complete this works. For the hours lost with him whilst I spent months reading and transcribing text. Your total support and belief in me has been unfailing and I thank you from the bottom of my heart.

# Table of Contents

# Preface

As a family we knew Mum secretly kept the diaries she had written during her younger years but we never knew where they were hidden, let alone seen or read them. In fact, she and our father kept virtually everything being the hoarders that they were. And not only items from their own lives but from most of their relatives' lives too. It was because of their inability to throw anything away that I am able to piece together such a unique and remarkably detailed history of my mother's adolescent life growing up in an ordinary British working-class family of the 1950s.

The diaries—discovered after she and my father had sadly passed away—I think are a truly amazing and rare insight in to the very private journey of a young, sensitive and spirited girl entering the adult world, particularly as they interestingly touch delicately on what was socially acceptable and politically correct at that time. Mary's first diary begins in 1952 when she is predominantly fourteen years of age. Being rather small in size, her initial entries were restricted to just a few sentences but as the years roll on her diaries grow in size resulting in an enormous increase to her writing capacity.

It was her routine to write something every night without fail, sometimes recording a whole essay on a day's events. Reading and enjoying them so much compelled me to partly transcribe and partly summarise her experiences in this work, principally completed for my siblings to enjoy. With their feedback and that of others, I began to realise that they may also relate and strike an emotional chord with many other people. Through Mary's eyes and subsequent writing, they describe in a very innocent and personal way, her daily life, her hardships and successes, the challenges she had to face, her seemingly endless worries, raw emotions and happinesses.

In most instances I have transcribed her exact text so presenting her copied hand as authentically as possible although some sections have been shortened or summarised where repetitions occurred. Please allow for school girl grammar as I thought correcting this may deflect from their charm.

This book covers the years 1952 to 1956 but her diaries, written considerably more in-depth in later years, continue to the beginning of 1962 after getting married to my father in 1961.

Being a nostalgic person myself, it has also been an absolute delight sitting for hours sifting through old photographs and documents to insert along the way, some tucked carefully into the covers of her diaries, thus adding an interesting visual element.

I must admit, I have been truly enlightened, surprised, emotional and totally entertained to read about my mother's life growing up in the fifties and sixties, experiencing first hand all the drama's you might expect and some you certainly don't, from a young girl finishing school, getting her first job, maturing to adapt to the adult world and eventually meeting the man that my sister and brothers would eventually call Dad.

So, even though clearing out the family home took what felt like forever and I know my siblings can vouch for this, having found these treasures I wouldn't have had it any other way and I thank and appreciate both my parents for who they were. I guess this is my way of keeping their memory alive and kicking and I really hope you enjoy reading them as much as I have.

Alison

# Introduction

First let me fill you in on the heart of Mary's roots.

Mary's parents were Kenneth, born 1906 in Beccles, Suffolk, UK and Margaret, born 1907 in Reading, Berkshire, UK. They were married in March 1931 at the London Road Liberal Christian Church in Reading then moved into their first abode being a semi-detached house which they fondly named 'Kenmar' in Tiptree in England's county of Essex. This was close to where the Anchor Press was located founded in Tiptree in 1900 and a cornerstone of industry in the village at that time and also where Kenneth was currently employed. His job as a Compositor

entailed inserting each letter of a word into a frame for printing and also proof reading for the company. In December 1934 he received a diploma in the operation of the 'Monotype' keyboard for 'straight setting at a fast speed' from The Monotype Corporation Limited in London.

Kenneth and Margaret moved to a slightly larger home in the first half of 1939 which they named 'Lavington' still in Tiptree, probably to accommodate their growing family.

With the outbreak of WW2 Kenneth served from July 1940 to July 1941 in B Coy 18th Essex Battalion Home Guard. He then signed up to be a Royal Air Force Volunteer Reserve at the RAF recruitment centre in Cardington, Bedfordshire, enlisting for the duration of the present emergency the country was facing. He entered service in July 1941. His RAF rank was L.A.C (leading aircraftman) or rank AC/2 aircraftman 2nd class in air mechanics. His RAF trade is later referred to as armourer and he was stated as being able to fire a rifle. At the end of August 1941 Kenneth was posted from RAF Skegness to 61 squadron at Luffenham in the East Midlands of England and records state that in January 1943 he was in 277 Squadron at Martleham Heath, Suffolk on an air sea rescue flight. At no point did he serve overseas.

Kenneth was demobilised at the end of October 1945 with his authorisation of release or last day of service being 19 December 1945. From the Air Ministry in London, he received the Defence Medal and War Medal for his contribution.

I believe the family moved to Reading in Berkshire, England in the early part of 1949 with Kenneth, having resumed his career in the printing trade, now working for Messer, Cox & Wyman Ltd where he remained until his retirement in 1971. For three years the family live with Margaret's seventy-five-year-old mother near Caversham in Reading, probably to give her a little help. Once back in the area Margaret was re-employed by the family business 'The English Leather Company' based in the town and owned by her elder brother. At that time, they owned a large portion of Queen's Road running to its junction with London Street. He also built The Queen's Garage. Margaret was always very proud of 'The English Leather Company' which ran for approximately seventy-seven years and at its peak helped keep our army well shod during two World Wars. They also supplied the Australian army, employed roughly one hundred and twenty people and were turning out about four thousand pairs of boots a week.

Sarah (Mary's older sister) and Mary at 'Lavington'

# Mary's Very Young Years

Mary was born on a Saturday in the latter part of November 1937 at home in 'Kenmar' in Tiptree. Her parents were Kenneth and Margaret and she had an older sister called Sarah who was three years old. Mary is baptised at St Luke's Church in Tiptree during June 1938 then during the first half of 1939 at the age of one and a half moves with her family to 'Lavington' remaining within the same area.

## World War Two

When World War Two breaks out on 1st September 1939 Mary is one year, ten months old. At some point during the six years the war endures, for their safety, Sarah and Mary are evacuated to Pembrokeshire in south west Wales where they stay with a lady called Dorothy, later to be known as Auntie Dot-Dot. I believe the family may have known her from before. Margaret accompanies her girls to Wales and Kenneth enlists so is away for a lot of this time although visits the family as often as he can when granted leave. Mary remembered and proudly told us about him being in the Home Guard and the RAF. She also recalled hiding under tables during air-raids, running to shelters and having to take her so-named Mickey Mouse gas mask with her everywhere she went. She was always chuffed that she had a Mickey Mouse gas mask whereas Sarah, being older, just had a plain black one.

After the war the girls and their mother return home to Tiptree where Mary was then registered with the local school—Malden Primary. She is now seven and three quarters. I remember her telling me how she was really quite wary and frightened when her father eventually came back to live with them after the war, as she didn't truly know him and use to say he felt like a stranger.

Photo of Mary taken at school in 1945 aged seven years, eight months

# Primary Education up to Eleven Plus

Once back in Essex Mary continues her education at Malden Primary school where she makes new friends and progresses well. In May 1946 at the age of eight and a half she is awarded a certificate for her handwriting at the Witham & District Sunday School Union.

Taken at school in November 1946 aged nine

Mary has incredibly neat handwriting and in May 1948 at the age of ten years, eight months is recognised for it again when she achieves first place for her illuminated text in the Witham & District Eisteddfod and Exhibition held at Tollesbury, Essex.

Witham and District Sunday School Union

## Certificate of Merit

Class:- Ⅴ c   Mary Deboll   (1st)
(Illuminated Text)

Eisteddfod and Exhibition

held at   Tollesbury   May 1948

Age 10 yrs 8 months.

Mary taken at school in May 1948.
She is ten years eight months old

During her spare time and when the weather is favourable one thing Mary loves to do above all else and is actually very good at, is diving and swimming. Here she is (on the left) with her sister Sarah on the right and a friend in the middle. This was taken at Martin's outdoor pool in Wokingham, Berkshire in June 1947 when Mary is nine years, seven months old.

This picture was taken in July 1947 by the River Thames in Abingdon, Oxfordshire. Mary is nine years, eight months old and it looks like the girls have been collecting feathers whilst on a walk by the river.

The family are still settled in Essex for Christmas of 1948 but in the first half of 1949, when Mary is eleven, her family move in with Margaret's mother sharing a semi-detached Victorian property in Reading only a short walk away from the river Thames. I believe this move was to aid Mary's grandmother who perhaps was starting to struggle being on her own. Consequently, Mary completes her final year of primary education at EP Collier School in Reading where she achieves her Eleven Plus, in addition to completing her swimming tests and proudly being awarded her first and second certificates.

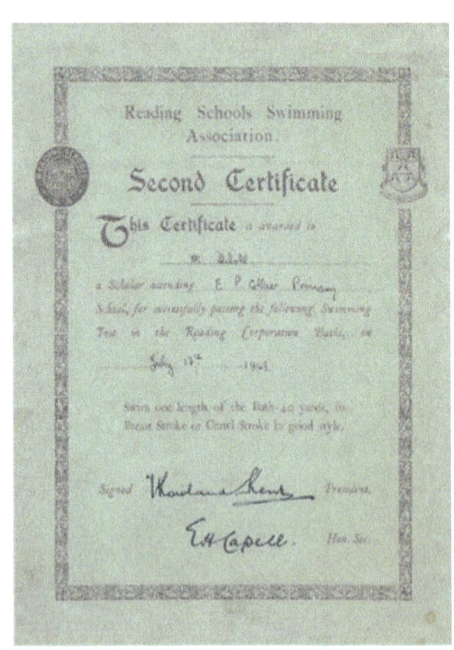

# My Christmas Holiday 1948

*Written by Mary on Sunday 26 December 1948 at Lavington*

'The day after we broke up for our Christmas holidays was Christmas Eve and my sister and I were very excited because we knew that that night we were to hang up our pillow-cases.

In the morning of Christmas Eve lots of people sent us presents but Daddy would not let us open them until Christmas Day.

Very soon it was dinner time so Sarah and I went out in the kitchen to wash our hands and when we had finished Mummy asked us if we would carry the dinner into the dining room for her, so we did. When Mummy, Daddy and Sarah had sat down there was not enough chairs for me to sit on one, so I went and got one out of the other room. When we had had our dinner, Sarah and I cleared away and washed up. After we had finished, I went upstairs and fetched my jigsaw puzzle and came downstairs again and did it, and it was a jigsaw with a lovely garden and pool on it. I soon finished it and I wondered what I could do now so Mummy said, 'Do you want to play Sorry?'

So, I said, 'Yes please, shall I go and get it.'

'It would be as well, wouldn't it,' said Mummy.

So up I went again and brought it down and got it ready and Mummy and I drew our chairs up to the table and we were ready to start the game.

It was about half past four before we realised it and Mummy said, 'gracious look at the clock it's half past four, come on Mary, go and tell Sarah to come and help you lay the tea,' so I went but when she came in, the tea was already laid out so she couldn't do anything. It was a lovely tea with Christmas cake and all kinds of nice things.

After we had finished our tea, Sarah and I washed up our dirty things and by the time we had done that it was seventeen minutes to seven so we put the wireless on for the Dick Barton Show and the moment we put it on we heard the end of music while you work so were just in time. When Dick Barton had finished, we all wanted to have a game of rummy, so we got the cards and started playing but Daddy said, 'We'll play until quarter to eight.'

Soon it was quarter to eight so Daddy said, 'go and say goodnight to Grandma and Grandad and Auntie and Uncle,' so we went.

When we got there, I asked Grandma if I could have a pillow-case and she said, 'you're not having Father Christmas this year because you don't believe in him.'

I said, 'well I will take the one off of my pillow then.' When Sarah and I were ready for bed, I went into my bedroom and then I took the pillow-case off my pillow and put it on my bed.

I have a monkey I never play with except at Christmas time and his name is Peter, so I took off my socks and on one of them put a piece of paper with 'Peter's stocking' on it and put it on my bed beside my pillow-case.

In the morning, I woke up at half past three and I got out of bed and switched on the light, and to my surprise I found my pillow-case back on my pillow and my sock on the floor and there was a little tiny stocking there for me and in it, it had: a drawing book, two hanky's, an apple, a bar of Bonds chocolate cream, two chocolate biscuits, 1 packet of Rolos and a bar of nougat, it made my mouth water so I got out of bed again and switched the light off and went to sleep again. When I woke up it was quarter to nine, so I got up and dressed myself.

When I was halfway down Sarah called to me from the bottom of the stairs and she told me to hurry up because she couldn't open her parcels until everyone was down, so I hurried up.

Very soon the postman came and Sarah and I went to the door and there were three parcels for me and three for Sarah, so we were very pleased. When we had opened all our parcels, I found I had: two books, one called 'Six Cousins at Mistletoe Farm' and the other one 'Peter Pan and Wendy.' I had a lovely fountain pen and a biro, three jigsaw puzzles, a box of Silver Lining chocolates, a bag of chocolate biscuits, £1'2s, a bag of sweets and a bubble set, so Sarah and I were very excited.

After we had had our breakfast, Mummy and Daddy washed up because it was Christmas Day. When it was done I started to do one of my jigsaw puzzles and by the time I had finished it, it was dinner time, so I went to wash my hands and then we all sat down at the table and had our dinner. I got a shilling out of the Christmas pudding so I was very pleased.

*After dinner I went round to the lady next door to ask if I could take the puppy out for her and she was very pleased because she said she could not get on with her work because it kept on pushing the papers onto the floor as soon as she picked them up. So, I took it on the recreation ground and had a game with it. Soon it was time to go home so I put the lead back on the puppy and took him home. When I got home I took the puppy back to his house and then went back to my house and Mummy was waiting for me so I hurried and washed my hands and then I went into the front room and had my tea which was very nice.*

*After tea we played charades until 10 o'clock and then Sarah and I went to bed and on the next day I stayed in bed until 1 o'clock.'*

# Secondary Education to End of 1952

Between Mary's academic years of 1949 to 1952 she undertakes the remainder of her education at Caversham Secondary Modern Grammar School in Reading. This is her school photograph taken in 1949 when she is eleven years, six months old.

She continues to enjoy her swimming lessons at school and is pleased to be awarded her fourth, fifth, sixth and seventh certificates in July 1951 at the Reading Corporation Baths, now known as the Central Pool. These are for swimming forty yards in back stroke, neat diving, gliding half a width, diving from a four-foot springboard, surface diving and swimming forty yards in forty-five seconds' free style.

## Mary's First Diary

The earliest diary we found of Mary's is for 1952 and for the most part of this year she is fourteen years of age. What she accounts gives us a pretty good idea of what life is like for her at home and at school during this time. Within its first few pages she lists all her school friends and her teachers' names along with boys that she likes and doesn't like. Most of their names shall appear as initials.

She also lists family and friends' birthdays in addition to their addresses at the back.

Currently Mary's father is working for Wyman's, a printing company in Addison Road, Reading and Sarah, her sister, is working for a hairdressing Salon in Tilehurst to the west of Reading. With Mary's extended family being based around the same area, there are always plenty of relatives who come to visit with Aunties and Uncles in plentiful supply. The family are living with Mary's Grandmother who, it becomes clear, is obviously struggling at this time, perhaps with her health. As time moves on Mary writes that she needs more in the way of care which subsequently leads to her grandmother entering a nursing home in Goring in the county of Oxfordshire, later in the year.

Mary normally gets up anywhere between 10am and 1pm at the weekends or on non-school days. She keeps herself busy by running errands for her mother such as scooting along to post a letter, buying cream from Cox's Creamery or a loaf of bread from the bakers. She helps out with the housework and grocery shopping and likes to go shopping in Reading town centre where on one occasion she spends her own money on a pair of grey slip-on shoes. Mary and her family and friends go to the pictures a lot, with some of the films starting to be in Technicolor. Afterwards at home she rates them in her diary as *"good"*, *"jolly good"* or *"smashing"*.

She also plays checkers or Monopoly with her mother and father, loves to sit reading her comics or the daily paper, knit and complete jigsaw puzzles. Being good at English she writes letters to Aunty Dot-Dot and enjoys listening to the wireless. Mary has her hair set fairly regularly even at this age, normally by her mother or Sarah and is already experienced at using home perm kits. She loves going to the pantomime, watching people sing and dance and longs more than ever to be a ballet dancer.

One of her favourite things to do is swim and when the weather permits can be found at Martins outdoor pool in Wokingham showing off her talented diving skills, especially if there's an audience of boys watching!

Sarah at this point is dating a boy called John who, in January, enlists in the army which makes her miserable all the time, leading to Mary noting this often in her diary. Normally though Sarah and Mary get on admirably as sisters and laugh a lot especially as Sarah can be *'quite daft'* and *'very funny'* at times.

At school in 1952 (unsurprisingly) her diary shows a lot of interest in boys, naming those whom she likes and doesn't like, in addition to who she quarrels with. Apparently if you are naughty or answer a teacher back you are *'sent under the clock'* as a punishment and if you're really naughty you can get the cane. Mary, at this stage, is a member of the school choir attending regular practices and states how she loves to sing.

Please note that from now on Mary's own words are in italics.

JANUARY

Tuesday 1st *'Stayed in bed till 10:45, then stayed in in the afternoon and cut out models.'*

Wednesday 2nd *'Got up at 10:45. Went out to Cox's Creameries, Clarks and Godfrey's soon afterwards. Wrote to Auntie Dot.'*

Thursday 3rd *'Got tummy ache. Got up at 9:00. It snowed during the night. Went out and had photos taken in the afternoon. They weren't bad photos. Uncle R came.'*

Friday 4th *'Mummy brought my breakfast up as well as a comic. Played Chinese checkers with Mummy (2-1 to me). Was sent out in rain twice just to get a loaf. Bought a savings book. Scooted along in pouring rain to post letter.'*

Saturday 5th *'Had hair set yesterday, it turned out quite good. Went to pictures in afternoon to see "Lady Godiva*

Mary taken 3 January 1952.
She is fourteen years, two months old

*Rides Again" and "The Black Widow", smashing. Pauline Stroud jolly good, Dennis Price good but has a wig. John McCallum smashing. Good film but not coloured.'*

Sunday 6th *'Got up at quarter to one. Had dinner. Sat in chair and read papers most of afternoon. Went to bed early as have to get up early tomorrow.'*

Monday 7th *'Start school today. Had note from DA. He told me to wait at school gate if I liked him. I didn't wait. I don't know whether I do or not. I don't think so.'*

Tuesday 8th *'Wrote letter to DA today. It said that I liked him but I don't really. I like JH best. Not bad at school today. Had to do a lot of dirty work in domestic science.'*

Wednesday 9th *'Had a quarrel with Jean but soon made up. DA and RS waited at school gate for us but I gave DA the slip. I think I wish I hadn't. I would not have minded walking with him.'*

Thursday 10th *'Wrote DA another note today. Gave him the slip again. I wish JH still liked me. I like him so much. Had a row with Mummy dinner time because I wouldn't wear my mack.'*

Friday 11th *'Decided I don't like DA. I like JH very much; hope he likes me. Anna is going to ask him. Had note from DA. I sent him one, I wish I hadn't now because I hate him.'*

Saturday 12th *'Got up at 9:05. Did errands. Uncle R and Auntie O came. Mummy fed up. Went up town in afternoon and booked seats in Palace for next Thursday. Looking forward to it. SJ has second leading part in "Goody Two Shoes". Her photo is outside the Palace. Wish I was her.'*

Sunday 13th *'Got up at 1:15. Had game of Monopoly with Mummy, Daddy and Auntie O. I lost; Auntie O won. I am sad because my pen has broken and Mummy and Daddy are ratty.'*

Monday 14<sup>th</sup> '*DA not at school today thank goodness. I seem to like JH more each day. I hope he likes me and not Ann or anyone else. He keeps giving me nice looks. I do hope that means he likes me.*'

Tuesday 15<sup>th</sup> '*I told RS to tell DA I hate him. Mummy found a photo I had of JH, very embarrassing. John came to tea for the last time before he goes into the army. Sarah is getting sadder.*'

Wednesday 16<sup>th</sup> '*JH doesn't like me for sure. Ann said he goes out with another girl. I think he likes her. Had my dinner at school today. I do wish JH liked me. MH likes Ann but he told me JH didn't like me.*'

Thursday 17<sup>th</sup> '*Sarah miserable. JH doesn't like me for sure. I am sorry. John went in forces today that's why Sarah is miserable. Going to Pantomime tonight.*'

Friday 18<sup>th</sup> '*Pantomime was lovely. SJ is ever so good. Wish I was her. AH is lovely. She doesn't swank at all not like SJ does. It was really very good. JH not at school today.*'

Saturday 19<sup>th</sup> '*Got up and did errands. Went to pictures in the afternoon to see "An American in Paris". It was lovely. Long more than ever to be a ballet dancer. I shall never be one though. Mummy and Daddy are very ratty today. Leslie Caron really beautiful. Lovely dancer. Gene Kelly jolly good. Oscar Levant very good. In technicolour so really lovely.*'

Sunday 20<sup>th</sup> '*Stayed in all day. Sarah daft and very funny. Had good fun in afternoon. Had a jolly good laugh. Played Monopoly and I came second.*'

Monday 21<sup>st</sup> '*DA back at school today. I told him I like him. I like MH too I think, he is very nice. Still like JH but I don't think quite so much, not much good, is it?*'

Tuesday 22<sup>nd</sup> '*Walked home with DA by myself. I'm really mad as JH was just behind me. I love JH. I am really angry and wish JH hadn't seen me.*'

Wednesday 23rd *'Finished with DA. Had it out with him. Told him I liked JH. I chose a song in music about—don't ever leave me, for him. I like MH too but mustn't take him away from Ann.'*

Thursday 24th *'DA still thinks I like him. MH told me that the note he had given me was written by BB. I asked BB and he said it was MH that had written it. I like MH but still like JH a lot better.'*

Friday 25th *'JH got sent under the clock from assembly. He answered Mr V back. I do like him so much. I must get him to like me again. I hope MH tells him nice things about me.'*

Saturday 26th *'Woke up to snow this morning, it is very thick. Tramped all around the whole town looking for a skirt and cardigan. I tried on ten skirts but none of them fitted me, worst luck. Supposed to be going to Auntie O and Uncle R next weekend. If it is fine, I will go but if it is snowy or wet, I won't.'*

Sunday 27th *'Got up at 5 to 12. Did nothing much in afternoon. Just mucked around. I am going away Friday until next Monday. First time been away alone.'*

Monday 28th *'MH not at school today. Ann is very sad. DA still likes me. I don't like him. I like JH. Wish he still liked me. Had a cardigan today and also bought a "Toni" perm.'*

Tuesday 29th *'DA still likes me. But I like JH much better. I do wish he liked me. I hope he likes me before I leave school.'*

Wednesday 30th *'Had hair permed today. Going away Friday until Tuesday.'*

Thursday 31st *'Hair looks nice but it's a bit short. Sarah very bossy. Going away tomorrow. Wondering what it will be like. I hope I'm not shy.'*

## FEBRUARY

Mary has her first ever experience of staying away from home on her own when she stays with her Auntie and Uncle who we think at that time were living in Lincolnshire, on England's east coast. She doesn't mention how she got there just that it was a 'nice ride'. I suspect she went by train. There's an entry of national importance made on 6th which Mary writes supplementary notes of at the back of her diary, which I have included.

Friday 1st *'Went away today. Lovely ride of 140 miles. Hair looks lovely. Lovely house, dear little bedroom.'*

Saturday 2nd *'Lovely day today. Did nothing in morning but Julie and Di came in from next door in the afternoon. They stopped until 9:20. Really lovely house. Wish it was ours. It is lovely staying there with Auntie and Uncle. Wish I lived there always. Lovely stay.'*

Sunday 3rd *'Di and Julie brought me two books. Read one of them but didn't quite finish the other. Home tomorrow.'*

Monday 4th *'Got up early this morning. Had lovely ride back. Wish I hadn't come back. Had to be quiet directly I got in, so I went up town.'*

Tuesday 5th *'Back to school today. Nothing much happened. JH still doesn't like me. I love him so much. I do wish he liked me. Not nice going to school after not doing anything.'*

Wednesday 6th *'His Majesty King George VI died today. He passed peacefully away in his sleep. He was found at 10:45am. Her Royal Highness Princess Elizabeth is now Her Majesty the Queen. Prince Phillip is now Prince Consort and Prince Charles is now Prince of Wales—heir to the throne. The Queen is now the Queen Mother. Had special assembly in the hall at school. JH still doesn't like me but I love him so much.'*

Thursday 7th *'Papers full of Royal family. I'd do or give anything for JH to like me again.'*

Friday 8th *'PH keeps winking at me. He's not bad but I love JH a lot better. Don't know whether he likes me or not. Papers are full with Royalty again.'*

Saturday 9<sup>th</sup> *'Went to pictures today to see "Texas Carnival" with Esther Williams and Howard Keel and "Cloudburst" with Robert Preston. Both jolly good. I do wish JH liked me. "Texas Carnival" really wonderful. Esther Williams very pretty and lovely. Howard Keel—smashing. Red Skelton really funny and Ann Miller lovely dancer. Lovely technicolour musical.'*

Sunday 10<sup>th</sup> *'Mummy away, does seem funny. John came home from the army. Sarah very pleased and happy. Not very nice while Mummy's away. Too much work!'*

The week commencing Monday 11 February sees Mary starting her mock exams at school in the following subjects: Arithmetic, Maths, RI, Geography, Literature and Handwriting, Composition, History, Needlework, Domestic Science, English, Science.

Monday 11<sup>th</sup> *'Had Arithmetic, R.I, Literature and Handwriting exams today. Not bad but could do better. I do wish JH still liked me. I love him so much.'*

Tuesday 12<sup>th</sup> *'Had History, English, Science and Needlework exams today. Got 95 out of 100 for Arithmetic. JH got 100.'*

Wednesday 13<sup>th</sup> *'Had Maths, Geography and Composition today. Came 7<sup>th</sup> in Domestic Science. Anna going to ask JH tonight. He seems to like me better today. Good.'*

Thursday 14<sup>th</sup> *'Had Valentines card. I think it came from DA. I do wish JH had sent it. I do hope he will get to like me before I leave.'*

Friday 15<sup>th</sup> *'Mummy came home today. Seems more like home. Anna said she was going to ask JH if he liked me.'*

Here is Mary's six-month report ending 15 February along with her year-end report on 31 July 1952.

Half-Year Ending 15·2·52

General Remarks

Mary has worked consistently well
throughout the term.
          J. A. Vickery.
            Form Master Mistress

    A good report - well done.
             E. F. Allwood
              Headmaster

Margaret Diboll.     Date 10/3/52.
Parent or Guardian

Year Ending 31·7·52

General Remarks

Keen, and consistent effort shown throughout
the year.
          J. A. Vickery.
            Form Master Mistress

    A good year's work.
             E. F. Allwood
              Headmaster

Margaret Diboll.     Date 30/7/52.
Parent or Guardian

---

## CAVERSHAM SECONDARY MODERN SCHOOL

### REPORT

Name   Diboll Mary

Form   III V

Grades used in assessing Form Work.
- A. Very Good
- B. Good
- C. Satisfactory
- D. Unsatisfactory
- E. Very Weak

---

| SUBJECT | Form Work | Marks Possible | Marks ob'ned | Position | Remarks | Form Work | Marks Possible | Marks ob'ned | Position | Remarks |
|---|---|---|---|---|---|---|---|---|---|---|
| | | EXAMINATION | | | | | EXAMINATION | | | |
| Half Year Ending 15·2·52 | | | | Form or Group II | Age 14·2 | Year Ending 31·7·52 | | | | Form or Group III V |
| Religious Knowledge | D | 50 | 23 | 29 | Fair | B | 50 | 35 | 19 | V.G. |
| English | A | 100 | 84 | 4 | V.G. | A | 100 | 85 | 2 | V.G. |
| Reading | A | 50 | 42 | 1 | Ex.G. | A | 50 | 45 | 1 | Ex. |
| Literature | A | 50 | 41 | 31 | V.G. | B | 50 | 33 | 40 | G. |
| Spelling | A | 25 | 22 | 3 | V.G. | A- | 25 | 20 | 15 | V.G. |
| Handwriting | A | 25 | 20 | 1 | V.G. | A | 25 | 22 | 2 | V.G. |
| Arithmetic | A. | 100 | 45 | 6 | Ex. | A | 100 | 100 | 1 | Ex. |
| Mathematics | A. | 50 | 42 | 1 | Excellent | | 50 | 48 | 1 | Excellent at all times |
| Practical Geometry | | | | | | | | | | |
| Technical Drawing | | | | | | | | | | |
| History | B- | 50 | 29 | 19 | Quite Good | C | 50 | 16 | 34 | Very disappointing result |
| Geography | A | 50 | 44 | 11 | V.G. | D | 50 | 32 | 35 | V.G. |
| Science | C | 50 | 33 | 14 | Should do better | C+ | 50 | 31 | 30 | Mary could do better |
| Art | B | 50 | 31 | 20 | V. Good | B | 50 | 33 | 19 | V. Good |
| Needlework | C | 50 | 28 | 17 | Fair | B+ | 50 | 44 | 4 | Has worked well with good result |
| Handicraft | | | | | | | | | | |
| Domestic Science | C | 50 | 37 | 7 | Could do better with greater effort | C | 50 | 31 | 16 | Disappointing. Mary can do better with |
| Physical Education | C | | | | Good | C+ | | | | Could do better |
| Games | C+ | | | | Could do better | B | | | | Tries hard |
| TOTAL | | | | | | | 546 | 76·8 % | | |

Number in Form 42         Position in Form 4x         Number in Form 42 65

Number of Absences 24         Conduct Gx         Number of Absences

Position in
See over for

Saturday 16<sup>th</sup> *'Went to the pictures to see "Meet Me After the Show" with Betty Grable and Rory Calhoun. Also "The Sword of Monte Cristo". They were SMASHING! "Meet Me After the Show" was really lovely. Betty Grable was smashing. Rory Calhoun is my favourite film star; he was really wonderful. Altogether it was a lovely program and in lovely colour.'*

Sunday 17<sup>th</sup> *'Stayed in all day. Didn't get up until 1 o'clock. It is a lot better since Mummy came home, just didn't seem right without her.'*

Monday 18<sup>th</sup> *'No school today, not until Wednesday. Half term. Had hair shampooed and set. Hope it turns out all right. Some hopes.'*

Tuesday 19<sup>th</sup> *'Hair not too bad. Could be better. Did nothing all afternoon except read comics. School in the morning. Good, I shall see JH.'*

Wednesday 20<sup>th</sup> *'Anna said JH stuck all my photos in his album yesterday. She wanted them but he wouldn't let her have them because he did. Had to take him sixpence that JR owed him. Lovely.'*

Thursday 21<sup>st</sup> *'GL wants to go out with me. JM came up to me today and asked me if I got RW's letter. I am now wondering if RW sent the Valentines card. I like JM but JH is best.'*

Friday 22<sup>nd</sup> *'Lovely day. Came 4<sup>th</sup> in class. JH beat me by 1 mark and came 3<sup>rd</sup>. Had to stand next to him. Lovely! Anna has promised to ask him if he still likes me.'*

Saturday 23<sup>rd</sup> *'Ray Day. Watched possession, very funny. Went to pictures to see "Elopement" with Clifton Webb, Ann Francis, and William Lundigan. Also "Take Care of My Little Girl" with Jeanne Craine and Dale Robertson. Both lovely pictures with second being in Technicolor.'*

Sunday 24<sup>th</sup> *'Didn't do much all day. Stayed in all afternoon while Mummy and Daddy went to see Uncle L in hospital.'*

Monday 25th *'JM and JL are very nice. GL wants to go out with me but I still like JH. He told Anna that he didn't know whether he likes me or not. I hope so.'*

Tuesday 26th *'JM and JL keep smiling at me in class. GL says he wants to go out with me but I still love JH so much.'*

Wednesday 27th *'I still love JH very much. People keep calling me ginger because of JM. I don't mind him but I love JH a lot more.'*

Thursday 28th *'JM and JL still smile at me and the girls still call me ginger. I hate it because I still like JH.'*

Friday 29th *'Went up nursing home today. JH still doesn't like me.'*

MARCH

By March Mary is noticing how she is getting very popular with the boys at school. They are offering to walk her home, putting their arm around her, wink and smile at her during class, write her notes and some are bold enough even to ask her out. At this stage she seems to rate how good her day has been depending on which boys have smiled or spoken to her.

Saturday 1st *'Went to pictures to see Rory Calhoun in "County Fair". He was oh so smashing. Also "The Man in The White Suit". Both were lovely pictures. Rory Calhoun is really wonderful. County Fair was in Technicolor but the other picture was ordinary. Both were lovely.'*

Sunday 2nd *'Went up to nursing home in the afternoon to see Grandma. A bit dim but not too bad.'*

Monday 3rd *'Getting good with JM, JL and GL. I wish I could say the same with JH.'*

Tuesday 4th *'JM wants to go out with me. DA started to walk home with me but I gave him the slip. Had some fun in choir practice. Almost forgotten JH.'*

Wednesday 5th *'DA tagged himself on to me again. Everybody keeps saying I like JM. I do really but not half as much as JH. He smiled at me today.'*

Thursday 6th *'Had fun in choir practice today with Archie somebody. He wants to go out with me. JH laughs every time he looks at me. I wonder why?'*

Friday 7th *'JH walked home behind me all the way up to St Marys Butts. He was talking about me I know. I hope he is getting to like me.'*

Saturday 8th *'Went up town in morning. Stayed in all afternoon. Had a letter from Margaret. I love JH very much. I do hope he likes me before I leave school so that we will be able to carry on courting. You never know what might happen.'*

Sunday 9th *'Went to Micheldever in morning and to pictures in afternoon to see Dorothy Lamour, Bing Crosby and Bob Hope in "Road to Utopia". Smashing.'*

Monday 10th *'JM keeps smiling at me. I don't mind him but I'd rather have JH. Looking forward to walking home with Archie tomorrow.'*

Tuesday 11th *'Heavenly day. Archie walked right home with his arm round me. Oh, it was heavenly. He wanted to kiss me but I didn't know who'd be watching.'*

Wednesday 12th *'Choir practice today. I don't think Archie likes me anymore. I hope he does but I am going to ask him tomorrow. He was mucking around with all the girls today.'*

Thursday 13th *'Not a bad day but dog tired. I saw Archie today. He smiled at me but I just couldn't ask him. I must pluck up my courage tomorrow.'*

Friday 14th *'Saw Archie but he was with three other boys so I couldn't ask him. Oh dear, I won't see him till Monday now. DA sent me a note; wrote and told him I didn't like him.'*

Saturday 15th *'Watched boat race. Went to pictures to see Gregory Peck and Susan Haywood in "David and Bathsheba" and Michael Rennie and Moira Lister in "Uneasy Terms" with Auntie O. "David and Bathsheba" was in Technicolor. SMASHING!'*

Sunday 16th *'Did nothing much. Had bath in afternoon. Listened to Lion Family on wireless. It was very good. Not bad weather today.'*

Monday 17th *'A wonderful day where boys are concerned. BB, JM, GL and PH have all been speaking to me.'*

Tuesday 18th *'Another good day. I seem to be getting very popular where boys are concerned. I still wish JH liked me as I still love him.'*

Wednesday 19th *'Another wonderful day. Been walking all up town behind JH for the last few days. Smashing!'*

Thursday 20th *'Really wonderful day. I had three letters from RW, JM and Archie. I walked to school with Archie and he made me read his letter in front of him. It was wonderful.'*

Friday 21st *'Lovely day. Lots of people want to go out with me. JM, GL, JL, Archie. I walked to school with Archie again today. I gave him an answer to his letter.'*

Saturday 22nd *'Went to the pictures to see Kerima and Trevor Howard in "Outcast of The Islands" and Vanessa Brown and Marshall Thompson in "The Big Decision". Kerima very wonderful, she didn't speak a word in the whole picture. Both pictures were really wonderful.'*

Sunday 23rd *'Did nothing much today. Stayed in all day. Had a bath and listened to the Lion Family. Wonder what will happen tomorrow.'*

The following week Mary details all the boys who want to go out with her with Archie actually asking her out to the pictures on Saturday, which she is stumped at what to do about. Luckily it doesn't stop snowing all day on Saturday 29 March so she has the perfect excuse not to go, commenting how freezing it is.

APRIL

Tuesday 1st '*Not friends with Ann or Edna because they sent me a love letter from JH saying that he wanted to go out with me as an April fool. I wish he'd sent the letter.*'

Wednesday 2nd '*Ann still won't speak to me. JH trod on my heel today and he said, "oh I'm so sorry" and I said, "that's alright." I hope it means something. Ann and Anna are not talking to me.*'

During Thursday and Friday Mary becomes friends again with Ann and Anna. PH tells her '*JH does want to go out with me again. He said "cross my heart, I'm not lying." I don't know whether to believe him or not.*'

Saturday 5th '*Bought coat or rather put a deposit on it. Went to pictures to see "The Greatest Show on Earth". It was really the best film I've ever seen. Betty was really wonderfully clever and Cornell Wilde was really bang on and Wizzo, Smashing.*'

Sunday 6th '*Did nothing much all day. John came to tea. Mummy not at all well.*'

Monday and Tuesday are good days with Mary's peers confirming that JH is still interested in her. A new girl called Joan starts school who '*is a good sport and lots of fun.*'

Wednesday 9th '*Broke up today. Everybody tells me that JH does like me but he doesn't like to tell me. But he himself says he doesn't. I'm very confused.*'

Thursday 10th '*Daddy brought my coat home today, it is lovely. Don't know what to do with myself now. I wish we were at school.*'

Friday 11<sup>th</sup> *'Had my hair permed. Coo it did pull. I got a sore head. Did nothing much all day. Very boring.'*

Saturday 12<sup>th</sup> *'Went to see Doris Day and Gordon MacRae in "On Moonlight Bay" in Technicolor and "Blind Man's Bluff". Both very good pictures. Doris Day is lovely; I don't like Gordon MacRae much though. I'd much rather see Cornell Wilde.'*

Sunday 13<sup>th</sup> Easter Day *'Woke up and was sick 6 times. I stayed in bed till after dinner so that I would miss Grandma's cooking.'*

Monday 14<sup>th</sup> Easter Monday *'Feel better today. Sarah bought me an Easter egg yesterday. Went to Henley today. Tried to go to pictures but full up. Had tea out today.'*

Tuesday 15<sup>th</sup> *'Went up town in afternoon and walked all the time. Saw JM in pictures queue yesterday and he smiled at me. Good.'*

Wednesday 16<sup>th</sup> *'Went to pictures to see Gary Cooper in "Distant Drums". It was very good. I went with Sarah.'*

Thursday 17<sup>th</sup> *'Went up town all afternoon. Had afternoon tea in Talbet in afternoon. Smashing. Lovely day. Seems like summer these days.'*

Friday 18<sup>th</sup> *'Went up town again today. Still a lovely day. I hope JH likes me when I go back to school on the 28<sup>th</sup>.'*

Saturday 19<sup>th</sup> *'Mummy went to optician today. Had to wait for her for about an hour. Gee was my seat sore. Still a lovely day.'*

On Sunday Mary passes the time playing Monopoly by herself then stays in all day Monday as it's pouring with rain. Wednesday she ventures to the pictures with her grandma to see 'The Blue Lamp' with Dirk Bogarde and Jimmy Hanley then rates them both as smashing. By Thursday the weather cheers up and the family go viewing some *'smashing caravans. I hope we have one.'* Then Friday she goes up to town with her mother in the morning and stays in all afternoon.

Saturday 26th *'Went to see Golden Girl with Mitze Gaynor. I didn't know she could ballet dance before. It was coloured and it was smashing. Mitze is very good and she is a clever actress. Wish I was her.'*

Sunday 27th *'Did nothing much all day. Played two games of Monopoly in the evening. Mummy won one and Daddy the other.'*

Monday 28th *'Back to school today. Joan likes JM but he doesn't like her. JH laughed when GL said "Hallo Mary" to him.'*

Tuesday 29th *'Grandma is very ill. Mustn't have the wireless on and must only speak in whispers. Don't feel very well today. Got a sore throat.'*

Wednesday 30th *'Had fun with GL, JM and JL in morning. Stayed away in afternoon to help Mummy. Caught a cold. Don't feel too good.'*

## MAY

May sadly sees a down turn in her grandmothers' health and Mary is enlisted to help care for her by running up and down the stairs frequently fetching things. Mary also gets sick herself which leads her to write one of my favourite entries on 2nd. She also mentions some pet caterpillars but not what happens to them.

Thursday 1st *'Feel awful today. I ache all over. I feel dizzy and don't know what to do with myself. Stayed away from school today as well.'*

Friday 2nd *'Don't feel quite so bad today but still stayed away from school. Knitted my doll a nighty and she look lovely in it!'*

Saturday 3rd *'Did work all day looking after Grandma. I hate it as quiet as this. It is awful. I wonder how long it is going to last. I do hope JH likes me before I leave school.'*

Sunday 4th *'Work again today. All I do is work, work, work. I do wish Sarah would do a bit more.'*

Monday 5th '*Stayed away from school today as still got horrible cold. Got stomach ache to go with it, as well as work.*'

Tuesday 6th '*Stayed at home again today. Having to keep running up and down the stairs for Grandma. I am getting very tired.*'

Mary stays at home looking after her grandma for the rest of the week commenting '*still working but at least it stops me going to school. Although I have missed seeing JH this week a lot.*'

Saturday 10th '*Work again. Went up town all afternoon and did shopping. My legs ache as if they are going to drop off. I do hope JH will soon get to like me. I like him so much. I wonder if JM still wants to go out with me?*'

Sunday 11th '*Horrible day. Mummy horrible, Daddy horrible, Sarah—well I can't say what she is. I want to run away but I don't know where. I should sleep.*'

Monday 12th '*No school today. I wonder if anybody is missing me. I don't expect so. People are better today.*'

Mary is kept very busy at home again on Tuesday and Wednesday looking after her grandmother. She goes to the pictures on Wednesday afternoon to see 'Star-Lift' and 'Fort Worth' which she notes are in colour and both very good. Also, on Wednesday '*Found two lovely caterpillars.*'

Thursday 15th '*Still got caterpillars. Found a baby one today but lost it in the dustbin. I wish I hadn't, it was such a dear little thing.*'

Friday 16th '*Stayed at home again today. Very busy but school again on Monday. Thank goodness. It's much too much hard work at home.*'

Saturday 17th '*Went to the pictures. Saw "Saturday Island" with Linda Darnell and Tab Hunter and "On Dangerous Grounds". Both lovely pictures. Linda very lovely. Wish I was her being shipwrecked on a desert island.*'

Sunday 18<sup>th</sup> *'Stayed in and did all the work. Getting very browned off. School tomorrow, thank goodness.'*

Monday 19<sup>th</sup> *'School lovely. Had fun with JM, JL, GL and they all want to go out with me.'*

Tuesday 20<sup>th</sup> *'Really smashing day with JM, JL and GL. I don't know which I like best. Still, I do have some fun with them.'*

Wednesday 21<sup>st</sup> *'Really wonderful day. Went swimming and JM was there. Had fun with the attendant who kept saying JM was my boyfriend.'*

Thursday 22<sup>nd</sup> *'Went swimming with Ann because we had holiday. It was lovely. Very cold at first but nicer afterwards.'*

Friday 23<sup>rd</sup> *'Went swimming with the school. Not bad but we had to do a lot of hard things. Edna gave up JH for good.'*

Saturday 24<sup>th</sup> *'Went to pictures to see "Ten Tall Men" with Burt Lancaster and Jody Lawrence. Also saw "Indian Territory" with Gene Autry. The first was in colour. Both were very good films.'*

Sunday 25<sup>th</sup> *'Went up to the hospital today and yesterday. Very dull. There's nothing wrong at all with Grandma.'*

The following week Mary continues to have fun at school with her friends, naming who wants to go out with her. She makes a decision on Thursday *'I have given up on JH for good. I don't like him a bit.'*

Saturday 31<sup>st</sup> *'Went to pictures yesterday evening with Mummy and Auntie O to see "Showboat" with Howard Keel, Joe Brown and Ava Gardener and Kathleen Grayson. It was lovely and in Technicolor. Howard had a moustache as well and I don't know whether I liked it or not.'*

JUNE

June arrives seeing Mary and her mother begin to frequently visit her grandmother in a nursing home in Goring, so I'm assuming that it got too difficult to look after her in the family home. Whether her grandmother is ill she doesn't really clarify but I would suspect this is the case as she passes away later this year. Whilst Margaret spends a lot of her time visiting her mother, Mary is expected to do more in the way of chores at home, including the grocery shopping. Mary is envious that Sarah never seems to get asked to help out.

Sunday 1st *'Went to Goring today and yesterday to visit a really wonderful nursing home. I wish I lived there.'*

Monday 2nd *'Went up to nursing home again today. That's three times running. I am getting tired of it.'*

Tuesday 3rd *'Bought some grey slip-on shoes out of my own money. I had £3 9s and the shoes were £2 1s 9d, they're lovely.'*

Wednesday 4th *'Went to pictures to see "The River" with Nora Swinburns and Esmond Knight. It wasn't bad.'*

Thursday 5th *'Bought lovely grey shoulder bag out of the rest of my money. It just matches my shoes. I am very pleased with it. It was 18/6.'*

Friday 6th *'Stayed in all day as it rained. Wrote letters to Margaret, Auntie Dot and Phillip.'*

Saturday 7th *'Went up nursing home today. Coo it is boring. I don't know how to stand it. I wonder whether GL still wants to go out with me? I don't know whether I shall go out with him or not.'*

Sunday 8th *'Went to nursing home again today. Very boring again. School tomorrow.'*

Monday 9th '*Had fun today with JM, JL and GL. Went swimming in the afternoon with the school. The degrees were only 60.*'

The rest of the week Mary has a good time at school and makes up her mind to go out with GL. '*Told MH to tell GL that I will go out with him. I don't know whether I'm glad or sorry.*'

Friday 13th '*Went to pictures with Edna in evening, first time I've been allowed to go alone. Saw Richard Todd, Ronald Reagon and Pat Neal in "The Hasty Heart" also "The Disc Jockey". They were both lovely pictures. Richard Todd is simply smashing.*'

Saturday 14th '*Went up nursing home again. Not so boring today as I took my comics.*'

Sunday 15th '*Not a very nice day. Everybody expects me to do the work and not Sarah. I have got to get the groceries in the morning before school.*'

Monday 16th '*GL and JM are not at school. GL is on holiday. It is a horrible day today; everyone is so ratty.*'

Tuesday 17th '*Not much fun today. JH seems to be getting friendlier. I hope and wish he would go out with me again.*'

Wednesday 18th '*Not much fun again today. GL and JM still not at school. Wish Monday would come, GL comes back.*'

Thursday 19th '*Not much fun either today. All work and no play. Got exams a week next Monday. Shall be glad when they are all over.*'

Friday is much the same with the comment '*Sarah miserable. GL back on Monday. Perhaps I shall have some fun then*' and on Saturday Mary has to go to the nursing home again stating, '*I don't know how I bear it for all that time.*' She then daydreams about GL returning to school on Monday and how hopefully this will liven things up a bit.

Sunday sees another trip to the nursing home with Mary noting, '*I get more bored every time I go up there.*'

The week commencing June 23 is the start of her final exams at school with needlework and domestic science being scheduled first.

Monday 23rd '*GL back today as well as JM. Had needlework exam. Not too bad but not too good.*'

Tuesday 24th '*Had domestic science exam today. Horrible. Miss E chose best cakes.*'

Wednesday 25th '*GL doesn't want to go out with me anymore. I don't know what's the matter with me?*'

Thursday 26th '*GL doesn't want to go out with me at all because JH has been telling him horrible things about me. Oh, I hate that JH now but GL has still been smiling at me.*'

Friday 27th '*GL asked me to sit next to him when we were having a lecture in the hall. I would have done if he had been alone. Had a baby mouse today.*'

Just to fill you in, I know Mary kept pet mice when she was younger which relates to this last entry. I remember her saying though that her father went and drowned them all in the river one day when she was out as he never liked them in the house. She never wrote about this though.

Saturday 28th '*Went up nursing home again today. Scorching hot outside. I hope it keeps like it for our holiday.*'

Sunday 29th '*Nursing home again today. Absolutely scorching today. Don't know how to stand it. Exams this week.*'

Monday 30th '*GL keeps smiling at me. I wonder if he does like me. Carol said he likes a twelve-year-old girl.*'

## JULY

This month Mary attends the swimming heats at Reading Corporation Baths. She does extremely well and wins all three relays coming first in the junior championship and second in the senior championship. She also manages to come fourth in diving. Mary always loved swimming and in later life admitted to us how it was a secret ambition of hers to one day swim the English Channel. Breaking up from school in July the family embark on their annual holiday.

Tuesday 1st *'GL smiles at me but doesn't like me, he likes someone else. I've given up on all boys.'*

Wednesday 2nd *'I don't know whether GL likes me or not. Still, I don't care. I've given up all boys.'*

Thursday 3rd *'Have had art, needlework, spelling and handwriting exams and part of domestic science. I am very worried I don't know anything.'*

Friday 4th *'Went to pictures with Edna to see Jean Simmons and Don Houston in "The Blue Lagoon" and Scott Brady in "Bronco Busters". Both were in Technicolor.'*

Saturday 5th *'Had swimming heats. Did very well. Won all three relays. Came first in Junior Championships and second in Senior Championships. Also came fourth in diving. Went up nursing home in afternoon. Very boring. More exams next week.'*

Sunday 6th *'Went up nursing home again today. Got caught in rain without even a cardigan on. Exams tomorrow.'*

Monday 7th *'Had Maths, History, Geography and Composition exams today. Got 48 out of 50 for Maths. Didn't know anything in History.'*

Tuesday 8th *'Had RI, Dom science, Arithmetic exams today. Think I got 100 out of 100 for Arithmetic. Came first in Composition.'*

Wednesday 9th *'Had Literature, Science and English exams today. Came bottom in Literature. Lifesaving exam tomorrow.'*

Thursday 10th *'I passed my elementary and intermediate certificates today. I am thrilled. Came 1st in Arithmetic with 100 out of 100.'*

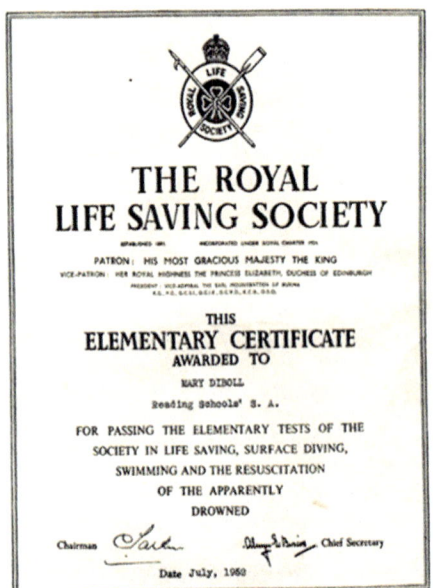 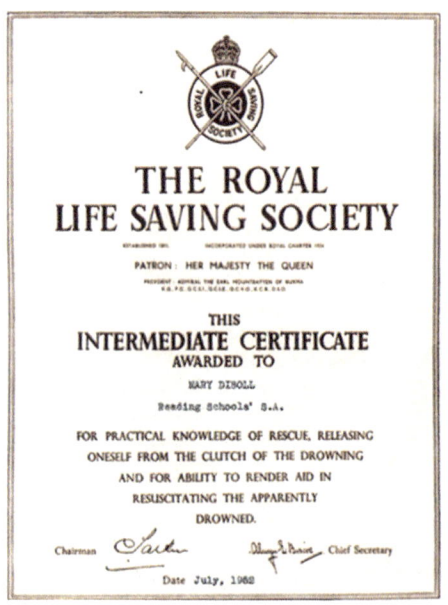

Friday 11th *'I love GL very much. Mucked around with him all day today. I had to shake hands with Mr V. I almost wish I weren't going away.'*

Saturday 12th *'Did packing. In an awful muddle. Don't know whether I want to go away or not.'*

On Sunday 13th Mary and her family drive to the Christchurch area near Bournemouth arriving at 11:10 to stay in a caravan for a week's holiday. Mary mentions how *'it's much the same as last year'* which would indicate they have been here before. She goes onto the beach in the afternoon then writes to her friends Ann and Edna from school. It is near to Aunty V and they visit whilst in the area, also having tea at Grandma's house somewhere in the vicinity too, this being Kenneth's mother. They visit Highcliffe with Mary stating, *'not very nice weather, hope it's going to be nicer than this on the rest of our holiday.'*

Tuesday 15<sup>th</sup> *'Went swimming in the sea. It was freezing and the wind was blowing very hard. Didn't stay in long as too cold. Then went for tea with Auntie V and Grandma. Said a prayer before we ate our tea. It was horrible.'*

Friday 18<sup>th</sup> *'Went to see Rory Calhoun in "There's A Song in My Heart". The three best parts were Rory, Rory and Rory!'*

Thankfully the weather improves with Mary commenting on Saturday 19<sup>th</sup> *'roasting hot day. Went swimming and it was hotter in the sea. Went to the pictures to see Margaret Rutherford and David Tomlinson in "A Castle in the Air". It was very funny.'*

The family take an additional dip in the sea at Hengistbury Head on Sunday where Mary *'took lots of snaps as lovely views. Sat on a bus without a top on.'* Now the weather is very hot they spend more time swimming with Mary saying *'getting lovely and brown, if a little sore.'* They catch the ferry to Swanage where they have a picnic and take a load more photos. An Aunt joins them on Wednesday when they go swimming at Highcliffe and Mary comments again on the water being *'lovely and warm.'*

Friday 25<sup>th</sup> *'Went to Auntie V's. Had a knickerbocker glory in Fortes. Lovely grub. Daddy miserable because he didn't have a swim.'*

These photos are from the family's summer holiday in 1951.
Mary is thirteen years, eight months old.

And these pictures are from the family's caravan holiday in 1949 near Hayling Island.

Mary is eleven years, eight months.

The holiday ends on Saturday July 26 with them arriving home at nine fifteen in the evening with Mary pleased she has caught a bit of a tan. There's a letter waiting for her from EC *'he keeps saying how much he wants me and that he wants to go out with me in the evenings.'*

Sunday 27<sup>th</sup> *'Stayed in all day and read comics which came while I was away.'*

Monday 28<sup>th</sup> *'Lovely day. EC came to meet me from school. I don't like him. I like GL. They keep teasing me about sharks.'*

Tuesday 29<sup>th</sup> *'PH seems to be taking an interest in me. He calls me Mawy. He is not bad but I do not like any boys now.'*

Wednesday 30<sup>th</sup> *'Went to pictures with Sarah and Valerie to see Tony Curtis and Piper Laurie in "No Room for The Groom" also "Something Money Can't Buy".'*

Thursday 31<sup>st</sup> *'Smashing Day. Mucked around with JM, JL and RB. And JL chased me into the girls' lavatories. BW wants me to go out with him. Went swimming with him.'*

## AUGUST

August seems like a very relaxing month for Mary with fairly good weather allowing her to partake in many outdoor activities. She is generally hanging out with friends, going to the pictures and swimming a lot. She still enjoys her knitting and playing games. I am very impressed by the entry on 12<sup>th</sup> although it doesn't state who she went with but I imagine it was with Edna from school as she's been getting very friendly with her lately and who I know becomes a lifelong friend.

Friday 1<sup>st</sup> *'Went swimming with BW. I like him but I'd much rather have GL. Valerie and I are going to see if we can find him and JL tomorrow.'*

Saturday 2<sup>nd</sup> *'Went round to Valerie's for the afternoon. Wanted to go to see Danny Kaye in "Wonder Man" but her mother wouldn't let Valerie come as she had to look after the children.'*

Sunday 3<sup>rd</sup> '*BW came round and asked Pop if I could go out with him. I got into awful trouble, horrible day.*'

Monday through to Wednesday it rains and Mary doesn't do much except go to the pictures to see a repeat of 'On Moonlight Bay' and goes swimming Wednesday afternoon when the weather finally cheers up, finding the pool surprisingly lovely and warm.

Thursday 7<sup>th</sup> '*Hiked to Henley. Stayed all day, it was smashing. We bused back although we were not tired.*'

Friday 8<sup>th</sup> '*Went round Edna's in afternoon. Played Monopoly, I won. But Edna won at cards.*'

Saturday 9<sup>th</sup> '*Went round Edna's again. I won two games of Monopoly and Edna won about two out of eight card games. I won the rest.*'

Sunday 10<sup>th</sup> '*Stayed in all day. Had bath and then read books.*'

Monday 11<sup>th</sup> '*Went up town with Valerie and Edna. Mummy cried over Grannie as she's not doing very well.*'

Tuesday 12<sup>th</sup> '*Walked to MAIDENHEAD and BACK. My, were we tired. That's 26 miles. Not bad, eh?*'

Wednesday 13<sup>th</sup> '*Very tired and got whopping blister on my foot. Went swimming in afternoon with Sarah.*'

Thursday 14<sup>th</sup> '*Went round Edna's and did one of my jigsaw puzzles. Edna not very good at it.*'

Friday 15<sup>th</sup> '*Stayed at home all day and did biggest jigsaw puzzle ever.*'

Saturday 16<sup>th</sup> '*Edna came to tea. Didn't go until half past ten. I like Edna very much. Better than Ann who is sulky.*'

Sunday 17<sup>th</sup> *'Stayed in all day. Did Sarah's knitting. Lovely day. Sun is bright.'*

Monday 18<sup>th</sup> *'Edna came to tea again today. Played games all the afternoon.'*

Tuesday 19<sup>th</sup> *'I went to tea with Edna today. Played games all the afternoon again.'*

Wednesday 20<sup>th</sup> *'Stayed in all the afternoon. Edna had to go to her sisters to look after baby.'*

Thursday 21<sup>st</sup> *'Went to Auntie M and Uncle B. Auntie C gave me 10/- and Auntie M gave me a half pound box of chocolates.'*

Friday 22<sup>nd</sup> *'Went blackberrying with Edna. Got a whole tin full but my legs are covered in scratches. They are so sore.'*

Saturday 23<sup>rd</sup> *'Went to pictures to see "Las Vegas Story" with Jane Russell and Victor Mature and also "Rancho Notorious" with Marlene Dietrich and Mel Ferrer. VICTOR SMASHING. Bought Mummy's birthday present.'*

Sunday 24<sup>th</sup> *'Stayed in all day. Did Sarah's knitting all the afternoon.'*

Monday 25<sup>th</sup> *'Went up town with Edna. She starts typing school a week today.'*

Tuesday 26<sup>th</sup> *'Went up town again with Edna. Went to Tilehurst to meet Sarah from work.'*

Wednesday 27<sup>th</sup> 'Went to pictures to see John Gregson in "Angels One Five", also the Bowery boys in "Crazy Over Horses".'

Thursday 28<sup>th</sup> 'Stopped in in afternoon. Did Sarah's knitting and read my comics at the same time. Clever what?'

Friday 29<sup>th</sup> 'Edna came to tea. I am going to hers on Sunday. It is her birthday party. She starts typing school Monday.'

Saturday 30<sup>th</sup> 'Did nothing much all day. Edna had to make some cakes for tomorrow so she didn't come round. Start school a fortnight on Monday.'

Sunday 31<sup>st</sup> 'Had a lovely time at Edna's birthday party. Went round Jenkins and watched TV. It was pitch dark and B was there.'

## SEPTEMBER

Mary gets her first taste of work this month when she accompanies her sister to the hair salon and there is a sad entry on 8<sup>th</sup> which impacts the whole family. Mary hates to see her mother upset but notes how she is finding it hard to speak to her presently. She is glad when school starts again on 15<sup>th</sup> which sees the boys being every bit as interested in her as they were the previous term. And there's an obvious importance for her to learn short hand now, as this is the month she signs up for and starts night school classes. Mary being a typical teenager who hoards lots of stuff is also ordered by her father to clear out her messy bedroom this month.

Monday 1<sup>st</sup> 'Edna started typing school today, she likes it very much. She came round in the evening.'

Tuesday 2<sup>nd</sup> 'Edna's birthday today. I gave her a tiny little cake and Mummy gave her a Chinese checkers board.'

Wednesday 3<sup>rd</sup> 'Went to work with Sarah today. Had to sweep cubicles out and I helped Sarah with a perm.'

Thursday 4th 'Went to work with Sarah again. It's a lovely shop. Was I tired when I got home.'

Friday 5th 'Went to work with Sarah again. I seem to get all the dirty jobs given to me.'

Saturday 6th 'Went to work with Sarah again. Mrs S gave me half a crown and Sarah gave me three shillings. John came to meet Sarah. Wore lovely flared skirt today.'

Sunday 7th 'Turned out my drawers. What a mess. Got a whole sack full of rubbish out of ONE draw.'

Monday 8th 'Grandma died today. Auntie V found her early this morning. She died about half past four. She is now at rest and is out of all pain. God bless and keep her.'

Tuesday 9th 'Mummy very upset. I went up the town with her to order a wreath for Grandma. Also, I bought a black sleeve band for my arm.'

Wednesday 10th 'Mummy still very upset. She is awfully tired. Don't know how to speak to her.'

Thursday 11th 'Mummy still upset. Funeral is tomorrow. I'm not going though.'

Friday 12th 'Funeral today. Mummy's gone away with Auntie V for a short time now.'

Saturday 13th 'Went to pictures with Edna and Pamela to see "Gone with The Wind" with Vivian Leigh and Clark Gable. It was a five-hour picture but, is Clark Gable smashing! Boy!'

Sunday 14th 'Helped Sarah cook the dinner today. My hands are awfully plum stained. I wish I could let my nails grow.'

Monday 15<sup>th</sup> '*School today. I am in Miss C's class. Had drama with Mr B with GL. I had to go out and act in front of him. How embarrassing.*'

Tuesday 16<sup>th</sup> '*Had netball at school today. I like GL but I like JM best, anyway Margaret goes out with GL.*'

Wednesday 17<sup>th</sup> '*Had art with Mr B also physical therapy. Had a letter from O today.*'

Thursday 18<sup>th</sup> '*Absolutely SMASHING DAY. Had beautiful fun with GL, JM, JL, BP and DS. I only hope every day is like today.*'

Friday 19<sup>th</sup> '*Really super day again. GL keeps winking at me. I wish he would go out with me. I still like JM.*'

Saturday 20<sup>th</sup> '*Went to the pictures with Daddy and Edna to see Betsy Drake and Cary Grant in "Room for One More".*'

Sunday 21<sup>st</sup> '*Went to Auntie M's. Had a lovely time. Saw Judy's brother Les, he's super.*'

Monday 22<sup>nd</sup> '*Went to night school. Horrible time. Had to enrol and then wait outside in the playground with hundreds of scouts.*'

Tuesday 23<sup>rd</sup> '*Night school not too bad tonight. Did a bit of shorthand, also English. I am the youngest.*'

Wednesday 24<sup>th</sup> '*Super day. Been mucking around with a lot of boys. Walked home with PH. BF wants to go out with me.*'

Thursday 25<sup>th</sup> '*Super day again with GL, BP, RB and all that little group. BP wants to go out with me. I like him but I like GL (I think) best.*'

Friday 26<sup>th</sup> '*No school today. Saw MG and he said, "Hallo Mary". I like him but I like all the others too. Fairly nice day today.*'

Saturday 27th *'Went to Edna's to tea today. Went up Tilehurst to fetch C then went to Edna's brothers to look after the children while Edna's brother and his wife went to a dance.'*

Sunday 28th *'Stayed in all day. Gave bedroom clean and turned bookcase out. Daddy turned out half my things.'* Not sure if this was the infamous day the mice met their fate!

Monday 29th *'Smashing day. DS made me lose my temper. He took my grey shoe and filled it with water. I HATE him.'*

Tuesday 30th *'Super day again today. Mucked around with all the boys. Night school again today. I don't know whether I like it or not.'*

## OCTOBER

By October Mary's grieving mother is feeling a little better and there is the first mention of the family starting preparations to move into their own apartment. Both Mary's parents have their birthdays this month and although she states what she bought her mother, there's no mention of anything for her father. School is going very well with Mary now starting dance lessons in her dinner hour on Tuesdays. The boys are getting ever increasingly cheeky with one getting the cane on 21st and the word of the moment is *"super"*.

Wednesday 1st *'Went to pictures with Sarah to see "Macao" with Jane Russell and "The Half Breed" with Jack Buetel. He was beautiful as the half breed.'*

Thursday 2nd *'Super day again today. Talked to Clifford today dinner time and I think he's super. Everybody at home is in a bad mood.'*

Friday 3rd *'Super day again today. Had to sing "Early One Morning" by myself. I didn't even go red.'*

Saturday 4th 'Mummy's' birthday. Went to see "Ivanhoe" with Edna and Margaret. In it were Robert Taylor and Elizabeth Taylor, both were absolutely SMASHING. Gave Mummy a tea set today.'

Sunday 5th 'Stayed in all day today. Lovely day. Sun shining brightly. Going dancing Tuesday in the dinner hour.'

Monday 6th 'Had super day again. Had fun with all the boys in our class. They are a super lot.'

Tuesday 7th 'Went dancing today. Had to dance with JH. I think I liked it. I'm not sure. I like JM now.'

Wednesday to Friday are all "super" days at school seeing Mary continue her antics with all the boys.

Saturday 11th 'Went round Edna's all the afternoon. Went to her sisters in the evening but went up town with Edna in the morning. Saw Archie today.'

Sunday 12th 'Stayed in all day. Started packing glass dishes for when we move to our lovely flat. I hope we go very soon.'

Monday 13th 'Super day again today. Had to do the staffs coffee and tea today. Got to do it all this week. Might have to sing a duet.'

Tuesday 14th 'Went dancing dinner time. Super time. RB wanted to dance with me but CC wouldn't let him, so he pushed him away. Learning all sorts of dances.'

Wednesday to Friday are more 'super' days with Mary continuing to note how she gets on with all the boys really well.

Saturday 18th 'Edna came round to tea. She was here all the afternoon and didn't go until about half past ten. We had 21 games of rummy. Was I tired of it? Phew!'

Sunday 19th *'Stayed in all day today because I came on and got an awful stomach ache. But it went off because I had a tablet.'*

Monday 20th *'Super day. I told JF that I liked him. I don't quite know whether I do or not. I think I do.'*

Tuesday 21st *'CC put sanitary towel in my desk today. He got the cane poor thing. I danced with RB at dance class today. It was super. I like him.'*

Wednesday 22nd *'Super day again today. I like JF as well as all the boys in our class. I'm having the happiest days of my life at the moment.'*

Thursday 23rd *'Getting very popular with the fifth-year boys. I like them all as well as the boys in my class. I don't know who I like best.'*

Friday 24th *'Daddy's birthday. Went dancing again today. Danced with RB. On Monday, JF wants me to sit with him at the town hall.'*

Saturday 25th *'Went to pictures with Edna and Pamela to see Jane Wyman and Bing Crosby in "Just for You" in Technicolor. It was super. Lecture on Monday at the town hall, worst luck.'*

Sunday 26th *'Stayed in and stuck pictures of fashions in a school book for Mrs L.'*

Monday 27th *'Super day. DJ put his arm round me the whole time we were in the town hall. It was super. Dancing tomorrow.'*

Tuesday 28th *'Went dancing. Everyone calls me DJ now because he told them about putting his arm round me. Had super taffeta frock from Auntie V.'*

Wednesday 29th *'Super day. Walked home with GL at 7:30pm by the prom. It was pitch dark. SMASHING.'*

Thursday 30th *'Mucked around with all the boys again today. JF keeps telling people he wants to go out with me.'*

Friday 31st *'Super day again today. Went dancing today. It is super. I had to dance with Mr N.'*

## NOVEMBER

Sarah receives her qualification this month in hairdressing and the family finally move into their lovely new apartment along the Bath Road. Mary receives her first kiss and has her fifteenth birthday. She also attends job interviews due to the fact she is scheduled to leave school in December. One interview is with a lady who will try and secure her a job in a wages office but it doesn't say where and no more is written about it afterwards so it's obvious nothing comes of this one.

Saturday 1st *'Edna and I went up to our flat so I could show her. She likes it. Then she came to tea. Went to pictures in evening to see "Meet Me at Eight" with Nigel Patrick and Valerie Hobson. It was very good.'*

Sunday 2nd *'Went to pictures to see Betty Grable in "Mother Wore Tights". It was very good but we got into awful trouble.'*

Monday 3rd *'Went to night school. Came out with Tony. He is very nice but I like GL and JF best.*

Tuesday 4th *'JF and GL came to meet me from night school. They came to the fish shop with me then right home again.'*

Wednesday 5th *'Sarah's birthday today. She got her diploma today in hairdressing. She had some wonderful presents for her birthday. I feel fed up.'*

Thursday and Friday are very similar *'super'* days then Edna comes to tea on Saturday and they go off to the pictures afterwards to see 'Son of Paleface' which she rates as *'very good and Jane Russell is SUPER.'*

Sunday 9th *'Hard work today. Scrubbed filthy kitchen table. Turned bedroom out and took carpets and lino up. Phew, what a day!'*

Monday and Tuesday pass quite ordinarily apart from a boy called Richard escorting Mary home from night school on Tuesday. Then on Wednesday *'didn't go to school in afternoon as went up flat to clear up a bit. Super morning at school today.'*

Thursday 13th *'Didn't go to school at all today. Had to help pack and get things ready to move tomorrow. I'm so looking forward to it.'*

Friday 14th *'Phew! What a day. We moved to No.9. All work and no play. The flat is beautiful. I am very tired after my days' work.'*

Saturday 15th *'Another very busy day. Very wet and nasty today. Had to go out and get some milk because milkman did not come. Still in an awful mess.'*

Sunday 16th *'Busy day again today. We are not straight just yet but we're doing very well.*

The Family's new flat in Florida Court. Mary and Sarah can be seen in the doorway.

Monday 17th *'Super day again today. A boy called Dick brought me home. He kissed me twice. It was heavenly.'*

Tuesday 18th *'Dick brought me home again tonight. He kissed me four times this time. I like him but I like JF best.'*

Wednesday 19th *'Super day again! I mucked around with all the boys. JR is jealous of me.'*

Thursday and Friday are very similar apart from walking home in a group of about ten boys on Friday!

Saturday 22nd *'Edna came to tea. We played Monopoly. I won. Then we went to the pictures to see Ginger Rogers and Clifton Webb in "Dreamboat".'*

Sunday 23rd *'Stayed in bed all morning. I have a terrible cold. Feel like drowning myself. Dick takes me home tomorrow.'*

Monday 24th *'Dick took me home today and kissed me about 6 times. He asked me if I ever used my arms. I said no.'*

Tuesday 25th *'Dick took me home again today. Kissed me lots of times. I think I like him but I don't know.'*

Wednesday 26th *'Had my interview today. The lady is going to try and get me a job in a wage's office.'*

Thursday 27th *'My birthday. Super day. PH took me home. He walked with his arm round me and kissed me. RB keeps putting his arm round me too.'*

Saturday 29th *'Had birthday party today. Edna came to tea. Lovely day. Had super ice cream cake and lots of jelly and lots of lovely things. Edna bought me a film book and Mrs R some hankies.'*

Sunday 30th *'Stayed in all day today. Not a very nice day. Very wet and horrible.'*

## DECEMBER

Mary mentions that her school puts on a play at the beginning of this month in which she may have to sing a duet but I can't establish whether she actually did or not. As she attends choir I assume she is probably singing in the play to some degree. Her father loses his brother this month making it another sad event for the family and I don't get the feeling all in all that consequently it made for a very good Christmas.

Monday 1st *'Dick brought me home again today. I don't think I like him very much.'*

Tuesday 2nd *'Dick brought me home again. I do NOT like him a bit. I like JF. I think he is very nice.'*

Wednesday 3rd *'School Play tonight, it is jolly good.'*

Thursday 4th *'Play again tonight. Very good night. JF there every night. He is nice. I do like him.'*

Friday 5th *'JH spoke to me yesterday. He is very nice but I think JF is best. Nearly all 47 boys want to go out with me.'*

Saturday 6th *'Play again. It is jolly good. I got a packet of chocolate biscuits off JF and he wouldn't give me my change. I like him very much.'*

Sunday 7th *'Stayed in all day. Slept at Grandma's last night. Helped paint the bathroom in afternoon.'*

Monday 8th *'Awful day. Not at school. I am very unhappy. One of these days I shall really kill myself.'*

Tuesday 9th *'Went to night school today. Dodged Dick because I hate him. Broke up from night school today.'*

Friday 12<sup>th</sup> *'Good day today. Had Christmas party at school. GL took me to tea then RB took me home. He kissed me lots of times. GL jealous.'*

Saturday 13<sup>th</sup> *'Stayed at home all by myself all day. Mummy and Daddy went to Uncle R's funeral. He died last Tuesday. Daddy is very sad.'* Kenneth's brother was only in his late forties.

Sunday 14<sup>th</sup> *'Stayed at home by myself again today. Mummy and Daddy round Vastern Road.'*

Wednesday 17<sup>th</sup> *'Super day. Went down the recreation ground with PS, BF and RB. They all tried to be naughty. They all kissed me.'*

Thursday 18<sup>th</sup> *'All 4<sup>th</sup>, 5<sup>th</sup>, 3<sup>rd</sup> and 2<sup>nd</sup> years, as well as my class know about last night. At school dance, RB didn't dance one dance with me.'*

Friday 19<sup>th</sup> *'Left school today. All the boys made fun of me because I cried. JF was very nice to me. He offered to lend me his hankie. RB likes me again.'*

Saturday 20<sup>th</sup> *'Met Hazel in morning. Did a lot of shopping. Waited for her for an hour in afternoon and she didn't come. Did Christmas shopping by myself. Got a date with RB tomorrow.'*

Sunday 21<sup>st</sup> *'Went for a walk with RB. It was super. I like him so much. Sarah saw us.'*

Monday 22<sup>nd</sup> *'Went up town. Went for my interview. The people can't tell me whether or not I have the job yet.'*

Tuesday 23<sup>rd</sup> *'Went up town with Mummy. RM keeps coming round asking for me. I simply HATE him.'*

Wednesday 24<sup>th</sup> *'Not bad today. I wish I was still at school. I wonder whether I'll get the job at Simmonds.'*

Thursday 25th 'Quite a good day. I had some powder and lipstick from Sarah. I didn't have anything from Mum and Dad.'

Friday 26th 'Grandma, Grandad and Auntie O came to tea today. Very mournful.'

Saturday 27th 'We, that is Sarah and I, went to pictures to see "Bloodhounds of Broadway" with Mitze Gaynor and Scott Brady, also "Rose of Cimarron". Both were in Technicolor and both were very good.'

Sunday 28th 'Went to meet RB but he didn't turn up. I had bought him a pen too because it's his birthday Tuesday. I like him.'

Monday 29th 'Edna came to tea today. She stayed until about 9 o'clock. I am going to hers to tea tomorrow.'

Tuesday 30th 'Went to pictures with Edna to see Bud Abbott and Lou Costello in "Jack and The Beanstalk", also "Waggons West". Both were in Technicolor and jolly good.'

Mary hears on Wednesday 31st that she has been successful at one of her interviews and will be starting her very first job at Arthur Newberys furniture shop on Saturday 3rd January stating, 'I wonder what it is going to be like?'

Mary's working life now begins; she is fifteen years of age.

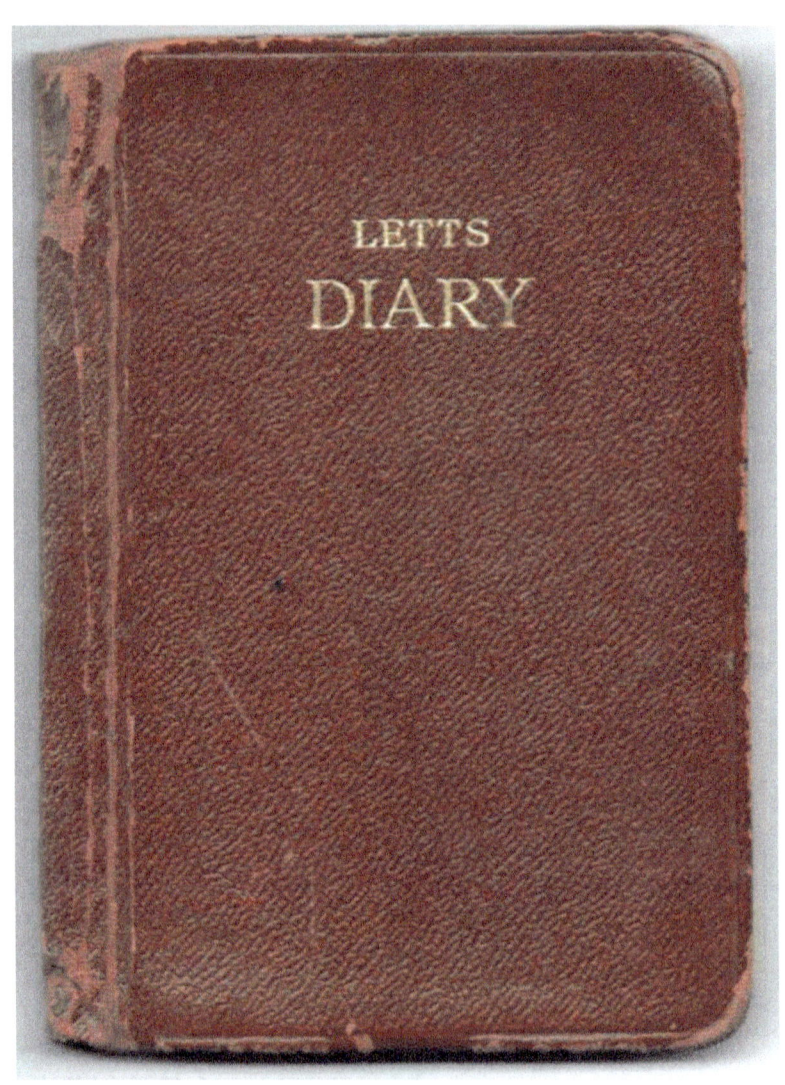

Photo of Mary's first diary 1952

# 1953 and Mary's Filmgoers Diary

A similar sized diary to 1952 with a week to view Sunday to Saturday. Every page contains a short write-up and an illustration of a famous film star. Within the front pages there are columns labelled "Films I Have Seen" which Mary has made full use of filling in the date and names of all the films she has watched and once again giving her personal comments to and rating them as super, smashing, not too good, heavenly or a bit queer. The diary lists London's West-End cinemas and gives postal information regarding post-war conditions. There is also space to enter addresses and telephone numbers. At the back there are blank pages for autographs, birthdays, books I have read and memoranda.

Mary starts work as a clerk at Arthur Newberys furniture shop on the corner of Queen Victoria and Friar Street in Reading on January 3, going up to town with her mother the day before especially to buy a new blouse to wear. Her two weeks rota consists of working Monday, Tuesday, Wednesday, Friday and Saturday the first week, then Monday to Friday the next, with an hour's dinner break every day. She is on the shop floor for the first few months then progresses to the cash desk where she often can't get it to balance correctly.

During this year she also does a lot of walking: to the Forbury, Prospect Park, down to the prom, to Horncastle and to Binfield Heath. When she's at home, Mary still likes to read her comics and listen to the wireless. At this point the family do not have a television so on occasion she can be found round her friend Edna's watching hers. On Sundays as Edna starts to come over more frequently they play games such as Ludo, Sorry, Monopoly and cards. The family also get a lot of visits from other family members including Uncle R and Auntie S (whom Mary likes very much), Auntie M and Uncle B, Aunty V and Uncle J, Aunty K and Uncle T with D, her cousin. She still likes to visit Martin's outdoor swimming pool when it's warm enough and enjoys showing off her diving skills in front of everyone.

Mary also helps her mother with the baking having now perfected the skills needed for making successful cakes and jellies. Even though Mary is only fifteen for most of this year, she feels very grown up especially now she is working. In amongst making new work acquaintances, she still meets up with her old school chums and likes to go to the pictures or to do a little shopping now that she's earning.

## JANUARY

Not a great start to the year for Mary as she has to endure a few minor health issues at the beginning of the month but commences her new job and excitedly receives her very first wage packet on 9th. Her bus fares total 4s 7d for the week and the rest, she enlightens, is put away for clothes and shoes.

Thursday 1st *'Edna came to tea today and we played games all the time.'*

Friday 2nd *'Went up town with Mummy. Bought a blouse. Start work tomorrow.'*

Saturday 3rd *'Started work today. I think I am going to like it. Had card from RB. Going out with him tomorrow.'*

Sunday 4th *'Went out with RB or Ray today. We went in the Forbury and sat down for a while. He brought his dog.'*

Monday 5th *'Work jolly good. Girls are very nice to me. Very helpful. I know I'm going to like it.'*

Tuesday 6th *'Work again today. My foot hurts. I don't know what is wrong with it.'*

Wednesday 7th *'Foot hurts terribly. It's all swollen and inflamed. It does hurt.'*

Thursday 8th *'Foot really bad. Can't walk. I got chilblains. My foot's about 3 times its usual size.'*

Friday 9th *'Foot bit better today, but now the other one has started to hurt. Got my first wage today £1 13s 6d. I have put £1 away for clothes. I wish I had a lot of money.'*

Sunday 11th *'Foot still hurts. I didn't go and meet Ray today as it hurt too much.'*

Monday 12th *'Work again today. I think it is jolly good except that I get all the dirty jobs.'*

Tuesday 13th *'Got a whitlow coming on my finger. It is terribly painful. I hope it will soon be better.'*

Wednesday 14th *'My finger is really bad. Mummy pricked it. I'm afraid I cried. Sarah held me while Mummy pricked. I was wet with sweat.'*

Thursday 15th *'I pricked my finger today. Got quite a lot of the poison out.'*

Friday 16th *'Daddy went away. Pricked my finger again today. Got more poison out. It is nearly better now.'*

Saturday 17th *'Edna and Pamela came yesterday to tea. Edna coming to sleep with me tonight as Sarah can sleep in with Mummy.'*

Sunday 18th *'Good fun last night. Sarah slept with Mummy. Edna slept in Sarah's bed.'*

Monday 19th *'Work again today. Bought a pair of shoes last Friday and a red skirt Saturday.'*

Tuesday 20th *'Work again today. Finger better now, thank goodness. Wrote to Hazel today.'*

Wednesday 21st *'Work again today. Not bad. Going to pictures tomorrow with Edna.'*

Thursday 22nd '*Pictures jolly good. "Road To Bali" with Bob Hope and Bing Crosby. Very funny. Dorothy Lamour SMASHING.*'

Friday 23rd '*Work again today. Jean very funny. Made me have a laughing fit.*'

Saturday 24th '*Work again today. Very tired. Went to bed at 5 to 9.*'

Sunday 25th '*Uncle R and Auntie S came. I like them very much.*'

Monday 26th '*Work again today. A man called Jim keeps giving me sweets.*'

Tuesday 27th '*Work again today. Had another sweet today.*'

Wednesday 28th '*Work again—I like it very much.*'

Thursday 29th '*Work once more. All I seem to do is work, work, work.*'

Friday 30th '*Work again. Had tummy ache all day. Going round Edna's tomorrow.*'

Saturday 31st '*Went round Edna's today. Saw the television. Wish we had one.*'

Mary doesn't mention anything about starting back at night school again this month but she is obviously learning to type as I found this note tucked in to her mother's diary of the same year stating that Mary used the typewriter for the first time on January 13th and typed her '*a lovely little letter, bless her.*'

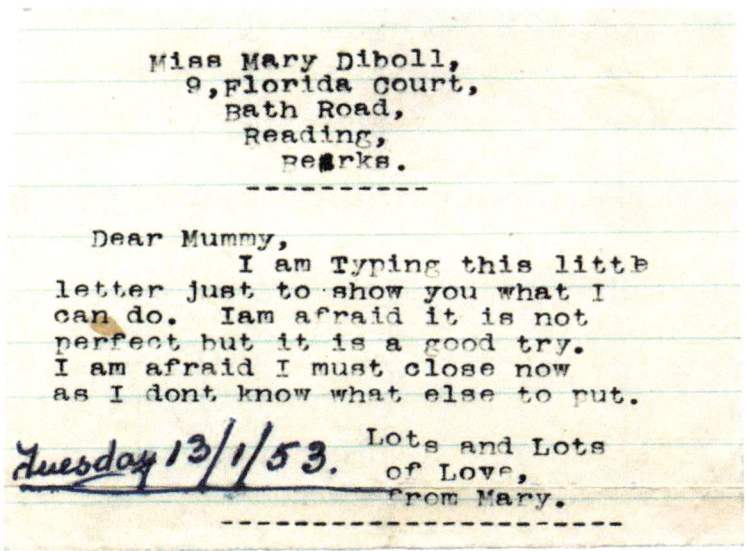

Miss Mary Diboll,
9, Florida Court,
Bath Road,
Reading,
Berks.
----------

Dear Mummy,
         I am Typing this little
letter just to show you what I
can do. Iam afraid it is not
perfect but it is a good try.
I am afraid I must close now
as I dont know what else to put.

Tuesday 13/1/53.     Lots and Lots
                        of Love,
                     from Mary.
----------------------------

## FEBRUARY

By February Mary is settling into her new role at Newberys and although she decides she hates doing stock taking, thinks that she will enjoy working there. She has made the acquaintance of the following ladies: Sheila, Joan, Shirley, Pam and Jean, who is very funny, and the boys who are: Jim, KQ, LB, KB, MC and AB all of whom she seems to get on really well with. Her first love turns out to be amongst one of these boys.

Sunday 1st '*Auntie M and Uncle B came round today. They are very nice.*'

Monday 2nd '*Work again today. Doing stock taking—terrible.*'

Tuesday 3rd '*Still doing stock taking at work today. I hate it.*'

Wednesday 4th '*Work again today. Jim keeps giving me sweets.*'

Thursday 5th '*Auntie V came round today. Auntie K came round yesterday.*'

Friday 6th '*Work again. More sweets from Jim.*'

Saturday 7th 'Work again. I like Jim very much.'

Sunday 8th 'Made some mock cream and cakes and jellies. Auntie V and Sarah's John came to tea.'

Monday 9th 'Work again today. Jim keeps putting his arm round me.'

Tuesday 10th 'Work again. More sweets from Jim.'

Wednesday 11th 'Went round Mrs F's to tea. Had favourite jam, bread and cake.'

Thursday 12th 'Work again. Still more sweets from Jim today.'

Friday 13th 'Had a coconut today at work. Miss P didn't know.'

Saturday 14th 'Jim says he is going to kidnap me on Monday. Edna came round today.'

Sunday 15th 'Auntie K, Uncle T and Dom came today. They keep saying how pretty I am! I wonder what will happen tomorrow about Jim.'

Monday 16th 'Nothing happened about Jim kidnapping me. I shall ask him why tomorrow.'

Tuesday 17th 'Jim said today that he didn't have anything to do with his wife but he would like to kidnap me. I had no idea he was married.'

Wednesday 18th 'Had hair washed and had a bath. I wish I'd got plenty of money.'

Thursday 19th 'KQ asked me to go to the pictures with him today. I had to say no!'

Friday 20th 'LB asked me to go to pictures with him today. I think he and KQ are having a competition to see which one can get me to go.'

Saturday 21st *'Pam away today. Had Joan in with me to help with the telephone. Had a long talk with Jim.'*

Sunday 22nd *'Did nothing much. Fed up with hair. It's all frizzy.'*

Monday 23rd *'Work again today. Jim keeps putting his arms around me. LB still asks me to go to pictures.'*

Tuesday 24th *'Work again. Sheila may have my green coat. I hope she does. I need a new one.'*

Wednesday 25th *'Sheila is going to have my coat. I don't know when I've wanted money so much as I do today.'*

Thursday 26th *'Work again. Going to the pictures with LB next Saturday.'*

Friday 27th *'Edna came round today. Pam leaves today. Buying new coat tomorrow.'*

Saturday 28th *'Bought lovely blue swagger coat today. It cost £9.7s. Walked round town with Jim. He is so nice.'* The picture is of Mary wearing her nice new coat.

## MARCH

During March a new lady replaces Pam at work and Mary's comment is really rather unflattering. She plucks up the courage to go to the pictures with one of the boys, specifying that she definitely cannot tell her parents and Jim oversteps the mark. Obviously being so young, receiving the attentions of a married man is confusing but to top it off she also receives her first proposal! This March hails the beginning of Mary's love affair with shoes as she purchases her very first pair of (many) high heels. She doesn't mention colour or price sadly but I feel this was the moment that her fetish for footwear began! My mother loved her shoes.

Sunday 1st '*Went to Spirit Church today. It was queer. The lady spoke to the spirits.*'

Monday 2nd '*Work again. All the boys here are so nice, I like them all.*'

Tuesday 3rd '*Went over to Post Office with KQ today at work. I do like him very much.*'

Wednesday 4th '*Went to pictures with Sarah today. MC at work said he liked my red skirt. He said he also liked what was in it.*'

Thursday 5th '*I believe I am falling in love with KQ. Or is it just a little girls fancy?*'

Friday 6th '*Going to pictures tomorrow with LB. I like KQ best. I also like MC. Walked with him today.*'

Saturday 7th '*Went to pictures with LB. I like him I think but I like KQ best. I don't want Mummy to find out.*'

Sunday 8th '*Auntie K came down with Uncle T. Going up there for Easter.*'

Monday 9th '*New woman came today. Talk about fat, she's monstrous.*'

Tuesday 10th '*Went for a walk with Jim this evening round the shops. I do like him.*'

Wednesday 11th '*Jim super today. He keeps putting his arms round me. He said he would have me if he wasn't married.*'

Thursday 12th 'Super day. Jim nearly kissed me. He keeps putting his arms round me. I do like him but he is married. Going to pictures tomorrow with KQ.'

Friday 13th 'Went to pictures with KQ to see "Decameron Nights". I was disappointed. He didn't even put his arm round me. Going with LB tomorrow.'

Saturday 14th 'Went with LB to the pictures today. He kissed me lots of times especially afterwards. MC wants to take me out, so does AB. It is very difficult.'

Sunday 15th 'I really don't know who I like best out of all the boys at Newberys.'

Monday 16th 'Super day again today. Jim is very friendly and keeps putting his arm round me. I do like him.'

Tuesday 17th 'KQ left yesterday. He didn't even tell me he was leaving.'

Wednesday 18th 'Auntie K came down again today. I am going to try to get Easter Saturday off.'

Thursday 19th 'I asked Miss P if I could have Easter Saturday off and she said YES! Thank goodness.'

Friday 20th 'Went to the pictures with KQ today. He rang me up yesterday to make the date. I do like him.'

Saturday 21st 'Went to pictures with LB today. I like him much better than KQ. He kissed me loads of times. Jim today almost told me he loved me!'

Sunday 22nd 'Stayed in and read comics all the afternoon. Very thrilling I must say.'

Monday 23rd 'Jim keeps saying that he'll kiss me. LB says he likes me, but I wish he would not flirt with Sheila. Makes me jealous.'

Tuesday 24th *'Bought pair of high heeled shoes yesterday. Jim kissed me today. It was horribly wet. I hope he doesn't do it again. Not half as nice as LB's. I do like LB.'*

Wednesday 25th *'Went to school to see teachers. Mr B made me feel a fool. Going to school dance on Tuesday. I almost wish I were back at school.'*

Thursday 26th *'Work again today. KQ hasn't rung me up yet as he said he would. Perhaps he will tomorrow.'*

Friday 27th *'KQ didn't ring me but he came to meet me from work, so we went to the Odeon. It was quite good but not so good as when I go with LB.'*

Saturday 28th *'heavenly evening. Went to the pictures with LB. Came out about ten to nine and got home at quarter to eleven. He said he loved me very much and he proposed to me. I said yes! He goes in the Navy soon worst luck.'*

Sunday 29th *'Did nothing all day but sit around and listen to wireless and dream of LB.'*

Monday 30th *'Work again. Oh, I do like LB. He tells me he loves me and that he will ask me to marry him.'*

Tuesday 31st *'Work again today. Sheila at work keeps flirting with LB. It does make me feel jealous.'*

## APRIL

Mary's family embark on a short vacation for Easter staying with an aunt near Brighton. There's upset with LB and her mother finds out about her picture outings with two boys. Things take a down turn towards the end of the month.

Wednesday 1st *'Sheila's birthday today. She still flirts with MY LB.'*

Thursday 2nd *'Went away today to Auntie K's. I do like her and wish I lived there always.'*

Good Friday 3rd '*Went to Brighton today. Went on the pier. It was cold but very nice.*'

Saturday 4th '*Went to pictures with Auntie and Uncle today. It was very good.*'

Sunday 5th '*Went to Brighton town for the day. Jerry, Alan and Edgar are all very nice.*'

Monday 6th '*Came home today feeling very fed up.*'

Tuesday 7th '*Work again. I do like LB very much.*'

Wednesday 8th '*Work again today. Sheila still flirts with LB. She is horrid.*'

Thursday 9th '*KQ keeps phoning me up. I do like him but I love LB.*'

Friday 10th '*Went to pictures with KQ. He is nice but I would much rather have LB with me.*'

Saturday 11th '*Both KQ and LB came to meet me today. We made an arrangement to meet KQ in the pictures but when he saw us, he said he didn't like to disturb us.*'

Sunday 12th '*Feel like killing myself today. Mummy's found out I go with KQ and LB and she says she's coming to meet me from work every day.*'

Monday 13th '*Work again today. Mummy didn't come to meet me. Had my hair permed.*'

Tuesday 14th '*Hair looks very nice although I say it myself. Sheila makes me sick. She still flirts with LB.*'

Wednesday 15th '*I do love LB. He is so nice, but I wish Sheila wouldn't keep flirting with him.*'

Thursday 16th '*KQ rang me today. I'm going to pictures with him tomorrow. I still like LB best and think I would kill myself if he ever gave me up.*'

Friday 17th '*Went to pictures with KQ. I think he is soft and a cissy. I much prefer LB.*'

Saturday 18th '*LB gave me up because I went to pictures with KQ. I've a good mind to kill myself. Wait until I hear from KQ, he'll wish he was never born. I love LB. I wish I would die.*'

Sunday 19th '*Terrible day. I had to be cheerful when I was feeling like killing myself.*'

Monday 20th '*LB still smiles and winks at me. I think he still likes me a little. I love him so much.*'

Tuesday 21st '*LB still smiling at me. I do feel ill. I don't know what's wrong with me.*'

Wednesday 22nd '*Stayed in all day. Auntie V felt hurt because we wouldn't go out with her and Mummy.*'

Thursday 23rd '*Feel like killing myself today. Auntie moping. Mummy moaning. One of these days I will.*'

Friday 24th '*Went to pictures with KQ. He isn't bad but I love LB and wish he would come back to me.*'

Saturday 25th '*Went to pictures with Edna. I did miss LB putting his arm round me. I wonder if he misses me?*'

Sunday 26th '*Good mind to kill myself today. Auntie crying again saying I hurt her feelings. Auntie K came today too and we did some painting.*'

Monday 27th '*Work again. LB said, "I don't suppose you'd let me take you to the flicks again."*'

Tuesday 28<sup>th</sup> '*LB being ever so nice. I think he wants me back.*'

Wednesday 29<sup>th</sup> '*Went to pictures with Mummy, Sarah and Auntie. Feel fed up.*'

Thursday 30<sup>th</sup> '*Wish I could kill myself. Mummy almost told me she was sick of me.*'

## MAY

May brings more depression as it seems like Mary and her family are going through a rough patch at the moment with everyone seemingly being miserable all the time. She writes that '*everyone keeps moaning*' a lot in her diary and that she feels very lonely of late, although this could just be down to being a hormonal fifteen-year-old. Still, she notes how a good cry always makes her feel better.

On the plus side LB asks her out again and work is going well, so much so that on 15<sup>th</sup> Mary gets her very first pay increase and goes out and buys (yes, you've guessed it) another pair of very high heel shoes. KQ comes into work to say a permanent goodbye on 6<sup>th</sup> as he is going in the army but promises he'll write to her. Mary now starts to date LB again and the weather has improved enough for the family to resume her favourite hobby, swimming at Martins outdoor pool.

Friday 1<sup>st</sup> '*Went to pictures with KQ. LB asked me if I would go tomorrow but Mummy made me stay in.*'

Saturday 2<sup>nd</sup> '*I could have gone with LB after all. Went with Edna. Still, I expect I'll go with him next week.*'

Sunday 3<sup>rd</sup> '*Went to Edna's to tea. Went for a walk with her. Saw GL. He is so nice but I like LB best.*'

Monday 4<sup>th</sup> '*Work again. Going with LB next Saturday. I'm so glad. I don't expect he could live without me.*'

Tuesday 5th 'Went to pictures with Sheila at work. I do wish she would stop flirting with LB. I do love him so much.'

Wednesday 6th 'KQ came to work to say goodbye today. He goes in the army tomorrow. Wish I could kill myself. Everybody at home is so miserable.'

Thursday 7th 'Everyone miserable at home; it really makes me want to kill myself. KQ went into the army today. Said he'll write so that I get a letter Saturday.'

Friday 8th 'Feel in fairly good mood today. Edna came round this evening. Going to pictures with LB tomorrow.'

Saturday 9th 'Heavenly evening. LB's come back to me. I do not feel quite so sure I love him now but I sure know I like him lots and lots.'

Sunday 10th 'Helped Daddy do some painting. Did all the skirtings. I hope LB doesn't change his mind about me again.'

Monday 11th 'LB says he still loves me. I'm so glad because I love him so much.'

Tuesday 12th 'Had letter from KQ yesterday. He is shy. I wish he was like LB.'

Wednesday 13th 'Haven't seen much of LB today. Bought new shoes yesterday—super. Very high heels. I love them.'

Thursday 14th 'LB now says he is going out Saturday, so I shan't be going. I do wish I was. I love him so much.'

Friday 15th 'Got my rise today of 3/6. LB says he can come tomorrow now after all. I am so glad.'

Saturday 16th 'Wonderful evening. LB says he loves me and I told him I love him too. I really do love him.'

Sunday 17th *'Stayed in all day. Played "Sorry" with Mummy. I do hope LB hasn't changed his mind again.'*

Monday 18th *'Horrible day. LB keeps flirting with Sheila. Mummy, Daddy and Sarah miserable. Had a good cry and felt a little better for it.'*

Tuesday 19th *'Wonderful day. LB says he still loves me. Had letter from KQ today as well as yesterday. I like him but I love LB.'*

Wednesday 20th *'Went to Maidenhead with Mummy and Sarah in afternoon. Went to Central Club with Edna to see Maureen in play. She is lovely.'*

Thursday 21st *'Saw LB putting up decorations from my window today. I do love him so much. He's going to London on Saturday.'*

Friday 22nd *'Jean said she saw KQ today. If he is home, I expect he will ring me tomorrow.'*

Saturday 23rd *'Went to pictures with KQ. He rang me this morning. He hadn't got enough money so I gave him some. I like him but I do so much love LB.'*

Sunday 24th *'Edna came round this afternoon. Walked to Prospect Park and sat down. I hope LB still loves me.'*

Monday 25th *'Went to Martins swimming pool with Mummy and Edna. I was mad because I couldn't go in. Had fun with 3 boys.'*

Tuesday 26th *'Feel fed up. No one will come swimming with me and I want to go so much. LB goes down the Thames. I wonder if I should go.'*

Wednesday 27th *'Feel fed up again. No one will come swimming with me and LB has been flirting with Sheila today. One of these days I shall kill myself.'*

Thursday 28th *'Absolutely fed up. I am seriously thinking of killing myself. I am so unhappy. LB still says he likes me but he still flirts with Sheila so much.'*

Friday 29th '*Feel so unhappy. Sheila has taken <u>MY</u> LB away from me. She waits for him everywhere. And now he says he has to go out tomorrow. I wonder where he's going?*'

Saturday 30th '*Very boring. I do miss LB. KQ came home today. I think I like him a bit more.*'

Sunday 31st '*Stayed in all day. Did painting for Daddy. I really feel lonely these last few weeks. I don't know what's wrong with me.*'

## JUNE

For the historians among you Mary's entry on 2nd notes Queen Elizabeth's Coronation and how she listens to it all day long on the wireless. She attends her school dance on 4th and finally gets to go swimming in the outdoor pool. Mary is now getting a little fed up with LB as he is coming across as very fickle. By the end of the month the weather is nice enough to sit out on the lawn at the front of Florida Court and she starts asking her father for a bike so she can cycle to work, probably to save some pennies.

Monday 1st '*Went to the pictures with Mummy and Daddy. It was good but I did miss LB.*'

Tuesday 2nd '*Queen Elizabeth II is crowned today. Listened to wireless all day. In evening saw fireworks display and procession.*'

Wednesday 3rd '*Went to pictures with Sarah. It was very good. Edna came round. I forgot all about her, so I only saw her for a short time.*'

Thursday 4th '*Went to school dance. It was quite good but danced with Hazel all the time. I haven't seen much of my LB today.*'

Friday 5th '*LB says he has to go out tomorrow. I am fed up with him even though he says he still loves me.*'

Saturday 6th '*LB apologised for not going to pictures with me. We've arranged to go out tomorrow. I do love him so much.*'

Sunday 7th '*Went out with LB today. I do love him so much but he doesn't seem to love me at all. I do wish he did. He brought his friend along.*'

Monday 8th '*Had some fun with KB today. I like him but I love LB. Jim says LB likes me a lot. I do hope that is true.*'

Tuesday 9th '*Very fed up with Sarah. She wouldn't do my hair for me and it's such a mess. I think I am beginning to like KB very much.*'

Wednesday 10th '*Went swimming at Martins Pool. It was fairly cold and there was only about a dozen boys and 3 girls there. They all watched me diving.*'

Thursday 11th '*Sheila's been flirting with LB again today. Also, Jean. They both get on my nerves. Jean is getting horrible lately.*'

Friday 12th '*LB says he's awfully sorry he's been mucking around with Sheila and Jean and has promised to take me to the pictures next week. I am so glad.*'

Saturday 13th '*Went to pictures with Edna to see "A Queen Is Crowned" and "Escape". KQ came home today. I really like him but love my LB best, although he isn't such a nice boy as KQ.*'

Sunday 14th '*Went for a walk with Edna. Saw GL. I still like him a little but I still love LB a lot better, although he is unfaithful.*'

Monday 15th '*Work this morning. LB not at work as he's training to be a sailor. I do love him so much.*'

Tuesday 16th '*Saw LB dinner time. He was in his sailor's uniform. He did look smashing. He says he will tell Sheila at work that I am his girlfriend.*'

Wednesday 17th '*LB didn't tell Sheila today. I wish I had the nerve to give him up but I love him so much.*'

Thursday 18th '*LB says I am still his girlfriend and that he will take me to the pictures on Saturday. I am so looking forward to it.*'

Friday 19th '*LB still flirts with Sheila. Still, I am going to the pictures with him tomorrow so I expect she will be jealous.*'

Saturday 20th '*KQ had to come home and spoil everything. LB was so mad that he let KQ take me. I was so disappointed.*'

Sunday 21st '*Don't know how to get through today. Feel very ill and wondering if LB will still like me. I wish I could kill myself.*'

Monday 22nd '*Wrote to KQ and told him I didn't want to see him anymore. LB says he doesn't know if he likes me or not. I wonder if I have done the right thing.*'

Tuesday 23rd '*Horrid day again. Today LB seems as if he likes me but he still won't tell me. He didn't post that letter to KQ thank goodness. He still flirts with Sheila.*'

Wednesday 24th '*Feel ill again today. I do wish LB would hurry up and come back to me. I wish it could be like it was at first. I wish I could kill myself until he comes back to me.*'

Thursday 25th '*Feel in smashing mood today. LB said he still likes me. I am so glad as I love him very much. He tore up the letter to KQ.*'

Friday 26th '*Still feel in good mood. I had a good time with KB today. I like him a lot. I have some fun with him.*'

Saturday 27th '*Went down to Edna's and went and sat on the prom. It was fairly cold but rather nice. KQ came home.*'

Sunday 28th '*Edna came up and we sat on the lawn outside. I keep asking Daddy for a bike.*'

Monday 29th *'Had fun with KB again today. I think he is very nice.'*

Tuesday 30th *'Bought new frock also had photos taken. Had fun with KB again today.'*

This is one of the photos taken on June 30th 1953.
Mary is fifteen years and seven months.

## JULY

LB at last commits to Mary this month but there are still bumps in the road ahead. She takes a week's holiday from work proudly jumping on a train by herself to stay with Auntie K where they visit London airport as a social attraction. On Wednesday 1st and Thursday 2nd Mary is still thinking of LB.

Friday 3rd *'Heavenly day. Mr S told LB to say goodbye to me and he kissed me on the landing. He says he will take me out after our holidays.'*

Saturday 4th 'Sheila said LB told her I was his girlfriend. He told Mrs F that he didn't like Sheila but that he liked me. I think he is beginning to feel that he has acted awful.'

Sunday 5th 'Another horrible day. I feel so lonely. I'm not allowed to do anything. Stayed in the whole day and it's my holiday too. One of these days I shall kill myself.'

Monday 6th 'It is horrible this lonely feeling. My holiday, did absolutely NOTHING. I wish I could die! Everything has gone wrong in the past few weeks.'

Tuesday 7th 'Went to Maidenhead in afternoon and to the Palace in the evening. Going to Auntie K's tomorrow.'

Wednesday 8th 'Went to Auntie K's. Uncle said I am easily his favourite niece. He says I am much better looking than Sarah. I do like Dom.'

Thursday 9th 'Went to Auntie V's. She's got a lovely room. I am going to Auntie K's for the weekend.'

Friday 10th 'Went on train by myself. Had a nice day. Dom is awfully nice. He teases me an awful lot.'

Saturday 11th 'Went to London airport. Saw some tremendous planes. I wish I could go up in one. Dom still teases me; I do like it and him.'

Sunday 12th 'Helped Dom in the garage today. Stayed up until midnight yesterday with Dom listening to the wireless. Aunty says he does like me.'

Monday 13th 'Work horrible this morning. Does seem terrible after being at Auntie K's.'

Tuesday 14th 'Mummy and Sarah and Daddy have all started moaning. It is different to Auntie K's.'

Wednesday 15<sup>th</sup> '*Made some toffee today. Turned out quite good. I wonder if LB is missing me. I am him.*'

Thursday 16<sup>th</sup> '*Work again. Keep getting teased about fretting for LB as he is on holiday. I am missing him.*'

Friday 17<sup>th</sup> '*Work again today. KB at work is awfully nice. I have a lot of fun with him.*'

Saturday 18<sup>th</sup> '*Went to pictures with Edna. Saw PS and JS afterwards. Just said hello! Then we went into the Regent and then for a walk.*'

Sunday 19<sup>th</sup> '*Daddy's cousins were supposed to come today. Mummy got tea ready and all, and then they didn't come.*'

Monday 20<sup>th</sup> '*LB back today. He's been talking and joking with Sheila most of the today. He says he hasn't changed his mind. Mr S mended my heel today in the Polyton shop and LB was in there.*'

Tuesday 21<sup>st</sup> '*Went to pictures with Sarah. Saw B, I forget his other name, but he played the trumpet in Cinderella. He wanted me to go and sit with him but Sarah wouldn't.*'

Wednesday 22<sup>nd</sup> '*Went round Sheila's this afternoon. Saw quite a nice boy but he wasn't half as nice as my LB.*'

Thursday 23<sup>rd</sup> '*Sheila told LB that I went out with the boy I saw yesterday and he almost gave me up, but I told him it wasn't true and he says he won't have anything more to do with her.*'

Friday 24<sup>th</sup> '*Going to pictures with my LB tomorrow. I do hope nothing prevents it again. KQ rang me up today and KB at work looked smashing.*'

Saturday 25<sup>th</sup> '*Absolutely wonderful evening. LB was naughty I'm afraid but he promised faithfully never to let it happen again. I didn't see much of the film* as he was kissing me most of the time. He told me after the film that he loves me. I'm so glad.'

Sunday 26ᵗʰ 'Wish I could kill myself. Stayed in all day with Auntie, Mummy and Daddy. Been thinking about LB today. I do love him.'

Monday 27ᵗʰ 'LB still won't tell me why he is sorry. Of course, I know it was because he was naughty. My shoe had to be mended and I stayed and talked to LB for ages and I got into trouble for being so long.'

Tuesday 28ᵗʰ 'LB still loves me at least that's what he says. He's going to tell me what he was sorry for on Saturday.'

Wednesday 29ᵗʰ 'Went to pictures with Sarah to see Robert Mitchum and Jean Simmonds. Saw new girl today at work. I've got to train her to go into the cash desk.'

Thursday 30ᵗʰ 'Feel fed up with Auntie V. LB still won't tell me why he's sorry and he says he still loves me.'

Friday 31ˢᵗ 'Sheila stayed in the Polyton shop with LB by himself for about 20 minutes. I wonder what happened. Oh, I wish she would leave. It is very hard not to be jealous. Jean left today.'

AUGUST

LB leaves Arthur Newberys on 14ᵗʰ to go in the Navy and although he says he'll keep in touch their nights out become fewer and fewer mainly because he doesn't show up. Mary feels heartbroken and quite depressed which may have contributed to her contracting an infectious skin condition during the middle of the month. She has to train up another girl at work and is still pestering her father for a bike. On the plus side though, work is obviously going well as she receives yet another pay increase on 18ᵗʰ.

Saturday 1st *'Super day. Went to pictures with LB. He was naughty again but I don't seem to mind him doing it. If anyone else tried to, I shouldn't let them. KQ came to meet me as well.'*

Sunday 2nd *'LB told me yesterday that he loved me and that he would ask me to marry him when he came out of the Navy. He said he'd never change his mind.'*

Monday 3rd *'Aunties lover came today. Went to pictures with Sarah to see Abbott and Costello in "Flight to Mars". I did miss LB putting his arm round me... All I've done over the weekend is dream of him.'*

Tuesday 4th *'New girl started today. She was sick and I had to clean up the mess. Haven't seen much of my LB today. Uncle J and S came today.'*

Wednesday 5th *'LB has promised to tell me what he is sorry for on Saturday in the pictures. I don't mind him being naughty so long as he doesn't go too far. I should hate to have a baby.'*

Thursday 6th *'LB told me today that he still likes me. I am so glad. I love him so much. I couldn't bear to lose him. Going to the pictures on Saturday.'*

Friday 7th *'Been down in the cash desk most of today. I do hope nothing goes wrong tomorrow; I just have a feeling that something is going to go wrong.'*

Saturday 8th *'Wonderful evening but I think Daddy must have seen me. When I got in, he said he had only just got in. Mummy and Auntie were waiting for me at the gate. They wanted to know LB. I walked home alone though.'*

Sunday 9th *'Edna came round and we sat in the sun and sunbathed. I have got quite brown. I do hope my LB hasn't changed his mind.'*

Monday 10th *'Saw LB today. He says he hasn't changed his mind. I asked him why he didn't seem so friendly on Saturday and he said he was terribly sorry but he was really tired.'*

Tuesday 11th *'My LB is still tired. He said he hasn't changed his mind. We have chosen a double bed for when we get married.'*

Wednesday 12th *'LB says he still hasn't changed his mind but can't come out now on Saturday as he has to go out.'*

Thursday 13th *'Sheila mucked around with my LB today. I wish she would leave. She said LB calls me names when I'm not there and that he is only pretending to like me.'*

Friday 14th *'My darling LB left Newberys today. I am broken-hearted. He doesn't know when he'll see me again. I think he is getting tired of me asking him if he still likes me. I must try to tell him I love him instead of asking if he loves me.'*

Saturday 15th *'Feeling dreadfully lonely. I do wish my darling LB would come back to Newberys. It is horrible this not knowing when I shall see him again, if at all.'*

Sunday 16th *'Went round to Sheila's today. Her mother is very nice. I wonder how on earth I shall live without my darling LB. I love him so much.'*

Monday 17th *'Went to doctors today. I have got ringworm. I feel so miserable and lonely. Everyone avoids me in case they catch it and I am missing my darling LB terribly. I wish I could die.'*

Tuesday 18th *'Getting a 13/- rise next week. Very pleased about it. But this evening Daddy won't let me have a bike and my ringworm is getting worse. Horrible evening. Had a good cry.'*

Wednesday 19th *'Treated Mummy to the pictures. Mummy upset because Daddy sent flowers to Grandma and Grandad from K and O. Did miss my darling LB putting his arm round me in the pictures.'*

Thursday 20th *'Sheila at work horrible today. She had a heat bump come up on her arm and she told Miss P she had caught my ringworm. They put Dettol on everything and made me use a special towel. KB was wonderful. He put his arms round me and told me not to worry.'*

Friday 21st *'Everyone a bit better today. KB smashing. I have a lot of fun with him and I like him too but do miss my darling LB so much.'*

Saturday 22nd *'Been down in the cash desk most of today. Start my work down there on Monday. Did miss going to pictures with LB. I hope he comes in to see me soon.'*

Sunday 23rd *'Stayed in all day. I am missing my LB terribly. I wonder if he is missing me. I wish he hadn't left.'*

Monday 24th *'Started work in the cash desk today. I don't know whether I shall like it or not. Got a new girl tomorrow. She will be 18 in December then she leaves.'*

Tuesday 25th *'Feel very fed up today. New girl is horrible. She went to Kendrick and she calls me dear. KB has been nice today.'*

Wednesday 26th *'Went to pictures to see "Sangaree" 3D film with Mummy, Daddy and Sarah. I do wish Daddy would let me have a bike. Also, I wish with all my heart that LB would come in to see me.'*

Thursday 27th *'Kendrick school girl still horrible. Still, I think it is Sheila's fault. I expect I will like her more when Sheila goes on holiday.'*

Friday 28th *'There's a rumour going round that little KB is leaving. I do hope he doesn't, as I have such a lot of fun with him.'*

Saturday 29th *'Went to pictures to see a X film also 3D called "House of Wax". It was GHASTLY. I wouldn't have minded if LB was with me.'*

Sunday 30th *'Went to Uncle J and met Stella's two brothers. Boy! Are they smashing. One is 21 and the other about 23. I still like my LB best.'*

Monday 31st *'It is true that KB is leaving. At least, he and Bill say he is. I do wish he wasn't; I like him so much and I have a lot of fun with him.'*

The photo is of Mary holding her Auntie's little dog—Sandy.

## SEPTEMBER

Mary gets a lovely surprise on 4th and uses a taxi on her own for the first time this month. Her friend KB leaves Newberys on 8th along with SH, thankfully. Can't tell you how glad I am about that!

Tuesday 1st *'KB says he is going to give me something and I asked him when he was going to. He said he'll think it over.'*

Wednesday 2nd *'I asked KB today if he thought of what he was going to give me and he said he knew what it was but he didn't know whether I would like it. I asked him to tell me what it was and he said it is nothing to tell but something he was going to do.'*

Thursday 3rd *'KB leaves tomorrow, worse luck and SH on Tuesday. It is a shame as I have such fun with KB. He says he's going to give me something tomorrow.'*

Friday 4th *'KB left today. I felt thoroughly fed up until I had a WONDERFUL surprise. My darling LB came into see me. We are going to the pictures tomorrow. I think he has changed.'*

**Saturday 5th** *'Heavenly evening! LB is wonderful. He was VERY naughty, but I love him all the same. He says he is learning to drive and that he will take me out when he has learnt.'*

**Sunday 6th** *'Went to Edna's today. Missed the last bus home and had to get a taxi. I was terribly scared. I wouldn't have minded if my LB was with me.'*

**Monday 7th** *'I got a 5/- bet on with SH that I wouldn't scream if he was to do anything to me. He says he is going to make me have a baby.'*

**Tuesday 8th** *'Mummy and Auntie went away today to Blakeney. SH left today, but I didn't see much of him.'*

The next few days are fairly humdrum but Mary is getting quite friendly with a girl called Shirley at work and they have started going to the pictures together some evenings after they finish for the day. Shirley is easy going and very often they walk round town together in their dinner hours with Mary noting, *'didn't have time for any dinner at all.'* She is looking forward to Saturday when LB says he will take her to the pictures again.

**Friday 11th** *'Had a letter from Edna today to say that she wouldn't be on the train I usually meet. Going to pictures with my darling LB tomorrow.'*

**Saturday 12th** *'My darling LB didn't turn up. I feel thoroughly fed up and miserable. I wonder if Sheila had anything to do with it. She knew he was coming today. She might have come about 25 mins past 5 and persuaded him to take her instead. As I didn't come out of work until 20 to 6. I do wish he had been there.'*

**Sunday 13th** *'Worse day of my life. Feeling absolutely fed up. Daddy keeps telling me I'm lazy. I have an awful stomach-ache and the feeling that LB took Sheila to pictures instead of me, or if he didn't, he still didn't come to take me.'*

**Monday 14th** *'Feel a bit better today. Apparently, LB didn't take Sheila as she went somewhere else, or so she said. I do wish he had come. I had even told Edna I couldn't go on Sunday so that I could go out with my LB.'*

Tuesday 15th '*Don't quite know how I feel today. Been having some fun with a man over winches and yet I am still feeling sad because of LB. I wonder why he didn't come?*'

Wednesday 16th '*Went to pictures with Shirley. She bought a smashing boy with her. He teased me quite a lot. I did feel mean because I should hate to take him away.*'

Thursday 16th '*Shirley said she had a row with John last night when he took her home. It was over me. He said I would treat him better than she did.*'

Friday 17th '*Shirley and I had some fun with some notes today. We keep writing to each other in a special code. She thinks I'm madly in love with John but of course I'm not.*'

Saturday 19th '*I was hoping my darling LB would come and meet me today but he didn't. I was so disappointed. I do love him so.*'

On Sunday Mary dwells on how much she actually misses LB and then remarks '*I don't seem to care very much whether he comes back or not, although I would be pleased if he did.*'

Monday 21st '*Going to pictures with Shirley again on Wednesday. She says she can't bring any boys because they will all be working.*'

Tuesday 22nd '*The nice man over in winches keeps waving and winking at me. I like him but wish LB would hurry up and come back to me.*'

Wednesday 23rd '*Shirley didn't turn up today so I went with Sheila to see "Hiawatha". It was smashing but I did miss LB putting his arm round me.*'

Thursday 24th '*Had two smashing boys in today to mend my telephone. They teased me a lot. Auntie K came today and said that Edgar wanted to know when I was going there again.*'

Friday 25th *'LB came to meet me today. He flirted with Sheila a lot but we are going to pictures tomorrow. Bought Mummy a tea trolley and tea set today. Spent £5:13s 0d on them.'*

Saturday 26th *'Absolutely SMASHING evening. LB says he loves me ever so much. He also says he is going to marry me. I asked him if I could be his bridesmaid and he said I could be his bride.'*

Sunday 27th *'Edna came round today. Went for a walk to Horncastle and then played Monopoly. I was dreaming of my darling LB all the time. I do love him so much. We are going out again next week.'*

Monday 28th *'Been dreaming of my LB at work today. I wish Saturday would hurry up and come. He goes in the Navy in February and he may join up for 7 years. I do hope he doesn't. I will miss him. He wanted to know if I would wait for him that long. I said yes!'*

Tuesday 29th *'PC says perhaps he will fight a duel with my darling LB for me. I do hope he doesn't.'*

Wednesday 30th *'Shirley found out she couldn't go to pictures with me after all, so I went with Auntie and Mummy. I'm glad I did as I didn't have to pay for myself.'*

OCTOBER

We all know Mary goes to the pictures a lot but the flick she sees on 7th I know becomes one of her absolute all-time favourites. Her romance with LB starts to dwindle but others take his place and impress her with their ownership of motorbikes. Emotions are up and down this month.

Thursday 1st *'Auntie went home again today. Mummy very lonely. I wish I could tell her about the trolley but I want it to be a surprise.'*

Friday 2nd *'Going to pictures with LB tomorrow, that is if he turns up. I do hope he does. Sheila told Jean that I don't have a boyfriend.'*

Saturday 3rd '*LB was so tired he didn't put his arm round me in the pictures and he wasn't going to go next week either. I was so disappointed. Then he changed his mind.*'

It's her mother's birthday on 4th '*gave Mummy the trolley and tea set today for her birthday. Daddy only gave her a box of chocolates and a card with best wishes on, she was so upset.*'

Monday 5th '*Mr M has offered to have me as his personal secretary if I can learn typing and shorthand. I would love it but I could never learn in time.*'

Tuesday 6th '*Cash keeps going wrong in cash desk. Feel very fed up. I wish LB would like me more and I hope isn't so tired on Saturday.*'

Wednesday 7th '*Went to pictures with Shirley to see "By the Light of The Silvery Moon" with Doris Day and Gordon MacRae. It was smashing.*'

Thursday 8th '*I do hope my darling LB turns up on Saturday, although I hope I can manage to get out early as Sheila wants to tell him something from Marie.*'

Friday 9th '*Going to pictures with my darling LB tomorrow. I've got a feeling something is going to go wrong though or somebody will see us or something.*'

Saturday 10th '*My feeling was right. My LB didn't turn up. I really don't know what to do about him. I love him so much; I don't want to give him up.*'

Sunday 11th '*Stayed in all day today and dreamed of LB. Got an awful stomach-ache and altogether, it's been a HORRIBLE DAY.*'

Monday 12th '*Feel quite cheerful today, goodness only knows why. Going square dancing on Wednesday.*'

Tuesday 13th '*Square dancing tomorrow. Shirley tells me about a certain boy named Ernie. She thinks I would like him.*'

Wednesday 14th 'Smashing time today or rather this evening. Shirley told Ernie and David to come and meet us from dancing and I went home on Ernie's motorbike. It was smashing.'

Thursday 15th 'Going out with Shirley, Ernie and David again tomorrow. I do like Ernie but I also like David.'

Friday 16th 'Smashing evening. Went for a super walk to some woods with Ernie. Shirley and David kept kissing and hugging in front of us so Ernie and I did the same in front of them.'

Saturday 17th 'Smashing evening. Went to pictures with Ernie. He is smashing but I still love LB a little. Ernie says he loves me.'

Sunday 18th 'Edna came round and we played Sorry, Ludo, cards and other boring games. Still, it wasn't bad. Going out with Ernie tomorrow.'

Monday 19th 'Smashing evening. Ernie put his hand right inside my knickers and tickled me. I don't know what will happen. I hope I don't have a baby. I am beginning to like Ernie more.'

Tuesday 20th 'Sarah found out about yesterday. She saw yesterday's entry and she has been giving me lectures and whatnot. I've never gone so red in my whole life. I told her it was a joke diary and I think she believed me. I hope she did.'

Nevertheless, Mary goes to the pictures with Ernie again on 21st 'smashing evening again. Ernie proposed to me and I said yes. He did what he did on Monday and I told him I didn't want to get into trouble and he said he promises he won't give me a baby. He said what he did won't give me one. I hope he is right. I think I still love LB.'

Thursday 22nd 'Stayed in and had my hair washed. Going out with Ernie tomorrow. I am beginning to like him very much but I can't get LB out of my mind though. I suppose I will in time.'

Friday 23rd *'Smashing evening again. We got soaked. Went for walk in the woods with Shirley, David and Ernie and it poured with rain. Nearly sat down in some mud and I lost my shoe as it got stuck in the mud.'*

Saturday 24th *'Went to pictures with Ernie and his cousin and his girlfriend. Saw LB. He did look lonely. I nearly left Ernie to go to LB. I was so fed up. Ernie, his cousin and girlfriend were all talking and nearly forgot I was there.'*

Sunday 25th *'Smashing day. We were going out with cousin again but we didn't thank goodness. We went for a motorbike ride all around Henley way. Then went to pictures and sat in the back row. It was smashing. Going out again tomorrow.'*

Monday 26th *'Ernie didn't phone me up so I don't expect I will be going out tonight. I think Shirley is coming to tea. I hope Ernie hasn't given me up, I was just beginning to like him.'*

Tuesday 27th *'Shirley came to tea yesterday and we stayed in all the evening. How thrilling. Had a bath this evening. Ernie didn't phone me up either. We wrote to Ernie and David telling them to meet us tomorrow.'*

Wednesday 28th *'Ernie and David didn't turn up. Shirley and I waited until 9 o'clock from 7 o'clock. We are wondering if they went to the wrong place.'*

Thursday 29th *'Feeling thoroughly fed up today. Wrote to Ernie and David asking them to phone us tomorrow. I hope Ernie has not given me up.'*

Friday 30th *'David phoned us up and said that he and Ernie were disgusted and insulted with us sending them a letter between them. Ernie has given me up but David hasn't given Shirley up.'*

Saturday 31st *'Shirley couldn't come out because she had a bad arm so I stayed in all the evening. I wrote to Ernie to apologise for writing that letter. I hope he comes back to me.'*

## NOVEMBER

The twists and turns of her relationships with boys and dating consume Mary this month when ructions occur between Shirley, Ernie and David which start to take their toll on her work, consequently getting her into trouble for being late. There's also a small brush with a few famous film stars on 3rd and Binfield Heath gets an awful lot of visits.

Sunday 1st *'Feel very miserable. Shirley is seeing David this evening. I wish I was seeing Ernie but he won't have any more to do with me.'*

Monday 2nd *'Shirley says Ernie and David told her yesterday they were going to the pictures with us tonight but they didn't turn up. David told Shirley Ernie is frightened to see me because he doesn't think I like him anymore.'*

On Tuesday 3rd Mary is feeling quite starstruck as she explains *'Had my photo taken with famous Anthony Steele and I had to ask him for his autograph. The manager of the cinema moved the crowd away and I had it taken. I expect my picture will be in the paper. I also saw famous Jack Warner.'*

Wednesday 4th *'Smashing evening. Ernie and David came but Ernie hardly spoke to me, so I went for a walk with David and Shirley. David had his arm round me all the time and he kissed me several times in front of Shirley. Ernie is jealous. David also took me home on his motorbike.'*

Thursday 5th *'Interesting evening. Ernie didn't turn up because he thought I wanted to go out with David and David when he took me home, told me he liked me a lot more than Shirley. I wish Ernie had turned up.'*

On Friday Mary goes round Edna's for the evening. She is still confused over what's happening between David and Ernie. She really likes Ernie but on Saturday 7th *'Absolutely HORRID day. Shirley rang me up and said she had finished with me. She also said Ernie had been going out with Heather the whole time and that David didn't like me anymore either.'*

Sunday 8th 'Stayed in all day. Edna didn't come round. Waited for her all afternoon. Read comics and listened to the wireless and dreamed of my Ernie.'

Monday 9th 'Ernie didn't ring me up but Shirley said he wouldn't have seen my letter until the evening so perhaps he will ring me tomorrow. Shirley came round and we talked.'

Tuesday 10th 'Ernie didn't ring me up today either and I am so disappointed. I was hoping he would so much. I think he has finished with me because David has finished with Shirley and he is frightened to come out with me alone.'

Wednesday 11th 'Went to Binfield Heath to try and see David with Shirley. We saw him but Shirley wouldn't go and speak to him. I wanted her to ask him about Ernie. I do wish he would come back to me.'

Thursday 12th 'David phoned me up today and said he had given Shirley up for good. He said Ernie wants to go back to me again so David is going to meet me from work Saturday to discuss it. I am so glad as I do so like Ernie.'

Friday 13th 'Went round Edna's today. David is coming to meet me from work tomorrow. I wonder if he'll bring Ernie. Shirley rang up, she is very jealous. I do hope Ernie comes.'

Saturday 14th 'Met David and he asked if I wanted to go to the pictures, so I went. I was very disappointed that he didn't bring Ernie, but enjoyed the pictures. It was smashing but I was jealous because Shirley met Ernie.'

Sunday 15th 'Stayed in all day and dreamed of Ernie. David said yesterday he loved me with all his heart but I wish Ernie would say that to me.'

Monday 16th 'Went over to Binfield Heath. Spoke to David and Ernie and almost convinced Ernie that I liked him and not David. In the end Ernie promised he would come back to me if I went for a walk with David, so I went with David while he went with Shirley. I was so jealous.'

Tuesday 17th 'Got into trouble yesterday for being late. Didn't get in until 10:45. Hope to go out tomorrow.'

Wednesday 18th '*Wrote to Ernie yesterday asking him if he was going to keep his promise and also asking him to come over tonight. He came over with David and said he was going to keep it and that he would phone me tomorrow.*'

Thursday 19th '*I am so disappointed. Ernie didn't phone me. I wonder if David's got anything to do with it. He was very jealous because I was talking to Ernie.*'

Friday sees Shirley and Mary go over to Binfield Heath yet again to seek out Ernie and David. Unfortunately, the boys have just gone out so the girls stop and talk to Ernie's father who says he will ask Ernie to phone Mary and ask David to go back out with Shirley. The girls pay Binfield another visit on Saturday where Mary is sure she sees Ernie but he just looks away.

Sunday 22nd '*Edna came round today. Mummy is not at all well today. She can hardly move. I feel very unhappy today as I think Ernie has given me up.*'

Monday 23rd '*Stayed in this evening as Mum not at all well. She is not to be left. Sarah at home all day today. Mrs H rang me up to ask if Sarah could go back to work tomorrow so I have got to stay.*'

Tuesday 24th '*stayed at home all day today to look after Mummy also stayed in all evening as Sarah went out with John who is on a week's leave. Ernie has definitely given me up.*'

Wednesday 25th '*Walked to Binfield Heath with Shirley in dense fog but didn't see anyone. Ernie has gone back to Heather. Wish I could hate Heather but I seem to like her, goodness only knows why. I am still really smitten with Ernie.*'

Thursday 26th '*Stayed in today and dreamed of Ernie. I wish he would come back to me. Shirley loves David but he has gone out with other girls. Boys can't have any feelings at all, I don't think.*'

Friday 27th brings Mary's sixteenth birthday and she has to work because it's a Friday but comments, '*Ernie didn't even phone me. I was hoping he would as* it's my birthday. He is the only present I really wanted although I had some very nice things.'

Saturday 28th 'Saw Heather for the first time and went out with her, Shirley and another girl named Margaret. Heather doesn't seem to care for Ernie at all. I wish he would come back to me.'

Mary stays in on Sunday to do some tidying of all her many things. She also stays in Monday and Tuesday evenings as Shirley tells her she can't go out with her. Mary notes, 'I wish she would tell me the truth as I think she is going out with David.'

## DECEMBER

A falling out between the girls at the beginning of this month, along with all the other recent emotional turmoil, probably contributes to Mary having a bad cold. Then she announces that work steps up a gear due to a company take over. Unfortunately, she doesn't mention much about Christmas this year even though she embarks on several shopping trips. And Mrs M at work sets up a blind date between Mary and her son on Christmas Eve to which he turns up wearing a skirt. How embarrassing!

Wednesday 2nd 'Found out Shirley did go out with David yesterday. Went over to Binfield Heath with Shirley and saw him, then we all decided to go to pictures in the evening. I'm glad Shirley is back with him.'

Thursday 3rd 'Feel as if I could kill myself today. Got a terrible cold and feel really ill. Shirley rang up and said David had told him I loved him but I don't, I love only one and that is Ernie.'

Friday 4th 'Feel terrible today. Got an awful cold. Went with Edna to school plays. They were very good. Shirley going out with David tonight. She absolutely HATES me now. I don't know why; I only love Ernie.'

Saturday 5th *'Shirley tells me she hates me. I would like to know what I have done. She thinks I want David but I only want Ernie. I'd be so happy if he would come back to me.'*

Sunday 6th *'Stayed in bed all morning then got up to have dinner. I stayed up in case Edna came but she didn't. Dreaming about Ernie today. I do love him.'*

Monday 7th *'Firm took over last Thursday. It really is too much work for me. I am beginning to feel really ill because of it. Missing my Ernie.'*

Tuesday 8th *'Stayed in this evening and dreamed about Ernie. I wish I could forget him, but it is impossible.'*

Wednesday 9th *'Went over Binfield Heath with Shirley but didn't see anyone. It would be so nice if Ernie came back to me and we could all go out as a foursome again.'*

Thursday 10th *'Stayed in this evening. Went out dinner time and did some Christmas shopping. Got a card for Ernie.'*

Friday 11th *'Did some more Christmas shopping today. Shirley is going out with David and Ernie tonight, the lucky thing. I do hope she tells Ernie how much I love him.'*

Saturday 12th *'Went round to watch Edna's television this evening. It was jolly good but I wish Ernie had been with me'*

Sunday 13th *'Edna supposed to have come today but she will come tomorrow now as she is going to help me home with Christmas tree.'*

Monday 14th *'Edna didn't turn up so Sheila let me take tree home on her bike. Saw Colin next door and he said he would pop in to see me at work tomorrow.'*

Tuesday 15<sup>th</sup> '*Colin came in today with Frank his brother. Both are smashing. They are coming in again tomorrow. Went round Shirley's this evening.*'

Wednesday 16<sup>th</sup> '*Went to Maidenhead with Shirley and her mum this afternoon. Had a lovely time but very tired. Stayed round Shirley's all evening. Jolly good.*'

Thursday 17<sup>th</sup> '*Stayed in all evening. Good day at work today, just a bit tired. I sent a card to Ernie today.*'

Friday 18<sup>th</sup> '*Worked until 7 pm today. Had a smashing time with RR the new salesman. I still like Ernie though.*'

Saturday 19<sup>th</sup> '*Went to pictures with Brian. It wasn't at all thrilling. He sat the whole time just watching the film not really noting I was there. I was thinking of Ernie all the time.*'

Sunday 20<sup>th</sup> '*Edna came round this afternoon. I do like her. We had such fun.*'

Monday 21<sup>st</sup> '*Went round Shirley's and brought her back home with me. She stayed for the evening. I wonder if Ernie will come back to me. I hope it will be soon.*'

Tuesday 22<sup>nd</sup> '*Had smashing time with two of the stock takers today. Yesterday was fun too.*'

Wednesday 23<sup>rd</sup> '*Worked all day. Went round Shirley's this evening and helped clean some silver. Still thinking of Ernie.*'

Thursday 24<sup>th</sup> Christmas Eve '*Went to pictures with Mrs M's son Bob. He is smashing. He wore his kilt and everybody stared at us. He does kiss funnily but he is nice.*'

Bob coincidentally goes off to Kenya for two and a half years in January 1954 after writing her a romantic poem by the famous author Robert Burns. He does write to her regularly thereafter and they remain friends.

Friday 25th Christmas Day '*Quite a good day today. The sun has been shining all this week and not a cloud in the sky. Mum and Dad have been teasing me about Bob.*'

Saturday 26th Boxing Day '*Grandma, Grandad, Auntie O and Sandy (her little dog) came up today. Played with Sandy most of the time.*'

Edna comes over on 27th and they play Monopoly most of the day, then they both venture to the pictures on 28th.

Tuesday 29th '*Stayed in today. Went round Palace after work and got two seats for tomorrow. I am going with Edna.*'

On Wednesday 30th, '*Had a letter from Bob today. Went to the Palace in evening to see Cinderella, it was good. I've been teased awfully about Bob. I do like him very much.*'

Her final thoughts on the last day of the year are '*promised to go to pictures with Brian tomorrow and a boy called Johnny on Saturday. I feel horrid about Mrs M's Bob. I hope she won't tell him.*'

# 1954

A slightly bigger and informative diary called 'Letts School-Girls Diary' which details within its first pages…know your road signs, careers for girls, tables of Latin and French verbs, logarithms, the metric system, weights and measures and a list of recommended books to read. There is also a section on…do you know, some interesting facts about past events, along with a list of all the countries of the world, details of Morse code, some tips on first aid, how to look after your cat and how to knit.

## JANUARY

In January Mary returns to work and quite a few boys platonically asking to take her to the pictures. Trouble is she's not allowed to go out with any of them alone forcing her into finding plausible excuses to tell her parents for going out each time. It's a fairly quiet month with days off often spent seeing Edna, reading the papers, listening to the wireless, playing cards or games and arguing with her mother and/or Sarah. Feeling a bit fed up at the moment, rows spark easily at home and she also argues with Sheila at work, leading to Mary wanting a job in London. She mentions several times about how nice the weather is for this time of year remarking on how blue the sky has been.

Friday 1st '*Went to the pictures with Brian from work. He is a very nice boy but not my type. He makes me sick. I still miss my Ernie although I don't know whether I like him as much as I did. I like Bob.*'

Saturday 2nd '*Went to pictures with a boy called Johnny. He is an electrician who is working at Newberys on our lights. He is fairly nice but it is very worrying having to find excuses to tell Mummy all the time. I don't really like anyone at the moment, not love any way.*'

On Sunday Mary stays in all day just commenting on the lovely weather.

Monday 4th 'Shirley came round this evening. She is funny. I went to Paxton House and saw her classroom. She says that Ernie keeps asking about me.'

Tuesday 5th 'Went to pictures with Sheila and another electrician. He is smashing. Sheila and I have had a lot of fun today and I think I am falling in love with Mr R at work.'

Mary has the morning off work on Wednesday 6th and goes to the Palace to watch a ballet with her mother, Sarah and Auntie V where she comments, 'jolly good, I wish I could ballet dance.'

Thursday 7th 'Stayed in today. Johnny wanted me to go out with him this evening but I said no! I am going out with him tomorrow.'

Friday 8th 'Mr R got me out in the yard yesterday and kissed me. Boy! Was that smashing. I think I am beginning to love him. Went out with Johnny this evening and we went down the prom. He almost undressed me. Blimey, I shall have to be careful with him.'

Johnny asks her out again on the 9th but Mary has to say no as she is frightened Edna might go round to Florida Court and she has been using her as an excuse to go out with him.

Sunday 10th 'I don't know whether I like Johnny or not. I think I do. I wish I were allowed to go out with boys. When I go out with them, I am worried all the time as to whether anyone will see me and to getting home on time.'

Monday 11th she goes to the pictures with her sister Sarah 'sometimes I quite like her but other times I feel I could strangle her. Still, I suppose I shall have to put up with her.'

Tuesday 12th 'Stayed in tonight. Supposed to be going out with Johnny tomorrow. I like him I think but I certainly am not going to get serious with anyone again.'

Johnny and Mary go to the pictures and then for a walk on Wednesday 13<sup>th</sup> '*I don't really know whether I like him or not. He says he loves me already but I'm not being taken in by that again. I'm going to play hard to get and I will see if he really wants me or not.*'

Work is very busy on Thursday 14<sup>th</sup> when Mary also receives a letter from Bob. '*He wrote me a poem and it was all about he didn't want to leave his Mary! He has gone to Kenya for 2½ years now.*'

Friday 15<sup>th</sup> Mary doesn't finish work until 7pm but she still goes out in the evening with Johnny and again with him on Saturday 16<sup>th</sup> stating, '*went for an awful long walk then went to Palmer Park. Boy! He's nearly as good as Ernie.*'

Sunday 17<sup>th</sup> '*Stayed in all day today and waited for Edna but she didn't come.*'

Monday 18<sup>th</sup> '*Stayed in again today. Going out with Johnny tomorrow. He is a very nice boy but I'm not going to get serious this time.*'

Tuesday 19<sup>th</sup> '*I came on today and when I was running over to the chemist I fell over in the middle of the road and cut my knee open and cut my knuckles nearly off. I've got an awful stomach-ache because of it but even then, I went to the pictures with Johnny. I was in agony.*'

Wednesday afternoon Mary stays in and nurses her leg which is causing her a great deal of pain. '*I feel really ill and my stomach is nearly killing me and I can't move my leg.*'

Johnny leaves to go to Salisbury on Thursday and she won't be seeing him again for a long while, suddenly spiking a feeling of loneliness. On the plus side though, her leg is feeling much better and she receives an invite to the pictures on Saturday from Brian.

Friday 22<sup>nd</sup> '*Went round Edna's today. She is talking about working in London. I wish I could, but I don't think I would be allowed.*'

Saturday 23rd *'Went to pictures with Brian. I've never had such a boring evening. We stood in a queue for nearly one and a half hours. I don't think I will go with him again.'*

Sunday 24th *Stayed in all day today. Edna didn't come round so I expect she will on Tuesday.'*

Monday 25th *'Stayed in all day again. Feel very lonely without Johnny. I think I like him but I'm not going to get serious.'*

Tuesday 26th *'Edna came round today and still talking about working in London. She is going to try and get me an interview.'*

Wednesday 27th *'Stayed in all the afternoon and evening. Very bored. Keep having rows with Mummy and Sarah.'*

Thursday 28th *'Really fed up today. Had row with Mummy and Sarah and also Sheila at work. Wish I could kill myself. I feel really ill.'*

Friday 29th *'Went round Edna's. She didn't ask about the job because she wasn't sure whether I would be allowed to go, so I will have to ask, then she will.'*

Saturday 30th *'Johnny came home today and I went to the pictures with him. He is very nice and he is crazy about me but I don't want to get serious as I have been heartbroken before now.'*

Sunday 31st *'Stayed in all day today. Daddy won't let me work in London. Sheila got sacked yesterday at Newberys. She will leave next Friday.'* Mary doesn't say why Sheila got fired but is apparently looking forward to her going as she states she will be able to work much better without her.

### FEBRUARY

Some relief for Mary this month as she is given the OK to date Johnny on the understanding that she doesn't take things too far, and an adversary leaves

Newberys much to her delight. The end of the month brings uncertainty over having her hair cut very short which I assume is an attempt to help make her look or feel more grown up now she is sixteen.

Monday 1st *'Was expecting Shirley to come round today but she didn't turn up. Feel very miserable, although I am looking forward to Sheila leaving.'*

Tuesday 2nd *'Stayed in again today. Wish Saturday would hurry up and come. I am really fed up with Sheila at work and will work much better without her.'*

Wednesday 3rd *'Expected Edna to come today. Waited for an hour for her but she didn't come. Could have gone to the pictures with Sarah and Rita.'*

Thursday 4th *'Going out with Johnny tomorrow. I do like him but I also like Bob. It will be awfully difficult when Bob comes home unless Johnny has finished with me by then.'*

Friday 5th *'Went for a walk with Johnny today. He is very nice but I'm certainly not going to let myself love him as I will only be heartbroken again.'*

Saturday 6th *'Went to pictures with Johnny. I wish I could make up my mind whether I like him or Bob best. I know Johnny better than Bob but I don't think that makes any difference.'*

Sheila leaves Arthur Newberys on 6th February and on 7th Mary writes, *'Sheila left yesterday thank goodness. She has been awful this week. Work is absolutely wonderful without her. I am so happy now that she has gone.'*

But on Tuesday 9th *'Sheila came to Newberys today. I thought I had got rid of her forever. She spoilt my day completely.'*

Wednesday 10th *'Mummy has found out I went with Johnny to the pictures last week. She says she doesn't mind as long as I don't do anything I shouldn't. I am so glad they know as I needn't worry any more. Mummy, Daddy and Sarah have all been teasing me this evening about Johnny. I gave him two photos of me last week and am beginning to like him more than ever.'*

Thursday 11<sup>th</sup> *'Going out with Johnny again tomorrow. I'm going to tell Mummy. Went to the pictures with Sarah yesterday and with Edna this evening.'*

Saturday 13<sup>th</sup> *'Went to the pictures for the fourth time running again today. I paid for Johnny as he was broke. That means I have paid for all the four pictures. Phew, it has left a hole in my pocket.'*

It's now a great weight off her mind that her parents and Sarah know about Johnny but they constantly tease her about him. The following week is a quiet one with Mary going round Edna's to watch television or just staying at home after work. She goes to the pictures again on Saturday 20<sup>th</sup> with Johnny, paying again as he only earns 27s per week. *'I wish he would give me up so I could concentrate on Bob who I like much better.'*

The week commencing 21<sup>st</sup> has Mary worrying about having her hair cut off. It suggests she is going from longish hair to really short. Perhaps this was a way of making her come across more grown up or maybe was the current fashion.

Monday 22<sup>nd</sup> *'Can't have hair cut tomorrow so am having it done on Thursday. I do wish I wasn't going to.'*

Tuesday 23<sup>rd</sup> *'Went to the pictures with Johnny. He nearly shot me because I told him about having my hair off.'*

Thursday 25<sup>th</sup> *'had hair off today. It looks absolutely horrible. I must have been out of my mind.'*

But, by Friday 26<sup>th</sup> *'hair looks quite nice today. Everyone been teasing me, I love it. I think I will like it when I get used to it being so short. Went to pictures with Johnny.'*

Saturday 27<sup>th</sup> *'Went to pictures with Johnny again today. He keeps teasing me about my hair as well but I think he likes it really; I think I do.'*

Sunday 28<sup>th</sup> *'Stayed in today and did nothing but listen to wireless and read papers.'*

## MARCH

Johnny is still very interested in Mary but she, on the other hand, seems not so sure about him and mentions several times that she wishes he would give her up. The start of March proves to be enjoyable at work as it is quiet but fun, especially with Ronnie and Gerald, two of her new co-workers and no Sheila. Ronnie asks her to go dancing with him but she says she couldn't. Having stayed in Monday evening, Mary ventures to the pictures with Johnny on Tuesday 2<sup>nd</sup> noting, *'I wish Johnny would give me up as I don't know whether I like him or not.'*

Wednesday 3<sup>rd</sup> *'Stayed in all afternoon. Very boring time. Nothing much to do.'*

Thursday 4<sup>th</sup> *'Stayed in again this evening and had my hair washed. I wonder what it will look like tomorrow.'*

Friday 5<sup>th</sup> *'Went to pictures with Johnny again today. Had fun at work with Ron and Gerald.'*

Sunday 7<sup>th</sup> *'Stayed in again today. Bit boring, although very nice not to have to do much work.'*

Monday 8<sup>th</sup> *'Stayed in again this evening. Been having some real fun with Gerald and Ron. Gerald asked me to the pictures with him today. Bought a new coat.'*

Mary goes to the pictures with Johnny in the evening of the 9<sup>th</sup> recalling, *'been having an awful lot of fun again today with Gerald and Ron.'*

Not sure why but on 10<sup>th</sup> March *'went to crematorium in the afternoon and to a mannequin parade in the evening with Pam and Edna, it was lovely.'*

Mary is still seeing Johnny regularly and paying for them both virtually every time they go out. She notes that she wants him to give her up but says '*he keeps telling me how much he loves me.*'

Sunday 14th '*Went round to Edna's to listen to the television. It was jolly good. I had to get a taxi home as I missed the last bus.*'

During the week beginning 15th Mary comes down with a terrible cold and states '*lost my voice, got an awful cold, feel very ill and can hardly breath. Been teased terribly at work because I couldn't talk. Stayed in and did jigsaw puzzles.*' By Friday she is feeling better though and goes to the pictures with Johnny on Saturday.

Sunday 21st '*Stayed in all day today and listened to the wireless. I do wish I was rich.*'

Monday 22nd '*Edna came round tonight and we played cards. It was so thrilling! She is nice though.*'

Tuesday 23rd '*Went to pictures with Johnny this evening. I do wish he would finish with me.*'

Wednesday 24th '*Went swimming this afternoon with Mrs M's daughter. Auntie K and Uncle T came.*'

Thursday evenings seem to be turning into hair washing nights as she has mentioned this happening for the last three weeks.

Friday 26th '*Went to the pictures with Johnny this evening. He is so nice but I wish he would finish with me.*'

Saturday 27th '*Went to pictures with Johnny again this evening. I had some fun at work with Gerald and Ron today. Ron is engaged, still Gerald is very nice.*'

Sunday 28th '*Stayed in all today and listened to wireless. I wish Johnny would give me up.*'

Monday 29th *'Stayed in all evening and cleaned silver. Auntie V is coming on Wednesday, worst luck.'*

Tuesday 30th *'Went to the pictures with Johnny this evening. He had to borrow money from his mother to take me as he was broke. He says he can't come on Friday, but I bet its money trouble.'*

Wednesday 31st *'Went swimming with Mrs M's daughter and three other girls. I don't like them very much as they are very common still it's someone to go out with. I do love swimming.'*

## APRIL

Easter comes and goes and it looks like Mary gets one of her wishes granted this month. Johnny tries to take their relationship to an unwelcome level and although another suitor heroically comes on the scene, Mary becomes quite depressed by the end of the month.

Auntie V turns up on Thursday 1st for a week's stay *'stayed in all evening. Very lively I must say. Not going out tomorrow, feel rather unhappy and miserable.'*

Friday 2nd *'stayed in this evening as I had to work until 7 o'clock. Auntie V came yesterday for a week and Auntie K came today.'*

Having visited the pictures with Johnny on Saturday evening, on Sunday Margaret and Auntie V go to church and Mary listens to the wireless, having a day in. Then on Monday Sarah does Mary's hair in readiness for her going to the pictures with Johnny on Tuesday.

Wednesday 7th *'Went to London today. Ivy Benson played while we had tea. I also saw Sandra Dorne. We went into a news theatre for an hour then went round the shops.'* Mary notes how she feels very tired the day after because of all this excitement and that Auntie leaves on 8th.

Friday 9th *'Went round Edna's this evening. Stayed until 9:30. I do like her. We are going to start hiking again soon.'*

Saturday 10th *'Went to pictures with Johnny again this evening. I am beginning to like him more; I wish I didn't.'*

Sunday 11th *'Edna came up today and we went for a long walk, we then played cards and listened to the wireless.'*

Monday 12th *'Stayed in this evening. Not going out with Johnny tomorrow but going on Wednesday instead.'*

Tuesday 13th *'Johnny rang up and said he is going to YMCA tomorrow so I won't be going out with him. Had a good cry. I didn't think I would mind if ever he let me down, but I do.'*

Wednesday 14th *'Went swimming with Pat and Betty today. It was lovely. I haven't heard from Bob for over a fortnight.'*

Thursday evening Mary goes to the pictures with Johnny then on Good Friday *'stayed at home all day. Very boring day but beautiful weather though. Wish I had lots of money and also lots of lovely clothes.'*

Saturday 17th *'Went to the pictures with Johnny this evening. He says he could never leave me as he loves me so much. I almost wish Bob would give me up as I am beginning to like Johnny better than him.'*

On Easter Sunday Mary visits her Grandma and Grandad in the morning, cycles to Theale and back in the afternoon then in the evening cycles to Edna's and back. As if that wasn't enough, she then goes for a ride around where they live. It seems like her father has finally relented and bought her a bike, as this very much sounds to me like someone playing with a new toy, perhaps one that was given to her for Easter.

Monday 19th *'Went to pictures with Mum and Daddy. Went for a cycle ride first and then again afterwards.'*

Tuesday 20th *'Went to the pictures with Johnny. Had a bit of a row about letting him do something. I wouldn't let him and he kept on and on. In the end, we just parted. Johnny was so miserable but it can't be helped. I don't know the facts of life so I don't know what would happen. I do wish I had been told.'*

Wednesday 21st *'Went swimming today and it was smashing. I wish I could go every day.'*

Thursday 22nd *'I fell off my bicycle today or rather got knocked off by a bus. It hurts terribly. The other electrician at work, LH, gave me a lift home on his motorbike.'* And now she is quite smitten with and likes him a lot more than Johnny, writing *'I'm afraid I've got it bad this time.'* She is now in a quandary, thinking about LH, Johnny, Gerald and KQ, who walks her home Saturday evening and gives her an Easter egg, some chocolates and also wants her to go out with him. She also gets a letter from Bob the same day! *'I wish I could die. I wouldn't have all this worry then.'*

Monday 26th *'went round to Joan's today. She has a baby girl called Christine. Such a sweet little thing with pretty auburn curls. I'm making a little coat for her.'* Seeing the baby makes her think about the facts of life which she admits to knowing nothing about but wishes she had been told.

Tuesday 27th *'Went to pictures with Johnny. Had another row about the facts of life. I think he nearly gave me up. I half wish he had and half glad he didn't. I wish I could make up my mind.'* She also goes to the pictures on 28th but with Sarah and Rita this time.

Mary goes through a bit of a low patch during the end of April and on Thursday 29th relates *'stayed in all evening and did some knitting. Everything has gone wrong today. Everyone is calling me a bad-tempered person. I do wish I had the nerve to commit suicide.'*

Friday 30th *'didn't go out this evening as I had to work late. Edna came round and I was rather annoyed as I was very tired and miserable. I just don't know what's wrong with me lately.'*

## MAY

A few firsts for Mary this month…some good, some bad! There are also a couple of new members to the family. She finds herself very busy at work due to climbing the ladder and is still contemplating her non-existent knowledge of the facts of life.

Saturday 1st *'Went to the pictures with Johnny tonight. He is so nice. He said I'll never know just how much he loves me. I wish I had the nerve to commit suicide. I have the feeling that everyone hates me except Johnny of course and that I am no good to anyone. I do wish I could die.'*

Sunday 2nd '*Stayed in all day. Feel very unhappy today. I just don't know what's the matter with me lately. I have been snapping everyone's heads off at the least little thing and I have been feeling so very tired.*'

Things soon improve though and something that helps is Pat at work getting the sack on Monday 3rd which Mary says she is really pleased about '*I'm so glad, as she gets on my nerves quite a lot. I think I am jealous of her and Mr R.*' Mary is then offered Pat's job of stock clerk for an extra 10s which now gives her a weekly wage of £3 5s 0d.

Tuesday 4th '*Went to pictures with Johnny this evening. I do wish I could give him up. Although I like him an awful lot, he is really too good for me.*'

Wednesday 5th '*Went to the pictures with Mummy today. Sarah gave us a free pass. It was very good but I did miss Johnny putting his arm around me.*'

On Friday Mary goes to the pictures with Johnny '*Sarah was on the same bus. She said she likes Johnny very much and so do I.*'

Saturday 8th '*Went to the pictures with Johnny again today. I like him very much. I think he is getting tired of me and I'm not at all surprised as I won't let him do anything. I wish I knew the facts of life but I have never been told. All I want to know is what does a boy have to do to the girl, but I just don't know.*'

Sunday 9th '*Bill left work on Friday and I do wish he hadn't as I was getting very fond of him. I shall miss him very much. Pat left yesterday. I don't think I'm sorry to see her go. Edna came round today to ask me to go to tea with her so I had to go. I was disappointed as I had to miss "Life with the Lions" on the radio.*'

Monday 10th '*Started my new job as stock clerk today. Phew, what a life. Never known such hard work before. Still, I shall be glad of the extra 10/- at the end of the week.*'

Wednesday 12th '*Went swimming with Pat today. It is wonderful. I would love to live on a desert island, wearing only a sarong and swimming all the time and not doing any work. I do wish I could get shipwrecked, ALONE though.*'

Thursday 13<sup>th</sup> *'We are terribly busy at work all this week. All I do is jump up and answer the phone and then sit down and it rings again so I have to jump once more.'*

Friday 14<sup>th</sup> *'Went to the pictures with Johnny this evening. He is very nice but he will keep on at me to let him do something but I won't let him. I do wish I hadn't started going out with him.'*

Saturday 15<sup>th</sup> *'Went to the pictures with Johnny again this evening. Afterwards he made me hold his thing. It was horrible. Big, slimy and wet. I just had to do it though, he was in quite a state because I said I wouldn't. I wish I knew the facts of life.'*

Sunday 16<sup>th</sup> *'stayed in all day and helped Daddy make a new hall table.'*

Monday 17<sup>th</sup> *'Edna came round this evening to ask if I was going to a play with her tomorrow. I had forgotten all about it so I will have to let Johnny down.'*

Tuesday 18<sup>th</sup> *'I did feel sorry for Johnny today. He tried not to mind me letting him down and he had bought me some chocolate. He said I could still have it even though I had to cancel going out with him.'*

Having been for a swim with Pat on Wednesday 19<sup>th</sup> Mary states *'went to the pictures after. A boy at the baths gave me a cigarette,'* which Mary smokes the day after *'smoked my first cigarette today. I was quite surprised I didn't even feel sick.'* The day after that she has three! She is wondering how to give Bob up now when he comes back as she's made up her mind that it's Johnny who she likes the best.

Sunday 23<sup>rd</sup> *'Johnny came round today for the first time. My mother and father like him very much and so do I. He told me not to fall in love with him. I don't know why. I suppose it's because he will give me up very soon and doesn't want to hurt me. I do hope he doesn't.'*

The following day, Mary buys a tortoise exclaiming *'it is a sweet little thing. I've named it Sleepy because it is nearly always asleep. I don't know whether it is a boy or girl.'*

She goes to the pictures with Johnny again on Tuesday 25th where she notes, *'I think he is cooling off me a bit, although I hope he isn't, as he is so nice.'*

Wednesday 26th *'Went swimming today. Then I went baby sitting at the Smiths next door. I watched television all evening.'*

Thursday 27th in the evening Edna comes round and Friday evening brings another picture night with Johnny.

On 29th she buys another tortoise *'they are both sweet'* but doesn't give its name. She takes them to show Grandma and Grandad in June. That evening she goes to the pictures again with Johnny. *'He is so nice but I wish Bob would write and give me up. Going round to Johnnys' tomorrow.'*

Sunday 30th *'Went round Johnny's today and met his mother. She is very sweet; I do like her and also feel sorry for her. Went to the pictures with Johnny in the evening. I do love him so much. I wish I didn't but I can't help it.'*

Monday 31st *'Stayed at home all evening and exercised my tortoise's, then had my hair washed. Going to the pictures with Johnny tomorrow. I do like him. He is so nice and I'm glad Mummy and Daddy like him.'*

## JUNE

June arrives and Mary starts spending even more time with Johnny, going to the pictures, walking in the park, playing Monopoly, watching cricket at the prom, going round to his house and him visiting hers, but it seems things are not to be. Mary this month is mainly consumed and worried about dating two really nice boys with her feelings swinging from one to the other. She does a few babysitting stints and still enjoys going for her bike rides around the area and swimming. Work is challenging at present and it doesn't help when her boss scares her on 12th or when she gets into trouble on 26th.

Tuesday 1st *'Feel very fed up. Johnny came to meet me from work and said he wanted to watch cricket, so we watched cricket all evening. Then we went for a walk along by the river. I wonder why I love him so much. I just can't guess but I do, so much.'*

Wednesday 2nd *'I went swimming in the afternoon and then went to the pictures in the evening with Pat. Got an awful stomach ache, feel dizzy and cold. I don't know what the matter is with me lately.'*

Thursday 3rd *'Stayed at home all evening. A boy called Danny (used to go to school with him) came to meet me from work today and asked me to go out with him. I had to say no. I like him very much but I like Johnny a lot better. I have felt really ill today.'*

Friday 4th *'Went for wonderful bike ride this evening until half past eight, then went down to Prospect Park and laid down on the grass. It was wonderful. I do love Johnny. I wonder if he loves me. I do hope so.'*

Saturday 5th *'Went to pictures with Johnny. Got caught in the rain without a coat so I borrowed Johnny's rain mac. He got very wet but he keeps saying he'd do anything for me. I do like him so much and don't know what I'd do without him. I think he loves me.'*

Sunday 6th *'Johnny came round at 2:30 and stayed until 5:45 then went to the pictures. I do like him so much and I don't know what I would do if he ever gave me up. I wonder if he really likes me.'*

On bank holiday Monday *'Johnny came round at 2:30 again today and we went for a walk in Prospect Park. Afterwards we went home for tea, and then went to the pictures. He said he wouldn't want another girlfriend. I wish I know whether that was true. I hope it is.'*

Tuesday 8th *'Went round Johnny's this evening and played Monopoly (I won). I do like him. Not seeing him until Friday now. It does seem like a long time. I wish it would hurry up and come.'*

Mary goes swimming in the afternoon of Wednesday 9th and states how freezing the pool is as it is not heated. She then goes babysitting for the Smiths in the evening just watching television and dreaming of Johnny.

Thursday 10th '*Stayed in this evening. LH was working at Newberys today. He took me home on his motor bike. I think I like him even more than Johnny. He is so nice. He said Johnny had told him he wouldn't mind a bit if anyone else took me to the pictures.*'

Friday 11th '*Oh my mind's in such a muddle. I told LH I would go to the pictures with him because Johnny told him he wouldn't mind if I did go out with anyone else. I really like LH very much but Johnny was so sorry for himself this evening, that I hadn't the heart to give him up. I just don't know what to do. I like them both.*'

Work is busy at the moment and it's not helpful when the boss comes to work drunk on Saturday 12th '*Mr W was drunk this afternoon. He did scare me as I had to work with him and he kept saying peculiar things and he wouldn't work properly at all. I had to keep prodding him all the time.*'

Sunday 13th '*Johnny made me cry this evening. I did feel a fool as I hate to let anyone see me cry. He said our friendship ought to end because he didn't earn enough to take a girl out. I didn't know just how much I liked him until I thought about it ending. Now I know he is the only boy for me.*'

Monday 14th sees Mary babysitting again '*went babysitting this evening. Edna came as well. Had to put Christine on her little pot. She is a sweet little thing.*'

Tuesday 15th '*Went down prom and watched cricket with Johnny. It was freezing. I have promised LH I will go to pictures with him tomorrow. I don't know whether I want to or not. I did when he asked me, but I have seen Johnny since then who I love very much.*'

Wednesday 16th '*Went to pictures with LH. He is very nice but I don't know whether I like him as much as Johnny. He kissed me lots of times (nicely). He asked me to go out with him again on Saturday. I wish things would straighten out.'*

Thursday 17<sup>th</sup> *'LH was at work again today. He took me home on his motorbike. I told him I liked him and he said he liked me. I wish Johnny would give me up although I still like him very much. I just don't know what to do. I often wonder if it is possible to love two people at the same time.'*

Mary and Johnny go to the pictures on Friday 18<sup>th</sup> where she admits that she feels sorrier for him than loves him. *'He is very nice and I like him a lot but I also like LH. Oh dear, I wish something would happen to make me drop dead. I'm in such a muddle.'*

On Saturday 19<sup>th</sup> she does indeed go to the pictures with LH and states how she doesn't want to hurt either him or Johnny but fears this might happen before long due to her inexperience in these matters. On Sunday still contemplating this, she stays in for much of the day only venturing out for a short while to show Grandma and Grandpa her tortoises.

Monday 21<sup>st</sup> *'Went babysitting this evening for the Smiths. Going out with Johnny tomorrow and then with LH on Wednesday. I do wish Johnny would give me up as I think I like LH best.'*

Tuesday 22<sup>nd</sup> *'Went swimming with Johnny. It was freezing only 63 degrees. I do wish I had a better figure. Then went home to Johnny's and we were alone in the house—boy, did we have some fun. Johnny said he loved me and I think I love him.'* She went swimming again on Wednesday afternoon with Pat and then goes to the pictures with LH in the evening, concluding, *'I think I am slightly in love with both of them.'*

Thursday 24<sup>th</sup> *'LH came to meet me on his motorbike. He wants me to go out with him on Sunday. I said I would try. I do wish I could make up my mind about him and Johnny.'*

Friday 25<sup>th</sup> *'Johnny gave me up today. I have realised it is him I love and only him. I am heartbroken. He said he couldn't afford to have a girlfriend. He didn't want to give me up and asked if I would go back with him when he had some money. I said yes. I wish we could have worked something out so that we could have seen each other at least once a week but there wasn't time. We just kissed, said no hard feelings and then parted. Oh goodness, what am I to do without him. I cried myself to sleep tonight, I just don't want to live without him.'*

On Saturday at Newbery's Mary gets in trouble for not doing her work properly probably because she is thinking about Johnny and notes how she has been crying most of the day. *'I just don't know how I got through the day today. I want Johnny to come back to me more than anything in the world. I really must go round and see him.'*

But not to worry as in the morning of Sunday 27th she pops round to his house to ask him to come back to her and he does. *'I went round to his house to ask him and when I got there, I just couldn't bring myself to say any of the things I had planned such as "Johnny I can't live without you" and "I love you" and "I can't let you go." Instead, when he asked me why I was there, I just said I don't know and can't you guess. Still, he is back now and I am so thrilled.'* The same day she takes an afternoon river trip with LH and frequents the local picture house with him in the evening, all the time thinking of Johnny!

Monday 28th *'Feeling wonderfully happy today. My darling Johnny's come back to me. I wish he wouldn't worry about money so much. It wouldn't worry me if he hadn't even a penny, I like him so much. I do hope he likes me.'*

Tuesday 29th *'Went to the pictures with my Johnny this evening. I was mad at him though as he showed the letter, I wrote to him on Saturday to his brother and his mate. I do wish I didn't love him so much because I'm sure he doesn't like me all that much. I think he and his pals have a good laugh at me.'*

Wednesday morning is terribly busy at work so Mary stays in all afternoon and evening with Auntie V and comments, *'very thrilling I must say!'*

## JULY

Thankfully things do sort themselves out this month leaving Mary heartbroken but not for too long especially as LH woos her with a trip to London at the end of the month. Her parents take a holiday without their girls and a tragic accident happens to one of the new members of the family.

Thursday 1st '*Went to the pictures with LH. When we were saying goodnight, Mummy and Edna came out. I had to get behind LH and hope that they didn't see me. Mummy stood right next to LH. I could have touched her and my heart nearly stopped. Still, they didn't see me. LH said Johnny had told him about what we do. He said he didn't believe it and I told him it wasn't true.*'

Mary goes to the pictures with Johnny on Friday night where he nearly gives her up again, making her wonder why she likes him so much. She then goes to the pictures with LH on Saturday night. This carries on for much of the following week with Mary going out with both on alternate nights, liking the one she is with the most when she is with them and trusting that things will straighten themselves out before long. '*I don't think I could bear it if Johnny gave me up and yet I would be sad if LH didn't take me out any more. I am in such a muddle. I think the only way to sort it out is to kill myself. I do wish I had got the nerve. If this goes on much longer, I think I will just have to.*'

Sunday 4th '*Went to work this afternoon for three and a half hours. Went to the pictures with Johnny tonight. He is wonderful, every time I look at him, I get butterflies in my stomach. I do hope he won't give me up.*'

Wednesday 7th '*Went to school for open day with Edna. Saw RB but didn't stop to speak to him. I do love my Johnny. I like LH but love my Johnny best. I wonder if I will ever marry him.*'

Mary goes to the pictures Thursday evening with Johnny and Friday evening with LH. '*He is nice but every time I look at him, I wish he were Johnny. I can't help feeling sorry for LH, because he is such a nice boy, but there, I love my Johnny and that's all there is to it. He makes me go weak at the knees.*'

Saturday 10th '*Went for a bike ride with Johnny and stopped in some very long grass. Had a wonderful time. Oh, I do love him so much and think I would die if he gave me up again. He says he loves me but I wish I could prove it was true.*'

Sunday 11th '*Went for a walk in afternoon with Johnny then to pictures in evening. I wish I knew whether he really meant it when he told me he loved me.*'

Monday 12th '*Went round to Edna's today after work and we went for a walk along by the river. I wish Johnny had been with me. I love him so much. I wish he didn't have to play cricket so often.*'

Tuesday 13th brings heartache with Johnny giving Mary up again, '*Johnny gave me up today. I am broken-hearted. I really do love him. He said he liked me a lot but that he would have to play cricket nearly every day so it wouldn't be fair to me.*' This obviously makes her feel rotten as she explains on 14th '*feel very miserable this morning but brightened up a bit this afternoon. I went swimming with LH in the afternoon, then into Lyons for tea, then to the pictures and then for a ride down to Purley and sat down by the river.*'

By the following day she is feeling a lot brighter although relates that every time she thinks of Johnny her heart stops beating. There's nothing like a bit of retail therapy to help cure a broken heart so that evening '*went to London with Edna. Bought lovely frock. I do like travelling. I will have to do more of it later on.*'

Friday 16th '*Wonderful evening. Went to pictures with LH, Gerald, Brian and Pat, all from work. I do like LH and am wondering whether I like him better than Johnny. I think I will later on, but on second thoughts, I do now.*'

Staying in all evening on Saturday, Mary takes a warm bath and thinks about LH. He is taking her to meet his parents for tea tomorrow and she is a bit nervous.

Sunday 18th '*Wonderful day. LH came round for me then we went round to Purley to have a swim but it was too cold. We then went to Basingstoke to have tea. His folks are nice. Then we went to church and I saw LH in the choir.*

*Afterwards, we went for a walk, then back to his place for supper. After that I came home.'*

On Monday 19<sup>th</sup> Mary is feeling in a very good mood and notes that she thinks she is really in love at last, with the wonderful LH, as he hasn't left her thoughts once all day. A sad event takes place on the same day which Mary writes about in the back of her diary. Her lovely little tortoise "Sleepy" dies. (See end of the year)

Tuesday 20<sup>th</sup> *'Went to the pictures with LH. When we got to Florida Court LH felt really ill, he sat down in the middle of the pavement. He really makes me quite worried. I do hope he will get home alright on his motorbike.'*

Wednesday 21<sup>st</sup> *'LH came to meet me from work today. He didn't go to work as he was still feeling a bit unwell. I am so glad he got home alright on his bike but it took him one hour, fifteen minutes. He lives in Basingstoke. We went swimming at Purley and I had a wonderful time. He is so nice; I don't know what I would do without him.'*

Thursday 22<sup>nd</sup> *'LH met me from work today, then he came round to Florida Court and had some tea with Sarah and I (Mummy and Daddy were out as they are on their hols). We then went in the front room and I sat on his lap and we listened to the wireless. They had "Never" on it and when the line "My love, I love you so much" was sung, he just looked at me straight in the eyes as if he was saying it to me. LH is the sort of boy I would like to marry. You never know, I might do one day. He is so polite and well mannered.'* They go swimming together at Purley on Friday, where she comments, *'it was freezing and raining, but I still enjoyed it. LH is just so nice.'*

Mary finishes work on Saturday 24<sup>th</sup> for a two-week break *'thank goodness.'* She notes how bad the weather has been lately *'absolutely pouring down with raining.'* No change there with the typical British summer then! *'What a lovely start to a holiday! Mind you Sarah cheered me up. She brought a little kitten home this evening, it is a sweet little thing.'* The following day, *'stayed in again all day today and nursed the kitten. It is a little white one with a black tail. I do love it so much. Daddy doesn't know about it yet; it is rather worrying.'*

Tuesday 27th '*took kitten to Wokingham and back this afternoon. I carried it all the way. Weather still not at all nice, I do wish the sun would hurry up and shine.*' Mary goes to the pictures on Tuesday and Thursday with LH stating, '*weather still horrid*' and '*LH is really wonderful. I do like him better than I ever imagined I could like anyone. I like him better than I even like Johnny and I really did like him.*'

On Wednesday with the weather still '*horrid*' Mary goes to the pictures with her mother indicating her parents are back from their holiday.

Friday 30th '*Went for a row on the river with LH and stopped on a little island that no one else was on and we lay in our birthday suits for a long time. But I can trust LH implicitly, he didn't even touch me. I do like him.*'

Saturday 31st '*Went to London with LH to see Belita and Max Wall in the White Horse Inn on ice. Had hair done in the morning then went straight up to London. At 12 o'clock, had some lunch and then looked around some shops then went to Earls Court to get our tickets. Went and had some tea then to the show. Afterwards went to Piccadilly Circus to look at the lights and then caught the 9:25 train back. Had to stand both ways but it was worth it. LH had the van from work with him and we sat in it for a while.*'

Mary kept her programme for this event and this is a photograph of its front cover.

# AUGUST

A fairly settled month which sees Mary cope for two weeks without LH as he takes his annual vacation. It's also time for a new challenge as she applies for a new job.

Sunday 1st is a quiet day for Mary as she has been feeling tired due to her exerts yesterday. But it gives her time to think about LH.

Monday 2nd *'LH came round today at 10 o'clock and we went down the prom for a picnic lunch. Stayed there until 4 o'clock and then went to the pictures followed by a tea of beans and chips (lovely grub!) in Lyons tea bar. Saw Johnny in there with his mates, I did feel a fool.'*

Staying in on Tuesday she comments, *'weather still horrible. I haven't had one really nice day the whole of my holiday. It is awfully annoying and I expect it will be lovely next week when I'm back at work.'*

Mary goes with LH to the pictures on Wednesday evening *'he is so nice; I don't know what I would have done without him when Johnny gave me up. I am beginning to realise it was LH I liked all the time.'*

Thursday 5th *'Went to Blenheim Palace with Daddy, Mummy and Auntie. It is really a beautiful palace and I wish I lived there. It is a lovely ride there and back; I do so love the country.'*

Then on the Friday *'went for a ride with LH on his motor bike and got absolutely soaked as it teamed down. Sheltered for a long time and the road got flooded, then we went swimming. The bank was really muddy, got my mac, costume etc, thick with mud. I went swimming in the nude while LH sat and watched.'*

Mary has her hair cut short and permed on Saturday 7th *'I do not like it at all, I do feel silly. I do hope LH will like it because he said he didn't like short hair. I do like him; he is so nice; perhaps one day we will get married.'*

On Sunday 8th Mary, stays in *'helped Daddy make some pelmets for the windows. Hair not at all bad today. I think I am beginning to like it. I do hope LH will as well.'*

Monday 9th *'Went to pictures with LH. He likes my hair very much and even said it was an improvement. I am so glad. I wondered if he would stop going out with me as I had had it cut.'*

Tuesday 10th *'Back at work again today. Heard that Mrs M and several of the men are leaving Newberys and going to Wolfe & Hollander, so I wrote to them asking if they had a vacancy for a cashier. I do hope they have.'*

On Wednesday Mary wonders if she will get a reply to her letter and then babysits in the evening relating how *'Little Christine wouldn't go to sleep!'*

Thursday Mary does indeed get a reply from Wolfe & Hollander requesting that she attend an interview on Saturday afternoon and hopes she can slip out of Newberys un-noticed. She babysits again tonight exclaiming *'went babysitting at the Smiths, little Michael was very naughty and wouldn't go to bed!'*

Friday 13th *'Went to the pictures with LH this evening. Going round to his for dinner on Sunday. I am really worried as I am so very shy. I can't bear to eat in front of anyone. Mrs M gave her notice in today. We sat all the dinner hour scared stiff. I held her hand while she told Mr W over the phone.'*

Saturday 14th *'Went for interview this afternoon and got job. I am getting £3-10/0 per week. I am wondering if I really want to leave or not. I do for some reasons but not for others. I am going to be a cashier and start on the 30th. I will have to give my notice in next Saturday.'*

Sunday 15th Mary goes round to LH's for lunch. *'I did feel awful as I had to leave a lot of beans, as I was full up. Went for a walk in the afternoon and to church in evening. Played ball after church and then LH took me home in the van. He is so very nice.'*

Edna pops round on Monday evening along with Auntie V and her friend Mable. They play Monopoly that Mary wins, and have several card games. Mary also stays in on Tuesday evening *'played Sorry with Auntie, Mable and Mummy. I had a very nice time. Going out with LH tomorrow. I'm so glad as I do enjoy myself when I go out with him.'* Having gone to the pictures with LH on Wednesday Mary notes, *'I am wondering if I really do want to leave Newberys. I do for some reasons and don't for others. I wonder if I am doing the right thing.'*

Thursday 19th *'Went babysitting at the Smiths. Sat and thought of LH and about my new job. I am quite worried and really wish I knew whether it is the right thing to do.'*

Friday 20th *'Went to pictures with LH. I won't see him any more for a fortnight as he is going to France on holiday. I feel terribly lonely and I don't know who to turn to. I wish I knew whether I really wanted to leave Newberys. I have to give my notice in tomorrow.'*

Mary is still feeling unsure whether she should leave Newberys but nonetheless hands her notice in on Saturday 21st *'Gave my notice in today. I feel awful. I don't want to leave. I have so much freedom at Newberys. I wish I wasn't leaving. Went to the pictures with Auntie. It was very nice.'*

Feeling fed up on Sunday she remarks *'wish I could run away or better still I wish I could go with LH to France. It would be so nice. I do wish I had a lot of money, then I could go.'*

Monday 23rd *'Had a lovely row with my bosses Reg and Harold today! Nearly burst into tears. They offered me £4 per week to stay on. I do wish they would leave me alone; I am still leaving.'*

Tuesday and Wednesday Mary is missing LH and is feeling *'very muddled about changing jobs. I do wish I could feel either one way or the other, but there are some reasons I want to stay on and a lot of reasons I want to leave.'*

This card was found in Mary's diary.

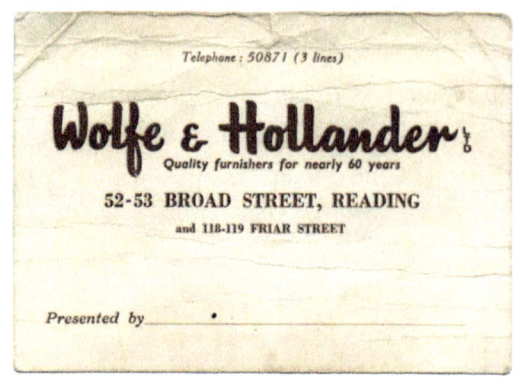

Thursday 26th *'Pat back today. We went to the pictures in the evening as she isn't seeing her boyfriend for a fortnight either. The film was very funny. It was one laugh from beginning to end.'*

Friday 27th *'Went for a bike ride with Pat this evening. I had a good time. We are both missing our boyfriends and we cheered each other up. We giggled most of the way. She is very nice but I wish she wasn't so common.'*

Mary's last day at Newberys is Saturday 28th where she writes *'can't believe I will not go there again. It will seem strange. I don't know whether I am glad or sorry. Partly both I think. Went to the pictures again with Pat this evening and I had a postcard from LH today. I do hope he will hurry up and write to me again.'*

Sunday 29th *'went to pictures with Pat but she went out halfway because she saw her boyfriend go out. Start work at W&H tomorrow. I wonder what it is going to be like.'*

Monday 30th *'Started work at Wolfe & Hollander today. Got office all to myself and my own telephone. My desk is a mass of pipes and tubes. I think I will get into an awful muddle.'*

Tuesday 31st *'I do like it at Wolfe & Hollander. There are some very nice people there. Feet nearly dropped off today as I had to stand*

134

*most of the morning and all afternoon stapling tickets on.'* Mary will work Saturdays and get Wednesday afternoons off in the week.

SEPTEMBER

Inevitably with starting a new job and making new acquaintances comes new love interests and this month is no exception. Mary is confused over the advances of yet another married man and has never prayed so much in her life for a certain young salesman who she really likes to ask her out. W&H open their doors for the first time and LH comes back from his holiday in France, all while Mary's neighbour's nights out escalate increasing her babysitting duties this month. She also enjoys a trip to the circus.

Wednesday 1ˢᵗ *'I do love it at W&H. There are so many nice people there, especially a nice young salesman. They are all terrible teasers. Edna came round today. Laid out in the hot sun all afternoon.'*

Thursday 2ⁿᵈ *'The young salesman is absolutely wonderful. I am almost sure I am head over heels in love with him. He sat next to me in Lyons today and then held my hand going along Broad Street. I really think it's the real thing this time.'*

Mary has made the acquaintance of a girl called Helen and goes to the pictures with her on Friday 3ʳᵈ. Trouble is Helen likes the young salesman too. *'She is very nice but I wish she didn't like the young salesman so much because I really do think he is wonderful. I wonder who he likes the best. I do wish he would ask me out.'*

Saturday 4ᵗʰ *'An awful day, everything went wrong. 1ˢᵗ I lost my pen. 2ⁿᵈ I got an awful stomach ache and feel really ill. 3ʳᵈ somebody stole £1-6.0 from my purse and 4ᵗʰ Helen said the young salesman, Dennis kissed her. I nearly committed suicide. No one was in the house when I got in from work so I had a good cry and had almost decided to do away with myself when Sarah came in.'*

Mary cheers up soon enough though and by Sunday is in quite a good mood when she sees Edna, especially as she is dreaming of LH coming home tomorrow.

Monday 6th 'LH came round at dinner time to W&H. He has had a wonderful time in France. Went into Lyons with Dennis this morning. Spent most of the morning with him. He is so wonderful but I do feel sorry for LH.'

Tuesday 7th 'Lovely day again. Went into Lyons this evening with Helen, Dennis and Mr C. Helen was very jealous because Dennis talked to me most of the time. He said, "if he proposed to me would I say yes?" So, I told him I'd have to think about it.'

Mary and LH go to the pictures on Wednesday 8th 'He is very nice but I am still madly in love with Dennis, he is so wonderful. LH bought me a bracelet. I do feel sorry for him because he is a really nice boy.'

Thursday 9th 'Wonderful day. Went into the Regent with Dennis all by myself. Then he took me home in his car. I do hope he likes me because I think he's wonderful. Shop opened today. Didn't stop doing receipts from 11 o'clock to 6 o'clock, am I tired, phew!'

Mary goes to the pictures with LH on Friday but wishes it was Dennis. She hopes LH will give her up soon so she can focus on him. On Saturday, at work 'Mr C kissed me on the lips at dinnertime. It was nice but I wish Dennis had as well. I do wish God would make him ask me out although I feel very sorry for LH.' She walks along Friar Street with Mr C and Dennis after work and finds out GDC is Dennis' full name.

Sunday 12th sees Auntie S, Uncle R, Mike and Rob come for a visit. 'I do like Mike although he is not half as nice as Dennis or even LH. I do wish Dennis would ask me out.'

On Monday she goes to the cinema with LH mentioning 'LH very nice this evening. I do wish he were more like Dennis to look at though.'

The week progresses with Mary going to the pictures on Wednesday 15$^{th}$ with Sarah and Francis (wishing it was Dennis taking her), babysitting until 11 o'clock on Thursday and then going to the Palace with LH on Friday. Each night she prays really hard to God for Dennis to ask her out. She even goes to the kitchen department on Friday during her dinner hour where he is based for a long time to chat to him and he teases her a lot. But she still doesn't know if he likes her or not.

Saturday 18$^{th}$ '*Went to pictures with Sarah. I do wish Dennis had asked me to go with him. He is so nice. I wonder if he likes me. I do wish he did. He seems to although he hasn't asked me out yet. How I have prayed to God to, but it hasn't made any difference.*'

Sunday 19$^{th}$ '*Went to LH's today on the train. Saw Doug, a mate of his before catching the train and he said he wants to take me out. Went for a walk with LH and sat down behind a haystack and had some fun, wow!' I still like Dennis best though.*'

On Monday 20$^{th}$ Mary comes out with a really bad cold and comments, '*feel really ill today. Got awful cold in my head. Don't know how I got to work. Stayed in kitchen department for half an hour this afternoon. I do wish God would make Dennis take me out, it would make me so happy.*'

The following day sounds like her cold gets even worse '*feel really ill today. Can't breathe at all and I ache all over. Went to the pictures with LH but couldn't really enjoy it. He said he had fallen for me. I do wish Dennis would ask me out. I do like him but I also like LH, although not quite as much.*'

On Wednesday Mary attends a mannequin parade with Arelle at the town hall but mentions how she is still feeling really ill, doesn't know how to breathe and how her head is all dizzy. By Thursday she is feeling slightly better and is still praying God would make Dennis ask her out but admits she has almost given up hope.

Friday 24th *'Went to the Palace with LH. He is a very, very nice boy, but I still like Dennis. Mr C took me out in to the yard this afternoon. Wow! I hope Dennis was jealous. Mr C said he wishes he wasn't married.'*

Saturday 25th *'Went to Chipper fields Arena today. It was wonderful. Went to see animals after and they were really and truly wonderful. I stroked them all. Wish I could have had one of the horses. I want one of those almost as much as I want Dennis to ask me out!'*

Sunday 26th *'LH came round for the day. The heel of shoe broke in half in the middle of Castle Hill on my way to the station to meet him, so had to get a taxi home and then back to station again. Whew! What a rush.'*

Monday 27th *'Went babysitting round the Smiths again with Edna. Tried to get the gramophone to work but couldn't. Mr C at work told me he had fallen for me. He was quite het up about it. He really meant it!'*

Tuesday 28th *'Went to Palace with LH to see Jane of the Daily Mirror. She is not half as nice as I expected. I still like Dennis very much. Mr C has told me he is in love with me.'* Mary states she is very confused and doesn't know what to do.

Wednesday 29th *'Stayed home all afternoon and had a bath in evening. Knitted a polo neck jumper in turquoise. I really have got it bad where Dennis is concerned. He is so wonderful, but I still like LH.'*

Thursday 30th *'Went babysitting round the Smiths and had the gramophone on all evening. Dennis spoke to me for quite some time over the telephone. He told me not to worry my pretty little head. I called him Dennis dear because he wanted me to speak to him nicely. Mr C is really in love with me, I don't know what to do.'*

OCTOBER

With the weather turning colder Mary decides to knit two jumpers this month, one for LH, who she realises is the one she likes best even though her crush for Dennis continues. She wishes she could talk openly about her worries with her mother but decides bottling them up is best. She also gets an invite from Edna to start going dancing.

Friday 1st sees Mary go to the pictures with LH '*He is a very nice boy. I don't like him half as much as I do Dennis. I do so wish he would ask me out but he just doesn't seem interested. I can't understand why, because nearly all the others are.*'

Saturday 2nd '*Went out to lunch with LH today. I wish it had been Dennis. I do like him. Mr C is very nice too and he is really in love with me. I do wish everything would straighten out, I'm in such a muddle. Oh, I do like Dennis but I don't think God wants him to take me out or else He would have made him long before now.*'

Sunday 3rd '*Sat at home and knitted all day long. Blimey, my arms, hands, fingers and seat are all sore. Still, it is worth it as I've finished a whole sleeve and a quarter of the other. I wonder if Dennis will ever take me out. I do hope so.*'

Monday 4th '*Mummy's birthday today. I bought her a pedal bin and a little green stool. She is thrilled with them. Mr C is still in love with me and I told him I liked him and Dennis.*'

Having stayed in Tuesday evening and LH coming for tea, Mary ventures out for a drive on Wednesday with LH and writes, '*went for a drive in the evening and stopped at a nice quiet spot. LH was quite naughty. I didn't think he was like that but I still like him as much as ever and I still also like Dennis.*'

Thursday 7th '*Stayed in all evening and finished blue jumper. Bought two lots of wool to make myself another jumper and LH a pullover. Sarah bought a boy named Dick home. She says she has finished with John. I still like Dennis and wonder if he will ever ask me out.*'

Friday 8th '*Had to keep getting up to go down to phone LH this evening. I went three times but he was out. I wanted to ask him about tomorrow dinner time. Got through in the end and I am going out to lunch with him. A very nice Irish boy, asked me to go out with him on Sunday.'*

Saturday 9th *'Stayed in this evening. Done quite a lot to both of my jumpers. I went out to lunch with LH. The Irish boy Paddy asked me out again today. I do like him although I still like Dennis as much as ever and also LH. Oh dear, I am in such a muddle, but still if I trust in God, He will help me out of it (I hope).'*

Sunday 10th *'Went round to Grandma and Grandads' this afternoon to see some relations of Daddy's, then I went to the pictures in the evening with Sarah. Saw Rory Calhoun. He is wonderful but I still like Dennis best.'*

Monday 11th *'Went to the pictures with LH. Paddy asked me again today if I would go out with him. Oh, dear it is so difficult to tell him I already have a boyfriend. Oh, I do wish I could talk seriously. I go through it in my mind and then when I see the person, I am frightened to say it.'*

LH comes to meet Mary from work on his motorbike on Tuesday and Mr C tells her that Dennis has a girlfriend which she hopes is untrue but wouldn't know what to do if her asked her out anyway.

Photo of LH on his motorbike at the back of Florida Court.

Wednesday 13<sup>th</sup> '*Went to the pictures with Paddy. Oh, I do wish I had had the nerve to say no. I didn't mean to go but I felt sorry for him. He looked so unhappy. He is very nice but I don't think I like him as much as Dennis and LH.*'

Thursday 14<sup>th</sup> '*Quite a good day today. Dennis has not got a girlfriend after all. He called me dear today and also said he would like to squeeze me. He has been phoning me up to tease me. He is so nice. LH came to meet me from work. He is also very nice. Paddy's been smiling at me all day.*'

Friday 15<sup>th</sup> '*Went to the Palace with LH this evening. I really do like him although I still like Dennis. I want Dennis to ask me out and yet I don't. I only hope that LH gives me up before Dennis does ask me out.*'

Saturday 16<sup>th</sup> '*Saw LH for about three minute's dinnertime. I was waiting for the bus to go back to work and he came to collect our radio as it has gone wrong. I am going round his for the day tomorrow. I've got to get up very early. I think I must be in love with him to give up my Sunday lie in!*' Mary says her day with LH was wonderful but didn't say what they did. '*I still like Dennis though. I didn't think it was possible for a person to be in love with two people at once.*'

Monday 18<sup>th</sup> '*Edna came round this evening and we just sat and talked. She said she would like to go dancing with me, but I am scared to because I know I would make a fool out of myself.*'

On Tuesday and Friday Mary goes to the pictures with LH '*he told me he really does like me. I still like Dennis and can't help thinking about him most of the time.*'

Wednesday 20<sup>th</sup> '*Stayed at home all afternoon and evening and finished the backs of both my jumpers. Paddy wanted me to go out with him tonight but I said no. He is alright but I have got enough to think about with LH and Dennis.*'

She babysits with LH for the Smiths on Thursday stating '*I think after all I really do like him better than anyone else. I do hope that he doesn't give me up. I think I am in love with him.*'

Friday 22$^{nd}$ '*Went to Palace with LH to see "Twinkle". He is so very nice and I really do like him very, very much. He is so kind and thoughtful, I think he is wonderful.*'

Saturday 23$^{rd}$ '*Went to the pictures with Edna to see "The Young Lovers". I thought about LH all the time and wished he was with me. I really have fallen in love with him at last. I had made up my mind not to as I have been hurt before and I don't want to again.*'

Sunday 24$^{th}$ '*LH came up for the afternoon. We went for a walk, then to church in the evening. He is wonderful. He wants me to go dancing but I can't dance properly. I do wish I could.*'

Monday 25$^{th}$ '*Stayed at home all evening and did some of my knitting, very thrilling I must say. LH is so nice; I wish I had the nerve to go dancing with him. I would like to.*'

On Tuesday 26$^{th}$ LH takes Mary to see Billy Cotton. '*The trumpeter kept making eyes at me and he threw a snowball especially to me. I wish I had had the nerve to go and ask him if he would teach me to play the trumpet.*'

Wednesday and Thursday she stays in completing more of her knitting commenting how very tired and fed up she is. '*I just don't know what to do with myself. I am so bored. I wish I could die. I would love to commit suicide.*'

Friday 29$^{th}$ '*Dennis saw me on LH's motor bike today. I just don't know what I am going to say to him in the morning. I do feel awful. I do wish he hadn't seen me. Mr C also saw me. Stayed in with LH all evening.*'

Saturday 30$^{th}$ '*stayed in all evening, very thrilling I must say. I really do like Dennis, although I like LH very much too. I am in such a muddle. I do wish I could tell Mummy about it like Sarah does but I just feel that it is better to worry about it rather than worry anyone else.*'

Sunday 31st *'came on today and I feel awful. Stayed in bed until quarter to four. Had dinner in bed. Oh, I was quite enjoying myself by that time, although I don't know how I got through the morning.'*

## NOVEMBER

Mary is now settling in to her new employment, with only a few glitches on 22nd and 23rd. She finally gets asked out by the infamous Dennis which he then disappointingly, proceeds to cancel. Edna gives up her job in London much to Mary's surprise and she celebrates her seventeenth birthday. LH is still by her side but although she is a little disappointed with his birthday present, he does declare his love for her for the first time and whisks her up to London again.

Monday 1st *'Edna came round this evening. She has resigned from the railway and leaves on Friday. I do think she's silly, as she had so many good chances on the railway. I feel a bit better today, thank goodness.'*

Tuesday 2nd *'Went to the Palace with LH to see "Sinbad the Sailor on Ice", it was wonderful and so is LH. I do like him so much and I like Dennis too.'*

Mary stays in on Wednesday to do her knitting commenting *'it doesn't seem to grow at all. Paddy asked me to go out with him again this evening but I said no because I don't feel like it.'* She also stays in on Thursday *'wrapped up Sarah's birthday presents ready for tomorrow. I have got her a cardigan and a scarf. Going out with LH tomorrow—nice!'*

Friday 5th *'LH has at last told me he loves me. I am thrilled. I told him I love him too, which I do. Oh, I am so happy. Saw quite a lot of Dennis today. He is very nice but rather slow. I like him though. Oh, I am so happy.'* Mary decides she loves Dennis too but in a different sort of way.

Saturday 6th is the day that Edna leaves her job in Paddington. Mary spends the evening with her.

On Sunday 7th LH comes round in the afternoon *'he said he really did mean what he said on Friday. I do wish I knew whether he really and truly meant it. I think I am in love with him; he is wonderful.'* LH has dinner and tea with Mary on Monday then stays the evening. *'I really do think that I have at last really fallen in love with him. He really is wonderful but I wish he would tell me he loves me more often.'*

Wednesday 10th *'Stayed in all afternoon and knitted. Went to pictures in the evening with Sarah. Mummy and Auntie have gone to London to see about a flat. Dennis gave me some dockets today and looked me straight in the eyes and said, "all yours" wow!'*

Thursday 11th sees Dennis ring Mary up at work *'he phoned me up and I asked what I could do for him and he said I could do a lot of things and he said he will tell me when I'm sixteen. Cheek! I suppose he means on my birthday.'*

LH takes her to the Palace on Friday evening and tells her he loves her six times but Mary still can't help thinking about Dennis.

Saturday 13th *'Stayed at home and knitted today and all evening, I am so very tired. Never had quite such a busy day. Haven't seen much of Dennis today worst luck. I do like him so much. Had a letter from Bob yesterday. I do wish I hadn't. I am so unhappy and in such a muddle. Dennis playfully said on Friday that he would have to get married one day and asked me to be his wife. I wish he was serious.'*

Sunday 14th *'Stayed in all day today and knitted and thought of Dennis, LH and Bob. I don't like Bob at all but I do really believe I am in love with Dennis and LH at the same time. It is so difficult. I am so unhappy, oh dear!'*

Monday 15th *'Heavenly day, Dennis asked me to go out with him this evening but I had to say no as LH was meeting me to go to the Palace. I was so disappointed. Mr C turned me upside down in front of Dennis and they both had a good go at me. I really do love Dennis.'*

Tuesday 16th *'Dennis wants me to go out with him on Saturday. I think I will go. He has been writing me notes all yesterday and today. I like him so very much. Mr C has been in a bad mood today but as long as Dennis likes me, I don't care.'*

Wednesday 17th *'Went to London this afternoon with LH. Went to a cycle expedition in the afternoon and then to the Folies Bergere to see Frankie Howard and Winifred Atwell. Didn't get home until 11:30 as the train got lost in the thick fog.'*

Thursday 18th *'Seen quite a lot of Dennis today. He is so wonderful. He put his arms all around me, oh it was heavenly. Mr C in a good mood today thank goodness. Stayed up in the kitchen dept until 2:45, supposed to have been back by 2:15.'*

Friday 19th *'went to pictures with LH. He is very nice but I really have got it bad where Dennis is concerned. I have seen quite a lot of him today. Got back early lunch time and he was all alone and put his arms all around me and his cheek against mine. Wow!'*

Saturday 20th *'Seen a fair amount of Dennis today. I felt very disappointed this evening as he wrote me a note on Tuesday to say he wouldn't probably be able to take me out this evening, but he hadn't said anything else about it and when I walked down the road with him after work, he said he was going out with the boys. Why is it that boys would rather go out with boys than girls?'*

On Sunday 21st having gone on the train to LH's, she notes that he is the *'far nicer of the two'* and still thinks he is a wonderful boy, stressing *'I would be absolutely heartbroken if he ever gave me up.'*

Monday 22nd *'Haven't seen Dennis or LH today. Do feel fed up. My cash was all wrong. Everything went wrong today. I do wish everything would straighten out. Stayed in all evening and had hair washed. Listened to a small radio in bed.'*

Everything goes wrong at work again on Tuesday and to make matters worse Dennis is off with the flu. *'I really am so fed up; I do wish I had the nerve to* commit suicide. I wish there was someone whom I could tell about my troubles. I know I will tell God about them and I shall feel a lot better.'

Wednesday 24th doesn't get much better *'everything gone wrong again today. I am just about ready to do myself in. Edna came this evening. It was alright while she was here but after she had gone everyone started moaning so I went to bed and cried my eyes out and eventually cried myself to sleep.'*

Thursday 25th *'Not quite so bad today although I wouldn't say I've had a good day. Dennis has changed this last week. He won't even stay and talk to me like he usually does. I went to pictures with LH which cheered me up a bit. I am so glad I have him, it's nice to know somebody loves me.'*

Friday 26th *'Feel in quite a good mood today. Had hair set. Made two big birthday cakes ready for tomorrow. I am looking forward to it. LH gave me his birthday present yesterday. I am disappointed. It is a torch. I don't want it really, but he is so nice.'*

Saturday 27th is Mary's seventeenth birthday and she has quite a good day. She takes some cake into work for Dennis and he says it is lovely. Edna and LH come round in the evening and they all have a good time. *'I had a lovely lot of things and 16 birthday cards. No one sent me a funny one though.'*

Mary and LH go out for a walk on Sunday afternoon, then they stay in for the evening.

Monday 29th *'Feel quite miserable today. Was going out with LH but he had to go to choir practice. Dennis has been a little better today. I do like him very much.'*

Tuesday 30th in the evening, LH takes Mary to the Palace to see Dickie Valantine *'he is smashing and is something like Dennis. Quite a good day today but not quite as nice as it could be.'*

DECEMBER

An announcement from Dennis on 11<sup>th</sup> leaves Mary very upset and LH redeems himself this month by buying her a lovely Christmas present. There's nothing said about what she got him. All in all, a busy month I imagine at work with Christmas looming and in Mary's case, she proves that getting your hair styled by an expert is not always worth it. She also has an unfortunate accident with some fish and chips.

Wednesday 1<sup>st</sup> '*Went to school to see their Christmas Play called "Toad of Toad Hall". I went with Edna. She doesn't like her new job at all so she will leave in three months' time.*'

On Thursday 2<sup>nd</sup> Mary stays in in the evening and starts more knitting, this time with mauve angora. '*Going out with LH tomorrow. I do like him but I still like Dennis who has been better recently. I do wish I could get him out of my mind.*'

At work on Friday, she has a lot of fun up in the kitchen department as '*Mr G and Mr Y were up there and were teasing Dennis about me and saying how nice I was.*'

Saturday 4<sup>th</sup> '*Stayed in this evening and did knitting and thought about LH and Dennis and everyone at work. I do wish I could get Dennis out of my mind but I just can't. I think it is because he is the only one who doesn't run after me.*'

The following week sees Mary mainly debating to herself who she likes best out of Dennis and LH, saying if Dennis doesn't like her she will just have to put up with LH. She cracks on with her knitting along with doing quite a lot of washing and having her hair done.

Thursday 9<sup>th</sup> '*Went baby sitting with LH at the Smiths. Wow! Nearly had it this time. Just stopped him in time. I really do love him. I think I am beginning to like him better than Dennis.*'

Friday 10<sup>th</sup> '*Stayed in this evening. LH came to meet me from work today. He said he wanted to bring a friend out with him tomorrow when we go out. I said I didn't mind so I shall have two tomorrow.*'

Saturday 11th '*What a day! Dennis gave his notice in today. I am very upset but didn't have much time to think about him as I went to the pictures with LH and his friend Jim. He is very nice but I really have decided at last that it is LH I really love. I still like Dennis though.*'

Sunday 12<sup>th</sup> '*Stayed in all day and thought a lot about LH, Dennis and all sorts of things. I do wish I lived alone. I am much happier when I can be alone and think and day dream.*'

Monday 13<sup>th</sup> '*Not too bad a day today although my cash went all wrong. Haven't seen much of Dennis which is a great pity. Went to Palace with LH. I really do like him. I am so glad I have him. I don't know what I'd do without him.*'

Tuesday 14<sup>th</sup> '*Stayed in all evening after going to Sarah's shop to have hair re-styled by London expert man. It does look flashy. I hope it will stay like this tomorrow. Won't see LH until Friday.*'

Wednesday 15<sup>th</sup> '*Hair looks dreadful, it is absolutely straight.*'

And on Thursday '*hair has never looked so awful. It is absolutely dead straight. I do feel ashamed to go out. LH came to meet me from work this evening. I don't think he likes my hair and I don't blame him.*'

Friday 17<sup>th</sup> '*Went to pictures with LH this evening. He is so wonderful; I have almost forgotten Dennis now. I really do love LH; I would do absolutely anything for him. Going over to his on Sunday.*'

There's a small note that Dennis leaves on Saturday 18<sup>th</sup> and that Mary stays in and has a perm '*thank goodness.*' She then sets her hair herself and hopes it will turn out right in the morning as she's spending Sunday with LH.

Sunday 19th *'Went to LH's for the day. Went to church in the evening and watched him in nativity play after. He was quite good. I do love him so much. I don't know what I would do without him.'*

On Monday back at work Mary notes that it feels strange without Dennis there but supposes she will soon get used to it. That evening she stays in and wraps up Christmas parcels.

Having a half day on Tuesday 21st to do some Christmas shopping she writes, *'Boy! Am I tired. I'm stony-broke. LH came round in evening. Went down to Edna's to take Xmas presents. Got fish and chips on way back and then I soaked mine in ginger wine. So, I had to sit and watch LH eat his. Oh dear!'*

On Wednesday Mary writes *'I have got half a crown left to last me until Friday week as I was paid early so that I would be able to buy my presents.'*

Thursday 23rd *'Went to pictures with LH this evening. Oh, I love him so very much, I have almost forgotten Dennis. LH gave me a beautiful powder compact as well as a box of Max Factors powder. He really is wonderful.'*

On Christmas Eve *'had a sort of party at work today. Had half a glass of port. Finished work at 3.45 and waited until 6.0 for LH to turn up. Nearly worried myself sick. I love him so much.'*

Unfortunately, on Christmas Day Mary states that she's not had a bad morning or afternoon getting quite a few gifts but has never had such a boring and miserable evening. *'I feel so unwanted and unhappy. I went into my bedroom and cried for about half an hour and then stayed there for a long time. Had quite a few gifts though.'*

Sunday Boxing Day is better however with LH coming round in the afternoon and taking her on a long walk round Prospect Park *'LH is really wonderful; I only hope that perhaps one day we will get married.'*

Mary and LH pictured together on Boxing Day 1954.

Monday 27th *'Quite a good afternoon and evening. Had Mrs C, Auntie O, Grandma, Grandad, John and LH up. Had a lot of noisy games. I do love LH so very much. I wish I knew if he really does love me as much as he says he does.'*

Being taken to the pictures by LH on Tuesday she writes *'LH really is wonderful. He tells me he loves me quite often now thank goodness and I am at last, beginning to believe him. I just couldn't bare it if he gave me up.'*

Wednesday 29th *'LH met me from work and took me home this evening but he seems different somehow. When he told me he loved me, I didn't quite believe him as he said it as if it was just something to say. Oh dear.'*

Thursday 30th *'LH brought me home again today. I really don't know what to make of him. He seems so different somehow. I do wish he would keep the same as when I first went out with him.'*

Friday 31st *'Went to dinner with LH this dinner hour. He really is wonderful. He came in before he went home at 4:30 because Ron had told me that LH had been taking another girl out. I was quite worried but apparently Ron told LH he had told me which had worried LH also, so he came in to tell me it wasn't true. I am so glad he did because I really was worried very much. I do love him so.'*

Thus ending 1954 on a really positive note.

### Notes at the End of Her Diary

*'My sweetest little tortoise died Monday 19th July. Christine, the little girl next door, let it out of the wire netting and her father ran over it with his car. It*

*was smashed to pieces. He bought me a great big ugly thing that will never take the place my little Sleepy had in my heart. I really loved my little tortoise and am heartbroken that she died. Please God look after her for me until we meet again. I didn't find out about it until Tuesday morning.'*

Packets of cigarettes I have bought:
3 x packs of 10 Players 1s 9½

# 1955

Another Letts diary by Charles Letts & Co Ltd of London which has a page per day for Mary to write on and fill it she does! Its first pages list notable dates for the year and show the calendars for 1954 and 1956. It also has the details for British Weights and Measures, Troy Weights, Jeweller's Weight and Measures of Capacity, to name but a few. At the back there are sections for notes on which she has listed all the music records she has bought and pages for cash accounts, showing this is much more of a grown-up diary.

A very tumultuous and emotional year for Mary this year as she experiences excruciating agony when she falls head over heels for a married man, causing quite the scandal at work. LH, apparently none the wiser, hankers to get engaged on her birthday in November with Mary exclaiming she has no idea how to handle that under the present circumstances.

With awkwardness building at work, Mary leaves W&H to begin her long and prestigious profession with the National Provincial Bank. There are still plenty of visits to the local picture houses although she does stop rating them from now on, but between work and juggling two men there's not much time left for hobbies this year. She still likes to go swimming when time allows, knit whenever she manages to get an evening free and this year treats herself to a gramophone on hire purchase to play all her records.

## JANUARY

The weather gets colder as Mary returns to work and all her hours knitting produce disappointing results. She starts to get a little possessive over LH especially as there is frequent talk of marriage and his health takes a dip around 13th. Mary makes a decision to enter a beauty contest to potentially help with her money worries and has a minor health issue to endure herself at the end of the month.

Saturday New Year's Day '*I stayed at home all evening and knitted. I was all by myself until 10:45. Mummy, Daddy and Auntie had gone to the pictures and Sarah was out with John. Feel a lot happier today than I have for the past few days as I had the feeling that LH was getting tired of me but when he came yesterday afternoon, he reassured me that he loved only me. I am so glad as I love him so very much. I don't know what I would do if he did ever give me up. I think it would break my heart.*'

On Sunday 2nd Mary catches the 11:45 train to Basingstoke to have dinner with LH. '*I am getting used to having dinner with his parents. After dinner, LH and I went into the dining room. Brian* (LH's younger brother) *wouldn't leave us alone. LH did get annoyed and I must admit I felt like sloshing him. He did go out in the end and LH and I had a lovely time. He told me he loves me from the bottom of his heart and I told him I love him too, which I do most sincerely.*'

On Monday Mary goes to the Odeon with LH to see Norman Wisdom in the comedy "One Good Turn". '*LH is so wonderful. I do wish we were older so that we could get married. I have always shuddered at the thought of getting married but I get very thrilled if I think of marrying LH. His toothache came back this evening, I am so sorry for him as it must have been hurting him an awful lot. It tried to snow today.*'

The weather outside is freezing so it's no surprise that on Tuesday 4th Mary wakes up to snow, the very day she is due to go back to work. After work she comments, '*I got fed up with work from about 4:30. My cash had all got muddled with stores trusts.*' The snow prevents Edna from paying her usual visit that evening but Mary is quite glad as she then can spend the time knitting.

Wednesday 5th '*Snow clearing up a bit today thank goodness, although it is very slippery. Edna did come round this evening. We had quite a few different games and I think she won most of them. I managed to almost finish my jumper before she came and then completely finished it after she had gone and I am very disappointed with it as it is miles too big but I am much too tired to bother with it now as it is past eleven. I haven't seen LH today at all. It has seemed a long time since I saw him last.*'

Thursday 6th '*Went to the pictures with my darling LH this evening. He really is wonderful. He hadn't got his motor bike today so we had to come out of the pictures rather early so that he could catch his train. I sat in the carriage for quite a while before the train went. Oh, he is such a darling and told me he loved me again and I told him likewise. I really do love him and I think, well I don't think, I know that it would break my heart if he ever gave me up. He keeps talking about when we are married. I feel so perfectly happy.*'

Friday 7th '*as I was going home this evening, Mr C started calling me names so I had a lovely fight with him and all day long the porters have been telling me how wonderful I am. I am afraid I shall have to keep a tight grip on myself or else I shall become big headed. I saw a job advertised today in Reading Standard for a girl wanted to help in a stable. Oh, I would love the job so much. Also, in the RS they are asking for girls and boys to go for a singing audition at the Palace. I do wish I had the nerve to go. If I'd seen LH today, it would have been the perfect day.*'

Saturday passes with work being very busy so Mary decides to stay in all evening and have a long bath… '*it was a lovely bath of about an hour and three quarters.*' She then listens to a play on the wireless while getting some things ready for tomorrow and daydreams about marrying LH so she could see him every day.

She spends the day with him on Sunday arriving in time for dinner. '*Thank goodness I am getting used to it now. After dinner, we went for a walk. He is going to a dance on Friday and I am awfully jealous and yet I can't say anything as he will think I am being too possessive. Oh, I love him so much and yet I get jealous every time he mentions anything at all to do with his club or other girls. I really will have to get out of it or I will lose him.*'

LH and Mary go to the pictures on Monday 10th '*he was very tired poor darling, but I like him a lot better that way as he seems more attentive to me when he's like that. He says he wishes we could get married and he also said that he could wait a lifetime to marry me. I do wish we were older. I have had awful chilblains today; my feet are swollen twice their normal size. I've put some ointment on them so I hope they will be better in the morning. They have been itching terribly.'*

Tuesday 11th *'stayed at home all evening and read newspapers and thought of LH. My chilblains nearly kill me with itching. Found a book at work today that I am supposed to have kept accounts in from the day we opened and I had forgotten all about it. It is absolutely impossible to catch up with it now so I have had to start from yesterday. It is an awful lot of work; I just don't know how I am going to keep it up, I'm sure. The men have been on at me again today to go in for Miss Reading contest. I wish I had the nerve.'*

Wednesday 12th *'Went to the pantomime this afternoon to see "Babes in The Wood" with Mummy. It was jolly good. Haven't seen LH all day today and it seems ages since I saw him last. My chilblains are a little better today but they still itch like fury. I have been wondering whether or not I should go in for the Miss Reading contest. I need the money so badly. I do wish Daddy would help me out but he doesn't. I wonder how I can get a lot of money. Oh dear, if it wasn't for money, I would really be perfectly happy.'*

Thursday 13th *'I was going out this evening but my darling LH rang me up this morning to say he couldn't come. He has been in bed since Tuesday suffering from exhaustion. I do feel sorry for him. I phoned him up after work this evening and he said he feels much better. I am so glad as I hate him feeling unwell. I love him so much; he is so sweet. I have been debating whether or not to go in for the Miss Reading contest. The way I feel at the moment I would like to. I do wish I had a lot of money then I would be able to go out and buy a lovely dress. Oh, how I wish!'*

LH and Mary go to the pictures on Friday 14th *'he really is absolutely wonderful. He told me that I was the right one and that he loves me enough to want to marry me. His train this evening was an hour late leaving and I stood on the platform all that time and there is deep snow all around. I was frozen. I decided today that I would go in for the Miss Reading contest and Mr W said he would get a photographer for me, but this man said he couldn't do it in time so I don't think I will bother after all. Saw Johnny from Newberys today.'*

Saturday 15<sup>th</sup> '*A day of ups and downs today, mostly downs. Haven't seen my darling LH and I had a lovely quarrel with Sarah and she said she hated me. Oh, how that hurt, I don't think I shall ever forgive her although she apologised afterwards. I am still in two minds as to whether I should enter the Miss Reading contest. Still, I have all day tomorrow to think over it. LH is at a dance this evening. I have been thinking and wondering about him, whether he took a girl home or whether he kissed one. Oh, dear I wish I wasn't so jealous, but I can't help it. I love him so very much it would break my heart if he ever left me for another girl.*'

When LH comes over on Sunday 16<sup>th</sup> he arrives unexpectedly early and Mary isn't dressed; it is 10:55. '*I am afraid I shall lose him if I go on as I have been— jealous at the least little thing. He says he loves me; I do so hope that is true. Went to church this evening. Quite a good service. Oh dear, if only I could explain my feelings but I just can't talk to people. I know what I want to say to them but it just won't come out.*'

Mary and LH go to the Palace on Monday evening where she states '*I do hope he won't get tired of me. I do so wish we could get married. I had my photograph taken twice today and Mrs A got hold of one and she has sent it in for the Miss Reading contest. I am fairly pleased and yet I am very nervous. It was a horrible photo too. LH seems quite pleased. I do hope it won't affect him too much. I should hate him any other way to what he is now, as I love him from the bottom of my heart.*'

Tuesday 18<sup>th</sup> '*Not too bad a day today although I am absolutely fed up with money. Daddy has told me I have got to give Mummy another five shillings and it is just impossible. I just haven't got it to give her. I am almost sick to death with worrying about it. Oh dear, there are so many things I must buy. I can only pray to God to make me win the Miss Reading contest so that I can have the fifty pounds I need so desperately. Haven't seen my darling LH today.*'

Wednesday 19<sup>th</sup> '*Stayed at home all this afternoon, had a bath, had hair washed, did some washing and ironing and plucked my eyebrows. I came out of the bath and slipped on the mat in the kitchen. Boy, did I go down with a bang. Cor blimey it's a wonder I can sit down. Sat and thought about the Miss Reading contest and how much I love LH and all the money I need. Oh dear, I have such a lot to think about.'*

Thursday 20th *'Went to pictures with my darling LH this evening. I fell over at work again today. I have hurt my leg terribly. Poor LH, he was quite worried about me. He gave me the money for a taxi. He is such a darling. I do love him so. Bought a jumper and a leather belt today ready in case, it is the quarter finals of the Miss Reading contest tomorrow. I wonder if I will get a letter from the people tomorrow to let me know. I am so nervous. I only hope and pray that I win so that I can have the £50 prize. I need it so desperately.'*

Friday 21st *'Very disappointed today, not even my name in the paper today. I really feel quite upset but haven't given up hope yet though as it said in the paper that the remaining girls will appear in next weeks, so I have got to wait another whole week which seems like a lifetime. Haven't seen my LH today but I don't stop thinking about him for a moment. It is his birthday tomorrow. I have got him a silver cigarette case and I have had his initials engraved on it. Also, I have put ten cigarettes in it. I hope he likes it. I may be going on holiday with him this year. I do hope so.'*

On Saturday 22nd Mary rises promptly getting in early to work so she can ring LH up before anyone else gets in *'but he was still fast asleep in bed, so I told his father I would phone later. I phoned about quarter to eleven and he was up this time. I do wish I could see him more often but it's either his plays or his club he's busy with. I just can't help feeling jealous. I do wish I could act as I did when we first met, when he ran after me then, but I'm afraid I run after him now.'*

On Sunday 23rd Mary goes round to LH's for the day and he is very pleased with the cigarette case. During the afternoon they listen to the wireless and then go upstairs to watch television. Having washed up the tea things they stay downstairs by themselves for a while, *'had a good time then went upstairs. There wasn't a chair for me to sit on so I had to sit on LH's lap in front of his mother, father and brother. Boy! Was I embarrassed. After church, LH and I sat on the settee with our arms around each other with all the others in the room. I am beginning to get used to it now.'*

Monday 24th 'My darling LH was really wonderful this evening. He came round and I tried to help him learn his play. I'm afraid I didn't help him much. When he felt that he knew it, we sat and had a serious talk on several things. He gave me a gentle hint that he would admire me more if I didn't run after him, at least that's what I took it to be. I really am trying very hard not to run after him. When we were in the train waiting until it went, he asked me if I would mind starting off married life in a caravan and we talked about whether he should come home to dinner and if I should carry on working. Oh, I am so perfectly happy. I love him so very, very much.'

On Tuesday 25th Mary waves to LH in the morning through Newbery's window on her way into work. 'He just saw me and waved. Went past Newberys again this evening to see if I could see him but all I saw was Ron. I stopped and talked to him for a little while. He told me he had caught LH upstairs with the office girl. I don't believe it at all but I have been worrying about it most of the evening. I don't know why; I just couldn't help myself. I don't know, I think about him all the time; I just can't think of anything else however hard I try. I don't expect he thinks of me very much. I wonder why I was made with a jealous streak because he is rehearsing his play tonight and I feel quite jealous at the thought of him with a lot of girls.'

Wednesday 26th 'Haven't seen my darling LH again today. It does seem ages since I saw him last. Went to the pictures with Edna this evening but could not really concentrate on the film. I was thinking of LH and wondering where he was and what he was doing and also wondering if he really loves me or not. I think if I don't hurry up and stop running after him and being jealous at the least little thing, he will soon get tired of me and give me up. I really must try hard. People are always saying that love is grand, but I think it is awful. I can't sleep properly; I'm getting all spotty and I'm always miserable if I'm not with LH.'

Thursday 27th 'Saw my darling Leonard this evening. I really must try and make an even bigger effort to stop being so possessive. This evening, he talked about other girls and I kept asking him if he would ever go out with anyone else. Then, we talked about other boys, all he said was—if I wanted to go with someone else, I was quite free to go. That slightly hurt my feelings. My lips today have been all swollen, sore and crackly. I look hideous. LH said it could be a

158

*disease which, if not stopped right away, would spread. He said it would have been caused by him if it happened to be this particular disease. I hope and pray that is it not as I would not only lose my fairly good looks but perhaps LH as well.'*

On Friday 28th she buys some Lypsyl as her lips are worse *'my lips have been awful today; I could hardly talk this morning and I couldn't smile at all but having put some Lypsyl on this evening they have now gone down an awful lot and hardly hurt at all. I am so glad as I should hate to have a horrible face as LH wouldn't want to go out with me anymore and that would kill me. I do wish I knew how to act so that I can keep him.'*

Saturday 29th *'My lips are a bit better today thank goodness although they are still quite sore. Haven't seen LH today but I phoned him up this evening. I was going to tell him I couldn't go with him to see his younger brother in hospital tomorrow as it would look as if I was running after him, but I just couldn't, so I will be going tomorrow. I am glad that I am going to see him though. LH told me on the phone that he was going to his club dance and party this evening. I feel a bit jealous at the thought of him with his arms round another girl but I mustn't let him know because I don't want him to think I am too possessive.'*

Sunday 30th *'Went round to my darling LHs today and then went in the van with him and his father to Southampton to see Brian in hospital. On the way, we went through Winchester. It was a lovely ride, I thoroughly enjoyed it. Still, I enjoy anything if LH is with me. He is so wonderful. His father is such a teaser. Oh, I am so perfectly happy, I do wish I was twenty-one so that LH and I could get married.'* Mary regards herself as being extremely lucky to have found LH who has now decreed, they should wait a year or so before getting married. There is no mention of why Brian is in hospital.

## FEBRUARY

During February Mary is still paranoid about her possessiveness towards LH. She receives a letter from Johnny asking if she'll go out with him but writes back by return saying she likes LH too much. Having wrestled with her conscience thinking she might hurt LH; she shows the letter to him on Thursday 3rd whereupon he hurts her feelings terribly by saying if she wanted to go back out with Johnny she was quite free to go.

'*I do wish he would change back to the way when I first went out with him. He was jealous of every little thing. I'm sorry to say the tables have turned now and it's me who is jealous. He doesn't seem to mind a bit if I talk about anyone else. I do wish he would. He did tell me this evening though that he loves me with all his heart.*'

Work is now starting to get busy with Mary expressing how she has never seen so much money going through the firm, leading to the inevitable happening on Friday 4th '*today has been a terrible day. Everything has gone wrong. Spent all morning trying to find £8. I discovered that Miss O had written out a receipt for £18 instead of £10. That is only one thing that has gone wrong today. It's so busy. Haven't seen my darling LH this evening. He is so wonderful. I really must make a bigger effort not to be so possessive and jealous. I really will try to act as I did when I first went out with him. He really did run after me then (how I loved it) but now he acts as if he couldn't care less if I went out with anyone else or not.*'

Her relationship with LH this month sees them going to the pictures, walking round the Forbury and Abbey ruins, talking about where they would like to have their wedding, reception and honeymoon, picking out furniture and even choosing baby clothes! LH also suggests they should get engaged on Mary's 18th birthday and married when she is 19. They also play chequers and card games and visit Brian in hospital in Southampton with LH's family. Although she never mentions just what's wrong his brother.

Saturday 5<sup>th</sup> '*A very busy day today. I don't think I have seen quite so much money before. I do wish it was mine and not the firms, then I could marry my LH. Haven't seen him today worst luck. I do wish I could see him more. As it is, I only see him at the most three times a week. Oh, I do wish we could get married and then I could see him every day and every night. It would be wonderful. When I was going out with Johnny, I imagined I was in love with him but now I am really in love, I can see that it was really imagination and was nothing like this.'*

Sunday 6<sup>th</sup> '*My darling LH came round for the day today. I cooked the dinner. It turned out fairly well. He is really wonderful. We went for a walk this afternoon round the Forbury and the Abbey ruins. We sat down at the side of the river and talked about getting married. Where it should be and whether it should be a white wedding. Also, where the reception should be and where we would go for our honeymoon.'* Later in the day they play chequers and cards, and LH becomes very tired. '*I do feel sorry for him. I think he ought to see a doctor.'*

Monday 7<sup>th</sup> '*Went to the Palace with my darling LH this evening. I do love him so much. After we came out, we talked again about getting married. He said it would be nice if we got engaged on my eighteenth birthday in November and then got married when I'm nineteen. He was quite serious about it. I'm so glad because I would really love to marry him. My lips are coming up again today. They have been awfully sore this evening and have been stinging terribly all evening. Oh dear. I may be going to London on Wednesday with Sarah to get a new coat.'*

Tuesday 8<sup>th</sup> '*Haven't seen my darling LH today worst luck. He really is a darling. My lips came up terribly again this morning but have gone down again this evening. I am so glad as I should hate to have got a disease. LH was rather worried about money yesterday as he has had to spend out £2 on his bike. I am going to London tomorrow with Sarah. I am going to try and get a coat and if I have any money left, I will try and get either a handbag or a jumper. I do wish I had a lot of money. It is such a worry.'*

Wednesday 9<sup>th</sup> '*Went to London this afternoon with Sarah. Bought a new coat, handbag and skirt. I am pleased with them but Mummy, Auntie and Daddy (of course) didn't like it. They never do like anything I buy; they say my coat is much too light. Had a row with them this evening. I said it was my money and that I could spend it how I like. Daddy said it wasn't mine because I don't pay Mummy half enough. But goodness, I work really hard for my little bit of money and I pay Mummy a lot more than I can really afford now. I had a good cry; I am so worried about it. I am glad I have got my LH.'*

Lifting her mood, she goes to the pictures with him on Thursday evening where they talk about married life together. '*He is quite serious about it. I would like to marry him, but not just yet.*' Mary thinks getting engaged on her birthday is '*a splendid idea.*' Sadly, her lips have been so sore all day that she could hardly kiss LH tonight but in bed later they start to feel better.

Friday 11th '*I bought LH a funny Valentine's card today and Mrs P is getting her husband to write on the envelope and Mr W is going to post it in London for me. I wonder if I shall get one from LH, I do hope so and shall feel quite disappointed if I don't. Going over to his on Sunday and I shall wear my new coat. I have had to wear it today as my other one is being cleaned. Darling LH said he will come in to Reading on Monday on the train as he didn't want me to get my coat dirty on his bike. I think that was ever so sweet of him.*'

Saturday 12th '*My lips have still been quite swollen today and they have been stinging terribly. Uncle R and Auntie S came round and Auntie thinks it may be "dermatitis", a skin disease which could spread all over my body if I don't hurry up and get it seen to, so I think I will be going to the doctors on Monday morning. I wonder what he'll say. I wonder if I will have to go to hospital?*'

Sunday 13th '*I went over to LH's for the day today in Basingstoke. Went to Southampton in the afternoon with him, his mother and his father to see Brian in hospital. Had a lovely ride. We sat in the back of the van with a blanket over us. It was almost like being in bed. LH is really wonderful and I do love him so very much. We have arranged to get engaged when I'm eighteen, married when I'm nineteen and to have a baby by my twenty first birthday. It is all so thrilling to think about. I only hope and pray that it will all come true. My intuition tells me it will.*'

Monday 14th *'Went to Palace with my darling LH this evening. I am a bit disappointed though because he didn't send me a Valentine's card. He did apologise and of course, I said I didn't mind, but I couldn't help just feeling the slightest bit disappointed. Still, I had three others, one from Bob, one from Johnny and the other one which I haven't the faintest idea who sent. I, of course, was pleased to receive these cards but I don't want these boys at all. All I want is LH and as long as I have him, I shall remain happy.'*

Tuesday 15th *'Haven't seen my darling LH today worst luck. I do wish I could see him more often, but I mustn't be selfish and take him away from all of his other friends, not that he would leave them anyway. Had my voice recorded today. The nice salesman in the radio department called me over to him and started talking and then he showed me a microphone which he had hidden. He played it back to me but it didn't sound like me.'*

Wednesday 16th *'Haven't seen my darling LH today at all. I do wish we could get married, but there are just two things to stop us—age and finance. I went to the doctors this afternoon with Mummy to see him about my lips. He said it was nothing at all to worry about. It is just "girlish spots" as he called it. He said most girls of my age get them during the process of changing from girl to woman. He said they should have gone completely within a week or ten days, thank goodness.'*

Thursday 17th brings a heavy snow fall by morning with Mary noting how the ground is covered and it is freezing cold outside. The snow has settled and is quite thick. Mary and LH still go to the pictures in the evening *'it is freezing cold but still, LH kept me warm all the evening and I expect he will on Sunday as he is coming down for the day.'* Mary prays for the summer to hurry up and come as she's longing to go swimming outdoors again, remembering how she had such fun last year.

Friday 18th *'My darling LH came into the shop today to ask me what time he should come on Sunday. He said his train gets into Reading at ten thirty and I said I would go and meet him from the station. Boy! I shall have to get up mighty early. That just shows what love can do. It has been snowing again today and is getting quite thick.'*

On Saturday 19th Mary states how she is 'rather worried about Sarah, she isn't the same as she used to be before she met John. She flies into a temper at the least little thing, she tells lies, she swears. Oh dear, I don't want to be old-fashioned and I do want to help her but she won't take any advice from anyone. Haven't seen my darling LH today. I feel so lonely when I am not with him. I do wish I had more self-confidence, then I would go dancing or some such thing to try and take my mind off him, but I am an awful coward, I just haven't got the nerve.'

To add to her worries LH's mother rings up on Sunday to say he won't be able to come for the day as he has a bad cold which makes Mary feel really disappointed and unhappy especially as she had got up early, had a wash, dressed, done her hair and made up all by ten o'clock. 'I don't know when I shall see him again, but I know I will be unhappy until I do. I have got an awful feeling that I shall never see him again. I do hope it is not true. If he doesn't come and meet me from work tomorrow, I will phone him up, although it will look as if I am running after him, but it's a chance I shall have to take.'

Work is going really well though and on Monday 21st 'had quite a good day today, in fact, I had a jolly good time most of last week. All the men tease me, especially the nice new radio man Norman. LH came to meet me from work today and I am so thrilled, as I had had the feeling all day that I would never see him again. He has an awful cold poor little soul; I do feel sorry for him.'

Tuesday 22nd 'Wonderful day again today. Had some lovely fun with all the men at work. They are all terrible teasers. I love it so much. Norman, the young radio salesman took me home in the firm's small van and is awfully nice. Pity he is married. I went out to lunch with LH today. He still has a bit of a cold but it has got a lot better thank goodness. I am so happy LH loves me and that all the men at work like me. I shall have to keep a tight grip on myself or else I will be getting big headed and I should hate that. All I want now is to be able to sing in a dance band.'

Having had another wonderful day on Wednesday 23rd Mary contemplates, 'Norman the radio man is really awfully nice. I do like him very much. Haven't seen LH today but I will be going to the pictures with him tomorrow. I think I *love him but after having so much fun at work I am just beginning to wonder. I am almost sure I do though, as he is so well mannered and thoughtful. He really is a very nice boy. Sat and knitted all afternoon and evening—very thrilling I must say.'*

Thursday 24th *'Wonderful day again today. I do get teased terribly. Mr C picked me up dinner time, laid me on the carpet stack and then Gerald and Norman pulled carpets all over me leaving me to climb out by myself. Norman said he would take me home again this evening but I had to refuse as LH was meeting me from work to go to the pictures. During the first half of the pictures, I kept wishing LH was Norman, but as the evening grew on, I was quite glad it was my LH. He asked me, quite seriously, to marry him when I get a bit older. I said yes, if he still wants me to by then.'*

Noting how happy she is lately she puts it down to being with all the men at work who are all so nice. Norman offers to take Mary home again on Friday but at the last moment Mr C says he needn't do any deliveries which means he doesn't have the van, so she can't have a lift.

Mary writes *'Norman said I can pay him what I owe him for the lift home on Tuesday next time he takes me home and he said it wasn't money he wanted!'* During her dinner hour she meets LH and they have something to eat in Lyons. She also writes how tired he seems again lately. *'He swears he still loves me but he just seems as if he couldn't care less. He ought to see a doctor.'*

Saturday 26th *'Heavenly day today. I went out with Norman or <u>Keith</u> as I now call him, this evening. Oh my heart, it's just leapt from me into him. He is really the man I have been looking for all my life, but just my luck, he's married. He is twelve years older than me and kissed me lots of times. We went out onto a very small and lonely road and we sat in the back of his car. Oh dear, I do wish he wasn't married. He said I was too beautiful and good to be true. Oh, I feel a little guilty but it is worth it to go out with him. He wanted me to go out with him on Monday but I shall be going out with LH so I expect I will go with him on Thursday.'*

Sunday 27th *'My darling LH came for the day today. He really is wonderful, although I still like Keith very, very much. I don't know, I am stupid, I love LH and want to keep him and yet at the same time I am fairly certain that I love Keith. I do wish I was wiser, then I would know what to do. Well, I know now in my heart what I ought to do, but I just can't do it as I like going out with Keith. Perhaps I will regret it someday but at the moment, I simply love it. Oh, I am so happy and unhappy at the same time.'*

Monday 28th *'I can't quite say what today has been except that it has been full of ups and downs. I cut my hand on Mr H's lino knife and had to be rushed to hospital and have a couple of stitches put in. They didn't even deaden it when they put them in. Brother, did that hurt! I was longing to scream but I had to pretend I was ever so brave. Poor Keith was ever so worried. Going out with him tomorrow. Went to pictures with LH this evening. Poor LH, he was worried too, in fact everyone was worried except me. Although inside, I feel awful and I can't help shaking. Oh, why do I have to be brave, I feel anything but at the moment.'*

## MARCH

With Keith continuing his advances, Mary finds herself completely besotted, harbouring feelings of guilt and heartache. Somehow she has managed to get herself in a pickle again loving two men at the same time. LH is just as wonderful and takes her to the Ideal Home Exhibition in London. She also has her stitches out on her hand and trouble brews at work even though she gets her first tip off a customer.

Tuesday 1st Mary goes out with Keith in his car and comments, *'wonderful, wonderful evening. He told me he loved me, and I (in not so many words) said that I loved him, which I do. I sat on his lap at the back of his car. He is so wonderful, how I do wish he wasn't married. When we said goodbye at the station, he was on the verge of tears and said he didn't want to leave me. He said he would cry on his way home. I must say I had a job to keep from crying myself. We will see each other at work tomorrow thank goodness.'*

Wednesday 2nd sees Mary staying in all afternoon and evening thinking about things and writing *'I must say I have been thinking of Keith all the time. Oh, it is awful just sitting and thinking. I don't know, I keep telling myself that I ought not to go out with him anymore and that I shouldn't fall in love with him but I'm afraid there's nothing I can do about it. I am already in love with him. I know people say that seventeen is too young to be in love but I expect there are quite a few exceptions. I do wish I had met Keith about four years ago. I might have been married by now.'*

She comments on Thursday, having seen a lot of Keith at work, that if he wasn't married she would marry him straight away and what a lucky woman his wife is. *'I seem to understand him somehow. He didn't feel too good yesterday evening, so he told me, poor boy. I do feel sorry for him, oh, how I would love to nurse him or better still wish we could just run away together and live happily ever after. I just don't know what's got into me lately, I do nothing but sit and think of him all the time.'*

Friday 4th *'Another day of ups and downs but on the whole, I don't think it's been too bad, except for the last part perhaps. Had sort of a row with Mrs M. She said I wasted too much time and to be honest with myself I think I do. But what can I do about it when Keith is downstairs. I just can't seem to get down to work knowing he is so near and yet so far away. The evenings are the worst, I just sit there thinking about him with his wife and son.'*

Saturday 5th *'Quite a good day today. Seen quite a lot of Keith. He is so nice and I'm going out with him on Tuesday. I feel sure that I still love LH but not quite so much as I used to. I haven't seen him since last Monday but thank goodness I have had Keith to think about as that stopped me wondering how LH was getting on. It is with very mixed thoughts that I write this. Half of them is for LH and the rest for Keith.'*

Having spent the day with LH at his on Sunday 6th Mary is almost certain that she loves him and likes Keith very much. *'Not too bad a day today. It would have been perfectly alright if I had not felt so ill. I have been aching all over and my throat is terribly sore. I have been coughing and sneezing all the time. It was so nice to see my darling LH again. I haven't seen him since last Monday and he said he had missed me terribly and that he loves me.'*

Monday 7<sup>th</sup> *'Went to the pictures with my darling LH this evening. He is so nice; I am almost sure I love him. But there is just the weeniest little doubt in my heart and with that doubt, I love Keith. It is very complicated, although I think I know who I shall end up with—LH. They are both so very nice, I wish Keith wasn't married, although I don't know what I would do if he wasn't. I really would be in a muddle, so I really think it is best that he is. I am going out with him tomorrow.'*

Tuesday 8<sup>th</sup> *'Went out with Keith this evening. Oh, I don't know how I managed to stop myself from telling him I love him. It is funny really, when I'm out with LH I am almost sure it is him I love and then I go out with Keith again and I am almost sure I love him. If the truth was known I don't think I really love either of them although I like both very much indeed. Keith says he wishes he had met me before his wife because he thinks I would have won from her and says he would have married me instead.'*

Mary goes to the pictures with Sarah on Wednesday afternoon and just thinks about Keith, not being able to get him out of her mind. *'He is so wonderful. I know I ought to finish with him now, before I fall completely into love with him, but I don't know, my sense is just not working lately. I know what I ought to do and yet I just can't make myself do it.'*

On Thursday she goes to the hospital to have her stitches taken out of her hand. *'I was scared stiff but had to pretend to be brave. It hurts terribly, I do wish I could have had a good cry, but I'm just not made that way. Went to the pictures with LH this evening. He is very nice and I should really be sorry if he gave me up and yet I still like Keith an awful lot.'*

Friday 11<sup>th</sup> *'Went out with Keith this evening. Oh, I do wish he wasn't married. I like him so very much. I don't know, I have been warned time and time again not to trust married men, that they never mean anything they say but I just can't make myself disbelieve him. I keep telling myself that he can't mean half of what he says but I just keep on foolishly believing him. It would break my heart now if he told me he didn't want to take me out any more.'*

Saturday Mary stays in all evening and comments how miserable and unhappy she is eventually concluding, after thinking all evening, that she will leave her present predicament to fate. She doesn't quite believe half of the things Keith says to her anyway. But she is much too fond of him to do what she ought to, which is finish with him now.

Sunday is a *'long and boring day'* as Mary stays in all day. She is very tired and wishes life would *'run smoothly for once as at the moment it is full of uncertainty and heartbreak. I try so hard to keep smiling but I am finding it awfully hard. I know my friendship with Keith can't come to anything and I'm sure he only takes me out so he can have some excitement but I do wish he really liked me. It would solve so many of my problems if he wasn't married. Oh, why can't we just go abroad or anywhere where we could be alone.'*

LH takes her to the pictures on Monday where afterwards she notes in her diary *'I do love him but at the same time I still think an awful lot of Keith. I just don't know what's got into me lately, perhaps it is just the longing for love and excitement. With Keith, I get both but with LH I don't. Edna is coming round tomorrow, then on Wednesday I am going to the Ideal Home Exhibition in London with LH. Thursday I am going to the pictures with LH, then on Friday I am going dancing with Edna until 7 o'clock and afterwards I am going out with Keith. I wish it would hurry up.'*

Tuesday 15th *'Edna came round this evening and we played a game of Monopoly (I won) and then talked about our dancing lessons which we are going to on Friday. Seen quite a lot of Keith today. Oh, why does he have to be married. I know our friendship can't come to anything, but I wish it could. I would love to go off and spend the rest of my life with him. I know he doesn't wish the same. I think he only takes me out so that he can have some excitement.'*

Wednesday 16th *'Went to London this afternoon with LH to the Ideal Home Exhibition and looked over some caravans. They were all very lovely. Saw Wolfe & Hollanders stand and shook hands with one of the TCR men and he opened up my cut, it was a "bloody" mess. My! Did it hurt. I thought I was dying. After all that, we went to the Prince of Wales Theatre and saw Terry Thomas in a play. It was very good and we got back to Reading about 10:15 and then I came home on LH's motor bike. I've been thinking of Keith quite a lot during this afternoon. Saw quite a lot of him this morning. Very nice.'*

LH also takes her to the pictures on Thursday 17th *'he really is very sweet but I still like Keith. My mind is like a cartwheel turning round and round and round. I just can't get him out of my mind and yet, at the same time, I think of LH. I just don't know what to make of myself lately. I know I ought to forget Keith but how can I when I see him nearly all day and every day. I will just have to carry on as I'm doing at present and leave the love affairs to fate.'*

Friday 18th *'Went out with Keith this evening. Oh, I wish he wasn't married as it would solve so many problems. He told me his wife was expecting another baby and I think now that he is only coming out with me because he wants love and excitement which he can't get from his wife at present. Oh, how I wish that wasn't true. I have had plenty of boys ask me out, but I have refused them. Why did I accept Keith? Why did I have to start going out with him? It can only mean one thing—love. If only, I had the nerve to kill myself. Everyone would be happy then!'*

Saturday 19th *'Stayed in all evening and did some knitting and thought all the time of Keith. I am so dreadfully unhappy. I do wish he wasn't married. I have seen quite a lot of him today thank goodness. I know I have LH but I don't love him, so what's the use? I would so love to go abroad and sit under the palm trees by a lake and forget about everything and everybody. Perhaps I will one day.'*

LH spends the day with Mary on the Sunday 20th and they go for a walk in the afternoon down the prom. She sees many boys she knows which makes LH so jealous. *'I am quite glad he is jealous because it must mean that he really loves me. I think I love him, I'm not sure. I don't really think I can be in love with either of them or else I would be really sure, which at the moment I am not. Oh dear, what a difficult and cruel world this is. Still, I expect things will all go right one day.'*

Monday 21st *'Awful day today. Everything's gone wrong. I was wrong in my petty cash and spent all morning looking for the mistake and then I was thirty shillings short in the till and spent most of the afternoon looking for that. But still, I have seen Keith quite a few times today which cheered me up no end.'* This evening, she goes out with LH to the Palace but is glad she is going out with Keith tomorrow night as this will keep her spirits up which are at the moment very low. *'I don't think I really love anyone at the moment.'*

Tuesday 22<sup>nd</sup> *'Went out with Keith this evening. He played a trick on me at first. He said he didn't want to go out with me anymore. He said he'd thought it over and decided that it was best to forget the whole thing. Oh, he was so serious about it all I believed him. I just don't know how I stopped myself from crying, I quite expected to burst out at any time but I managed to hold it in. Then he told me it was a test to find out if I really loved him or not. Oh, I was so relieved. I didn't realise just how much I did love him until I thought I was going to lose him. I had told myself I wouldn't mind if he gave me up but now it would break my heart.'*

Wednesday 23<sup>rd</sup> *'Quite a good morning. Saw Keith quite a lot and played a trick on him this time. I had been a pound short in the till and I pretended I had got the sack. He got so worried poor boy, I felt very sorry for him. But still, it proves he must like me or else he wouldn't have been so worried.'* In the afternoon, which she mentions is *'awful'* she does some needle work and knitting, thinking of Keith the whole time, explaining that this is the reason why there are a lot of mistakes in her diary for today.

Thursday 24<sup>th</sup> Mary goes to the pictures with LH *'he is very sweet and I would hate to hurt him but I just don't love him anymore. The whole of the time I am out with him, I think of Keith. That's all I do think of—when I eat, when I'm asleep and all the time at work. I am afraid my work is suffering. Oh, why does he have to be married? It would be so much easier if he wasn't. I will be going out with him on Saturday thank goodness. He was going to ask me to go out on Tuesday but I had to refuse as I'm going to the school dance. Oh, why can't I die?'*

Friday 25<sup>th</sup> *'Queer sort of day today. I went to dancing lessons at the Court School with Edna this evening. I liked it very much. I have seen quite a lot of Keith today thank goodness. I like him so very much. I am going out with him tomorrow. Sarah's in a bad mood again this evening. She keeps crying and Mummy fusses around her. Oh, it makes me sick. Perhaps I'm a bit jealous, but Mummy has always preferred Sarah. I often feel like crying but I keep it to myself so as not to worry anyone else and Mummy thinks I'm hard, if only she knew.'*

Mary ventures out with Keith on Saturday evening as planned and has the courage to ask him whether he only goes out with her for the love, excitement and thrills but is assured by him that it's because he loves her. *'How can I make myself believe him? It is so awful, knowing that when he leaves me, he goes back to another woman, oh how I wish I was his wife. It would be so heavenly. People say you are too young to really be in love at seventeen but I don't agree with them. I must keep smiling although I don't feel much like it. I do wish everything would straighten out. It would be so nice to tell everyone about it.'*

Sunday 27th she spends the day at LH's *'I do like him very much, but I like Keith just as much, if not more. LH is really in love with me but I just feel I don't want to love anyone at the moment. I don't know what's wrong with me just lately. I expect it is just the effects of growing up. I shall see both Keith and LH tomorrow. I do wish I could have them both for keeps. Perhaps everything will work out right one day.'*

Mary goes to the pictures with LH on Monday night. *'I was thinking of Keith all the time. I like LH a lot but I have cooled off him an awful lot lately. Poor Keith has been so miserable today at work. Everything has gone wrong for him. I do wish I could have taken him out somewhere and cheered him up a bit. I bought a record today called "Give Me Your Word" and gave it to him to play for me. I don't know how I kept myself from throwing my arms around him and kissing him. Oh dear, I can't go on like this much longer.'*

Tuesday 29th *'Heavenly evening. Went to the Old Scholars Dance at Caversham School. It was wonderful. I had every dance. JL and RB kept excusing each other in the "excuse me quickstep". Then they were quarrelling as to who should take me home. In the end I said JL could take me (I had the last waltz with him). He took me to the bus stop after going down the prom, as he thought I still lived down Vastern road. Boy! Can he kiss. I wish they had a dance there every evening.'*

Wednesday 30<sup>th</sup> '*I had my very first tip today. Today a man came in and wanted a radio so I helped him by taking him downstairs. Then he cancelled the order and I had to give him his money back. He said I had been so kind and helpful that he gave me 2/6 and told me to go and buy myself some sweets. Keith was very jealous today because I went to the dance yesterday. He said he had been thinking of me all the time. I am so glad as it must mean he likes me (really likes me I mean).*'

On Thursday Mary sees a lot of Keith at work '*he was in a fighting mood, wacko! I am going out with him tomorrow after dancing lessons. I went to the Palace this evening with LH. He certainly is sweet but I just don't seem to love him anymore. Not like I used to anyway. I think I love him a little but there again, I love Keith a little as well. I can't really love either of them or else I would be really sure of my feelings.*'

### APRIL

After a wonderful evening with Keith on 1<sup>st</sup> Mary writes '*Oh, how I wish I was married to him. I would love to fuss over him and look after him. Why couldn't I have met him three years ago? What's the use of wishing though, as that's all I seem to do all the time and what good does it do. When I'm with him I feel as if he is the same age as me, not twelve years older, which proves that age makes no difference at all. I wonder whether he will still want to go out with me when his baby is born in June. I hope so as it would break my heart if he didn't.*'

Saturday 2<sup>nd</sup> Mary stays in during the evening and knits, all the time daydreaming about Keith, stating how God must have meant them to meet for some reason and how much they have in common, apart from him being married and her not. '*I suppose I will just have to wait and see what God has in store for us. I hope it is that we could perhaps get married one day.*'

On Sunday she spends the day with LH and maintains that he is '*really sweet. I have been thinking about Keith quite a lot today, even when I am kissing LH. I wonder if other girls get into such muddles as I do. I expect so, but I wonder how they get out of them. Just carry on until fate and love finds a way I suppose. Anyway, that's what I will just have to do.'*

Monday 4th she is back at work with nothing extraordinary happening apart from seeing Keith a lot and thinking about her predicament. Going out with him Tuesday evening, she notes, '*I told him this evening that I was in love with him which I am, but I had decided not to because I should feel so stupid if he gave me up. But I just felt I had to tell him. It gets worse every time I see him and it would be so wonderful if we could tell everyone about us. I would love to tell everyone that I go out with Keith but at the moment* it is quite *out of the question. Life is so cruel and difficult. I do wish it would run smoothly for once.'*

Wednesday 6th '*Horrible morning. Haven't seen much of Keith worst luck. Afternoon not too bad. I went to Blackbushe Airport with LH on his motorbike. It was a lovely ride going. The sun was shining and it was quite warm, but coming back it started to rain and was quite chilly. In the evening, I went to my dancing lessons with Edna while LH stayed at home then I sat with him all the rest of the evening. He really is nice but I just can't help myself loving Keith.'*

Thursday 7th Mary goes out with Keith '*wonderful evening. It was unexpected as I didn't think I would be going out with him again just yet. He is so very nice; I just think about him the whole time. I do wish he wasn't married. He showed me some photographs of his wife and son. His son is so sweet, I almost wish he was mine. His wife is very nice too, she is very lucky. I wish I was her. Oh dear, I wonder where all this wishing will get me. That's all I seem to do just lately—wish, wish and wish. Perhaps one day my wishes will all come true.'*

Friday 8th being Good Friday she spends the day over at LH's house noting '*I went at 9 o'clock am and stayed until 9:30pm. LH really is sweet but even so I have been thinking quite a lot about Keith. I just can't get him out of my mind. I do wish I was wiser. I suppose I must be too young to be in love. What a muddle I am in. Oh well, the only thing I can do is to keep smiling and hope that perhaps one day, all my wishes come true.'*

Saturday 9th '*Stayed in all evening worst luck. I was hoping that Keith would ask me out although I knew he couldn't possibly come out again this week. I have*

174

*seen quite a lot of him today but I won't see him now until Tuesday. I wish it would hurry up and come. I do so wish Keith wasn't married, although I don't know whether he would want to marry me and I'm not absolutely sure that I would want to marry him. I think it would be rather nice. I shall be going out with him on Tuesday, I know I ought not to but I just can't help myself.'*

On Easter Sunday *'quite a good day today. LH came round. I felt very fed up when he first came round (I had been thinking a lot about Keith) but later on I felt a lot better. LH is so nice; I do like him very much but all the time I still have a very strong feeling for Keith. I just don't know which one I like best. My head tells me to finish with Keith before I get hurt, but my heart just tells me to carry on as I have been and I think my heart is winning. I've just got a strange feeling that God planned it all out and that he wants me to carry on going out with Keith.'*

Easter Monday *'quite a good day again today. Went to Goodwood with LH, John and Sarah to see car racing. Started off about 9:45 and arrived in Goodwood just before twelve. Stopped on the way to eat dinner—sandwiches. It*

*was boiling hot to start with, the sun streamed down, but later on, the sun went in and it turned a bit cooler. Got home about 9:15 and feel absolutely tired out and just don't know how to keep my eyes open. I feel a little upset as LH has just told me I can't see him until next Sunday. When I first went out with him, he came out a lot.'*

Tuesday 12th Mary is taken home from work by LH on his motorbike then promptly goes out to secretly meet Keith with whom she has a wonderful time. *'Quite a mixed-up sort of a day today. When I went out with Keith, it would have been so easy to have really let myself go but I just thought of his wife and managed to stop myself. The time does seem to go quickly when I'm with him and yet it seems to drag every minute, I am not with him. I wish I had met him three years ago but still, if I had, he wouldn't have liked me as I was a fat schoolgirl then.'*

Wednesday Mary goes swimming in the afternoon '*went with Pat, it was lovely and warm. I went round to Mrs M's afterwards and played some records, getting home around ten past six. Then I did nothing all evening but sit and dreamed about Keith. It all seems so hopeless and yet all the time I have a voice inside that tells me to carry on going out with him and that everything will turn out right one day.'*

On Thursday 14th having stayed in all evening again, Mary is so fed up that she goes to bed at 9.30pm and listens to the wireless. Keith has been feeling unwell again at work and Mary feels quite sorry for him saying how she would have loved to have taken him home and fussed over him. LH takes her home on his motor bike, '*I was quite glad as I felt too fed up to go on the bus.'*

After her usual dance lesson with Edna on Friday she goes out with Keith. '*He didn't feel too good this evening, I did feel so sorry for him. He told me he was worried because I didn't smile at him when I got to work on Tuesday. Oh, if only I had known I'd upset him, I would have apologised at once. I was so disappointed with myself on Tuesday morning, as I had looked forward so much to seeing him and when I did see him, he was surrounded by people and I'm afraid I just couldn't manage a smile. If I had known it would upset him, I would have tried harder.'*

Saturday 16th '*Had a wonderful surprise today. Keith took me out again this evening. I had the feeling that he was getting fed up with me all through the evening. I don't know why; I will just have to put it down to the fact that it was the thirteenth time I have been out with him. I do hope he is not getting fed up with me, it would just about break my heart. I wonder why it is that I love him so much. I just don't know. I don't know why people say one is too young to be in love at my age, but I think differently, in fact, I know differently.'*

Sunday 17<sup>th</sup> *'Wonderful day today. I went over to LH's. He is very nice and I am quite sure I am love with him and yet I still love Keith. I wonder if it is possible to love two people at the same time. I think it is. We went for a nice walk this afternoon in some woods—wow, we had a lovely time and managed to get a few primroses before we went back. After tea we had a game of tennis and while I was playing LH, his mum and dad and Brian were taking photographs of me. It was awful, they were all around me and I just couldn't keep my mind on the game!'*

On Monday 18<sup>th</sup> Mary states *'a jolly good day again today'* and goes to the pictures with LH in the evening. *'I am quite sure I love him and I feel quite happy today which is the first time for about six days now, as Keith hasn't been feeling well and I hadn't seen much of LH last week due to him having rehearsals for his play, which was on Friday last. I don't ever want to go through another week like the last one. It would drive me mad.'*

Tuesday 19<sup>th</sup> *'Wonderful evening. I went out with Keith. Met him in Pangbourne and then he took me to some woods where there was a beautiful lake. Oh, how I would have loved to dive in and have a swim. I would like to have built a bungalow beside it and lived there always with Keith. Later, we went to some more woods. Oh, why does he have to be married? People keep saying one is too young to really be in love at seventeen but I know different. When I am with him, I feel as if we are the same age instead of twelve years difference. I wish we could just go away somewhere and forget everything and everyone but ourselves.'*

Wednesday 20<sup>th</sup> *'Not too bad a day I suppose. I have seen Keith quite a few times which helped to brighten the morning up. This afternoon I went on a tour of Reading with Mummy and Auntie. It wasn't bad. After that, I went for a cycle ride to Theale. It was quite good except for the fact I was thinking of Keith all the time. He told me yesterday, amongst other things, that he couldn't ask me to wait for him, I wonder how long he meant. I think I would wait forever if I thought there was the slightest chance of his becoming free.'*

Thursday 21<sup>st</sup> *'Lovely evening. Went to the pictures with my LH. He is so very sweet. I do love him; I know I do and yet I have a very strong liking for Keith at the same time. I wonder what made me go out with him? I am convinced that God had some definite reason for it as I don't know what else could have made me. I know it is wrong and I am suffering terrible mental agony through it. But something very strong keeps urging me to carry on going out with him. I got a bit worried today. Mummy gave me a lecture on right and wrong and I've been wondering if she has found out anything. I don't think she has. I hope not.'*

Friday 22<sup>nd</sup> *'Lovely evening. Went to dancing classes with Edna and then we came home for tea and then went back to the ordinary dance. Oh, I do like it. I was scared stiff at first but when we got in it was lovely. Our dance teacher—Peter was there. He wanted the last waltz with me and to take me home after. He wants to take me to the pictures. I think he's rather nice (he's not married) but I don't think I will go as he is leaving soon so I won't see him for much longer. It's such a pity as I was just beginning to know how to dance.'*

On Saturday 23<sup>rd</sup> Mary meets up with Keith *'wonderful evening. He is so nice; I like him so very much. I do wish he wasn't married then we wouldn't have to tell so many lies and we would enjoy it so much more when we go out knowing that everyone knew about it. I would love to go round telling everyone that Keith was my boyfriend. He played a trick on me again this morning. He said he didn't want to go out this evening. Oh my heart, it was down in my shoes all morning and a lot of the afternoon. I didn't know how to stop myself from throwing myself under a bus. I am so glad he didn't mean it.'*

Sunday 24<sup>th</sup> *'Not too bad a day I suppose. LH came over for the day today. He is very nice but I just can't seem to feel any love for him at all after going out with Keith. I do try hard but it's no use. I wish I could die then perhaps nobody would get heartbroken. I shall just have to wait patiently for my call. Sarah has given John up and now she is so moody. Everything I say to her she tells me to shut up. She really is horrid to me. It does hurt so although I have to try not to show it. She really has changed lately. You can't say anything to her for fear she will snap your head off.'*

Monday 25<sup>th</sup> in the evening after going to the Palace with LH *'we were saying goodnight and he asked me very seriously if I would marry him. I told him* yes, but I don't think I would really, at least not for another five or six years. Oh dear, I don't know who I like best—LH or Keith.'

On Tuesday 26th Mary has a good day at work seeing a lot of Keith which always brightens her day, especially as he has been in a very good mood today. 'My LH came to meet me from work this evening. A very pleasant surprise but, Brother! Am I glad I wasn't going out with Keith. We stood talking outside Florida Court until 6:45. Coo crumbs my legs didn't half ache. Sat knitting most of the evening after Sarah had shampooed and set my hair. I feel quite happy today, I don't know why. I expect is it because everyone else is happy now including Sarah. She is quite back to her normal self, thankfully.'

Wednesday 27th 'Not too bad a day today. Haven't seen all that much of Keith which is a great pity, but still, I have seen him so mustn't grumble. I went to the doctors this afternoon about my hand. He said that apart from it being a bit puckered, it had healed very nicely. I wonder if I will get any compensation for it. Daddy has put in a claim. I think I may get about five pounds. I hope so anyway, I could just do with it. Going out with LH tomorrow, then with Keith after dancing on Friday. I don't know which I am looking forward to most as I like them both. LH is quite serious about getting engaged on my birthday but I don't know whether to or not.'

Thursday 28th 'Lovely evening. Went to the pictures with my LH, he is wonderful. I would really like to get engaged to him. I'm afraid I am cooling off Keith again. I still like him very much and if I was encouraged a bit, I think I could love him again, but at the moment, I really love only LH. I think Mummy is a bit suspicious as she has said a lot of queer things lately. I do hope she hasn't found out about Keith and I, as it would only hurt her and that's the last thing I want to do. I expect this affair will just die out and then no one will be any the wiser.'

Friday 29th 'Wonderful evening. Went out with Keith and, oh dear, all my old feelings came rushing back to me and I am so in love with him again and yet, I am still in love with LH. People say it is impossible to be really in love with two people at once but I don't think it is as I am really in love with both of them. They are both so wonderful in their different little ways. What's a girl to do? I wish I *had the nerve to kill myself. Bought a watch today and I am quite pleased with it. Went to my dance classes before going out with Keith. Wrote off for a job at Martin's Swimming Pool but don't know if I want it now.'*

Saturday 30th *'Not too bad a day I suppose but awful evening. My old beau Bob came into the shop today. He is very nice but I am too tied up at the moment. It was so awful having to say goodbye to Keith after work this evening, we both nearly cried. I do like him so much. Went to look at my tortoises this evening and found them both dead. I am really upset. Went in the bathroom and had a good cry. Felt a bit better after. I am awfully worried at the moment. I left my diary at work yesterday and then in the evening wrote the days happenings on a page of a note book. When I went to copy it in this book, I found it had been torn out. I do hope no one finds it. I wish I knew who had it.'*

## MAY

With suspicions circulating about Mary and Keith at work and her mother raising questions at home, the couple decide to play it cool for a while. She visits Madame Tussauds with LH and Mrs M at work sets her up again with her son Bob.

Sunday 1st *'Quite a nice day but spoilt by one thing, I went to LH's for the day and came on. Of course, I had nothing to put on so I just had to sit there all the afternoon and pretend there was nothing wrong. Then in the evening I had to go to church like it. It was terrible and I was glad when I got home. In church, I prayed hard that I might find that paper I lost yesterday. I fact, I have been praying to God ever since I found it missing not to let anyone find it.'*

Keith takes Mary home dinnertime on Monday 2nd in his car and she goes out to the pictures in the evening with LH. He is still saying he wants to get engaged on her birthday this year but Mary doesn't know if she wants to now. *'I am in love with him, although not enough to marry him. I don't want to hurt him but I don't feel I want to get engaged yet; I am much too young. I will just have to trust in God to lead me the way He wants me to go. I know I will do the right thing then. How glad I am that I have Him to comfort me.'*

Tuesday 3rd '*Not too good a day today. I was going out with Keith but I think Mummy was getting suspicious so we called it off until Friday. It seems an eternity to me but I will just have to be patient. Mummy said she came through the shop this morning and heard two people talking about one of the married men in our shop going out with a young girl. That seems too much of a coincidence to be true, but I do hope she doesn't really know about Keith and I. Went to Sarah's shop and had my hair done this evening and Edna came round after. She is very nice; I wish I was her.*'

Wednesday 4th '*Quite a good day today. Went up to London for the afternoon with LH. Went to Madame Tussauds and stayed there for about two and a half hours. It was lovely especially the 'Chamber of Horrors.' I wish I could stay in London and get a little room all by myself where I could do just what I liked and come in late without getting told off. Oh dear, I keep moaning. I haven't seen much of Keith today, worse luck, but still, I will be going out with him on Friday.*'

Thursday 5th '*Jolly good day today. Had some fun with Keith and Mr V this evening before going out with LH. I was alone with the two of them. Oh, how I do like Keith. How I wish we could go away together, somewhere where nobody would tell us how awful we are. Still, if God wishes it, I expect that it could happen. Went out with LH to the Palace this evening. He is awfully nice. I feel sure I love him. What a mess.*'

Keith and Mary step out together on Friday evening '*wonderful evening. Oh, how I wish we could run away together and get away from everything and everyone. But how could we? It is so stupid to wish such impossible things and yet I believe that God is on our side and that He will help things turn out fine for us. The time seems to go very quickly when I am with Keith and yet when I'm not with him, it seems an eternity. I would love to go round telling everyone that he and I are in love.*'

Mrs M arranges for Bob to take Mary to the pictures on Saturday night '*awful evening. I am so unhappy. Went to the pictures with LH, Edna and Bob. It was all arranged by Mrs M and Bob. What an awful time I had trying to get out of going but it was no use, so I rang up LH and asked him to come. I am so very glad. I had an awful time. Edna kept nudging me and giving me filthy looks (I bet I will get told off by her when I see her) and Bob kept insulting me all the time. Only dear LH was really nice to me and I shall always be grateful to him for coming with us. I couldn't have stuck it without him. Haven't seen much of Keith today worst luck. I love him so much and really wish we could run away.'*

Sunday 8th *'Quite a good day today. My LH came for the day. He is so sweet and I really don't know what I'd do without him, yet I still love Keith. Goodness only knows why, but there it is, that's the way life goes. What's the use of worrying about it, it won't help at all. I wish I could go far away and stay there the rest of my life, but then that's a coward's way out. I will just have to trust in God to do what He wants me to do. Perhaps He will let me know what it is one day. I hope so.'*

Over the next few days having gone out with LH on Monday evening and Keith on Tuesday, Mary writes how LH keeps mentioning about them getting engaged and she states that she would like to but in a few years' time. *'I just want to have some fun before I really tie myself down, which is quite natural.'* Keith on the other hand tells Mary he has been thinking about finishing their friendship but keeps changing his mind as soon as he sees her. *'I felt so awful when he said that because I knew I really loved him. I have been thinking of finishing it too, but I just couldn't.'*

Having said that, they have a wonderful surprise date on Wednesday 11th where they meet in Stoke Row, go for a walk and then sit in his car on Peppard Common. *'He is so wonderful; I really do love him. I wish he wasn't married as everything would be much easier then. I would love to run away with him, somewhere where nobody could find us and have him for always. Perhaps one day everything will work out nicely for us both.'*

Thursday 12th *'Quite a nice day today but awful evening. I have been so worried about Keith. He told me he had heard that his father was turning his mother and brother out so he wouldn't be able to come out very much with me this week. I feel so sorry for him and yet I have been worried in case he is making it up so that he won't have to go out with me. I do so hope and pray that it is not so because I really do love him. I couldn't ask him very much about it as Mr C came and interrupted us. I wish the morning would hurry up and come so that I could make sure. I just couldn't bear to lose him now; I love him so very much.'*

Friday 13th Mary is still worrying about Keith '*not too good a day today. I feel so sorry for him having such a lot to worry about. I do wish there was something I could do to help him, but I just can't. I managed to ask him if he was playing a trick on me so that he wouldn't have to go out with me anymore but he said he wasn't. I am so relieved, as I just couldn't bear to lose him now. I love him so very much. At the moment, every minute of the day and night I think about him. I really have got it bad.*'

On Saturday 14th Keith tells Mary that he has managed to smooth things over at home with his father and asks her to go out with him this evening. '*Wonderful day and evening. We went into some woods and sat in the back of his car. Oh, I just don't know how I managed to remember the time as I felt like staying there all night. I wish with all my heart that he wasn't married. I would so love to call him mine and to be with him always. I just feel so very happy when I am with him.*'

Sunday Mary spends the day round LH's stating '*quite a nice day today. He is very sweet and I like him very much but I am not in love with him. I am in love with Keith—goodness only knows why, but I am, right from the bottom of my heart. I do wish everything would go right for us.*'

Monday 16th '*Jolly good day today. Went up to London with Mummy and Auntie this morning to see a doctor about my bad hand (re: insurance). He was an awful man. I didn't like him at all. But still, I had a lovely time after that. We went into Lyons Corner House and had dinner and then we went round C&A's and I bought a frock. It is lovely, but I really wanted to get some shoes. When I got back to work about three, Keith said he had been thinking of me all the weekend and that he really had got it bad. Oh, I am so very glad as I love him so very much. I do hope that everything will turn out right for us.*'

Tuesday 17th '*Jolly good morning and early afternoon but awful from about three fifteen onwards. Mr C called me into his office and said someone had been complaining about me talking to Keith. I don't know who it was as Mr C wouldn't tell me but I think it was Mr W. Oh dear, I love Keith so very much, I just can't help myself going up to him and talking. He was called into Mr C after I came out so I think he was told about it too. Didn't see much of him after that, except* when he was just going home. He asked me to get in early in the morning so that we can talk. He said it hasn't changed his mind about me and I'm so glad.'

Wednesday 18<sup>th</sup> '*Awful morning. Only saw Keith twice. Oh, it has seemed such a long morning. I will have to see more of him tomorrow or I'll go mad. I just want to be with him all the time. I do wish we could go away somewhere where there wouldn't be people to gossip and make scandal. But still, I will have to carry on trusting in God to make everything turn out right for us, so that we can be together always. It has been terrible weather today. It has been snowing and raining.*'

Thursday 19<sup>th</sup> '*Not too bad a day. I haven't seen Keith much though which has spoilt it. When I say I haven't seen Keith much, I mean to talk to. We both think now that the people who told Mr C about us were Mrs M, the cleaner, and Mr W. We were trying so hard not to be seen together but we love each other so much it is very difficult. Perhaps everything will turn out right one day. Went to the pictures with LH this evening. He is sweet but I am not in love with him. I don't really know what I would do without him and yet I keep thinking of Keith all the time. This is so difficult.*'

Friday 20<sup>th</sup> '*Wonderful evening. Went out with Keith. He is so wonderful; I love him very much. How I wish we could be shipwrecked on a desert island where no one could tell us off. He told me his wife may have her baby in a fortnight. I wonder if he will change at all. Went to my dancing lessons this evening with Edna and afterwards we stood and talked to our teacher and a nice boy called Barry. He had his arm round me.*'

Saturday 21<sup>st</sup> '*not too bad a day today, although I haven't seen Keith much to talk to worst luck. Mummy, Daddy and Auntie went to Wembley today, so Sarah and I sat in all evening and listened to Radio Luxemburg as loud as it would go. I just sat with the music in the background thinking of Keith and imagining that we were down by the swaying palm trees, just the two of us. How I hope and pray that one day we will be really doing that.*'

Mary spends Sunday with LH as he comes round for the day which stops her from thinking about Keith to some extent. *'LH is awfully sweet and I like him very much, but I just don't love him anymore. It is Keith I really love.'*

By Monday 23rd Mary is still thinking about Keith and is disappointed not to have seen very much of him at work at all today. She comments how she would love to be with him all the time without being afraid someone will see them. *'It is awful having to hide the fact we are in love; it is also very difficult.'* She goes to the Palace with LH in the evening and is now adamant that she is not in love with him. *'I would hate to hurt LH in any way because he is such a nice boy, so I will just have to be patient and wait and see how things turn out, but all the time I am with him, I keep thinking of Keith and wonder what he's doing.'*

Tuesday 24th *'Seen quite a lot of Keith today, thank goodness. He came to meet me dinner time and took me back to work. Then he took me home again this evening. He really is wonderful; I do wish he was my boyfriend instead of LH. I would love to tell everybody about us, but it all seems so hopeless. If only we could run away somewhere but we can't because it would make his wife unhappy and that's the last thing I want to do.'*

Wednesday 25th *'Jolly good day again today. Haven't seen all that much of Keith but what I did see of him was lovely. I do love him so very much. I stayed in all afternoon and evening and did some washing and ironing. Auntie V brought some friends up to tea but they didn't stay very long. Sarah very miserable this afternoon and evening because her new boyfriend, Jerry, won't be able to go out with her until Sunday. She has been so moody and flies in a temper at the least little thing and some of the things she says to me really hurt. Oh dear.'*

Thursday 26th *'Jolly good day again today. Seen a lot of Keith which has helped to make it nice. Mr C hasn't been in today so I was able to talk to him quite a lot. Just before he went home, we waited until everyone had gone home and then we had a nice time for about ten minutes, kissing and hugging. I love him so much and yet I think I am beginning to like LH better now. Went to the pictures with LH this evening and then went and had some dinner after. I am going over to his on Saturday for the weekend. I am nervous as I don't like staying the night away from home. I am so shy.'*

Mary cheekily skips her dance class on Friday night to go out with Keith *'wonderful evening, met him at six o'clock and didn't say goodbye until 9:45, nearly four hours together. It was lovely. I love him so very much; I don't know how I managed to say goodbye to him. I would stay with him forever. It would make things so much easier if he wasn't married. If only something could turn out right for us. How I long for my wishes to come true. Perhaps one day they will.'*

Saturday 28th *'I am writing this in LH's house. I am staying here for the weekend. I am so nervous; I am frightened to move. LH is just in the next room. It is twenty past eleven and I am longing to get into bed and go to sleep. I only hope I can wake up very early tomorrow morning before anyone brings me a cup of tea. It's been a busy day today at work. Seen a fair amount of Keith, but not as much as I would have liked to. We both nearly cried when we said goodbye this evening. Saw Johnny today.'*

Sunday 29th *'Well, I managed to get through the night alright but how I got through the day I just don't know. Went to church this morning and then went to a friend of LH's mothers for the christening of her baby. Had some tea with the lady, then the christening and then after that a lot more people came round the house. Altogether there were fourteen people in the room. All, except four, I had never seen before. Boy, was I scared. We didn't get back to LH's until eleven fifteen and then we had some supper and then got ready for bed. I am just getting into my bed now and its twelve fifteen. Thought a lot about Keith today.'*

On bank holiday Monday Mary has a lovely day going into Basingstoke in the morning to help put up some loud speakers for a fete, then onto a horse show. *'I do wish I had a horse. After the show, we went back to the house for tea then back to the fete to take the speakers down. By that time, it was ten twenty, so we had a quick supper and LH drove me home in the van as there were no trains owing to the strike. Poor LH was so tired and I must admit so was I.'*

Tuesday 31st *'Wonderful evening. Went out with Keith. Oh, how can I stop myself from loving him so much? I just long to be with him all the time. If only he wasn't married. I just think of all the things we could do together. LH came into the shop today to offer me a lift home but of course I had to refuse. I do like him, but I just can't like him as much as Keith.'*

## JUNE

Wednesday 1st *'Not too bad a day today except for gnat bites. I am simply covered in them. The reason being, I laid in the long grass with Keith yesterday. But still it was worth it as I love him so much. Haven't seen very much of him today except when he was just about to go home. Went to an ice circus with LH this evening and for a walk this afternoon. He had the day off from work today and asked me quite seriously to marry him. I was quite amazed and I just didn't know what to say. I can't love him or else I would have been thrilled, but I'm not.'*

Mary doesn't see much of Keith at work on Thursday which leads to her saying the day could have been better. She frequents the Palace again with LH this evening saying *'Oh dear, he really is serious, I do wish he wasn't as I don't want to get engaged to him for the simple reason that I am not in love with him. I saw the boy who goes dancing today. He asked me to go out with him but I just can't get Keith out of my mind.'*

On Friday 3rd everything goes wrong in the morning at work; *'first, I went to work without the safe key and had to go home and get it. Secondly, my weekend summaries went wrong. Thirdly, I was a pound over in my banking and lots of other things like that. But still quite a good afternoon and evening. I went dancing this evening, I do like it very much. I also like the boy who goes—Barry, his name is and also Don, my teacher. Both of them are trying to get off with me. Seen quite a lot of Keith today, thank goodness. I phoned him up just before I went dancing to arrange for us to go out tomorrow. Oh, how I wish God would make things straighten out.'*

Saturday 4th *'Wonderful evening with Keith. He says his wife will have to go into hospital on Monday and he wants me to go out with him a lot, which of*

187

*course I can't. I wonder what he will be like after his baby is born. There is so much to wish for and think about. I don't know where I am or what I am doing. The only thing I really am certain of is that God is with me and helping me, which is such a comforting thought. I do wish Keith and I could be together forever and yet I don't really want to break up his marriage. Oh dear!'*

Sunday 5th *'Quite a nice day today. The weather has been beautiful. The sun has been shining and the sky has been bright blue and also it has been really hot. LH came round and we went and sat on the prom from about three fifteen until about five forty-five. Got home and had tea then sat out the front on the lawn. It was lovely. I could easily have gone to sleep out there. I was dreaming about Keith most of the time, wondering where he was and what he was doing. LH is really serious about getting engaged on my birthday this year. I don't know what I will say.'*

Monday 6th *'Quite a good evening. Went to the pictures with LH. It was an awful film though—all about a cobra who turned into a woman, awfully creepy. I hope I don't dream of it tonight. Afterwards, we had some dinner at the Oxford Café, then LH took me home. After he had left me, I ran down the road to the phone box and phoned Keith as he asked me to at work today. We had a nice long talk. He is alone in the house now as his wife is in hospital about to have her baby at any moment. I wonder if it will change Keith at all.'*

On Tuesday evening *'wonderful evening. Went out with Keith. Oh, how I love him. We went to Wallingford at first and I walked round the town while he went and saw his wife in hospital. Then we went into some woods and sat in the back of his car. I do wish everything would turn out right for Keith and I. At the moment, everything seems hopeless. His wife is supposed to have her baby this evening. I have been so jittery.'*

Wednesday 8th *'Horrible day today with nearly everything going wrong. I don't know whether it is because I am so tired, that I feel so unhappy or whether it is because I love Keith and can't have him. I was going out with him this afternoon but I had my hair cut and permed instead. It does look a sight. I do hope Keith will still like me tomorrow as he hates short hair. I phoned him up this evening and we had a nice long talk. I think I will go crazy soon if things don't turn out nice for us. Sometimes I wish I could die but know this is just a coward's way out.'*

Thursday 9th *'not too bad a day I suppose but could have been a lot better. Went to the Palace with LH and then into the Oxford Café. He tells me he loves me over and over again and I know he really means it but I just can't bring myself to love him. All the time I am with him, I'm only thinking of Keith whom I do love very much. His wife had her baby this morning—a boy. I think poor Keith was a teeny bit disappointed as he had hoped for a girl. I phoned him up this evening after LH had gone and he told me he loves me and always will.'*

Friday 10th *'Wonderful evening. Went out with Keith. I love him even more than ever and enough to spend my whole life waiting for him. I felt so sorry for him this evening as he had been looking forward to going out with me tomorrow and I had to tell him I was going away. He said I had hurt him terribly; I did feel awful as that is the very last thing I wanted to do. He said he would like to take me to Canada and the way I feel now I think I would go with him.'*

Saturday 11th she writes from LH's house where she is staying once again for the weekend. *'I am so unhappy and am thinking of Keith all the time. I love him so very much. He took me home in his car dinner time and then picked me up outside Florida Court after dinner and took me back to work. He is so disappointed that he couldn't take me out this evening and I do wish I could have gone out with him. On the way to Basingstoke with LH, I made an excuse and managed to phone Keith. It was wonderful to just hear his voice. I feel so very different about him than all the others I've known. This is real love.'*

On the Sunday she goes to Portsmouth with LH's parents to meet his grandmother, three aunts and one uncle, but still wishes she was with Keith. LH brings Mary home quite late on Sunday after they stop along the way. *'Not too bad a day I suppose. It was a lovely ride but I kept thinking of Keith and wishing I was with him. Daddy is in an awful mood. He told me off dreadfully. I feel quite ill, my head feels as if it is going to drop off, my throat is as sore as can be and I ache all over. I have told LH I won't be able to go out with him tomorrow (I am going out with Keith) and he was so disappointed.'*

She then proceeds to go out with Keith on Monday and Tuesday evenings saying she feels so happy and unhappy at the same time and fears she may have a breakdown before much longer as life is so cruel. '*I am so madly in love with him I just can't help myself. I ought not to be but love is something that just comes and it can't stop and turn off just like that. If only he wasn't married. How I long to be far, far away—somewhere by the sea under the palm trees with music in the background. We wouldn't have to be so careful in case anyone saw us. It would be wonderful.*'

Wednesday 15th '*Haven't seen much of Keith today worst luck, but I phoned him up this afternoon and then again this evening. I love him so much. It is getting worse. There isn't a minute that goes by without me thinking about him. Life is so cruel. At the moment, I feel like throwing myself in front of a bus or something. I won't be going out with him tomorrow and it will seem an endless evening. Went round Edna's this evening.*'

Having gone out with LH on Thursday evening, '*I couldn't concentrate properly as I was thinking too much about Keith. I have been worrying because when LH and I went into the Odeon Car Park Keith's car was right in the entrance. I thought perhaps that he was waiting there to see if I really did go out with LH. I was so worried in case he gave me up as I think he would if he did find out. I phoned him up afterwards for about 20 minutes and he didn't say a word about it so I don't think he could have seen us. I am so glad.*'

On Friday Mary goes out with Keith stating she had a '*wonderful evening. We had such a lovely time. It would make me so very happy if we could see each other every evening and I would love to tell everyone that we were in love. It is awful having to keep a secret and having to tell so many lies in order to get out. I will just have to go on hoping.*'

Saturday 18th '*Wonderful evening. Went out with Keith again. We went right past his house. It is beautiful, I wish I lived there. He told me this evening that he had seen LH and I go into the Odeon car park on Thursday. I felt so awful and yet I just couldn't say what I felt. I was so near to tears. I would do anything in the world not to have lied to him but I was so afraid he would give me up if I did. But still, it is such a happy relief not to have to tell him lies anymore. It was so painful having to tell lies to one I love above everything and everyone else in the world. I think I would die if he really did give me up.'*

Sunday 19<sup>th</sup> *'Awful day. All I've done is watch the clock and think of Keith. It's been such a long day and I really have got it bad. I am truly in love with him. I have thought I was in love lots of times but it was never like this. There isn't one minute that goes by without me thinking of him and wishing he was mine forever. I phoned him up this evening and he said he hadn't been feeling well today. I do hope he will be alright tomorrow. I would die if anything happened to him, or if he gave me up now.'*

On Monday Keith takes Mary out in the evening *'I love him so much. oh, it is such a cruel world to be in love with someone whom you know you can't have. It's just heart-breaking. I do wish he wasn't married. I would give the whole world for him not to be. I know I will do something desperate soon like throw myself in front of a bus.'*

Their current situation is obviously affecting Keith too as on Tuesday 21<sup>st</sup> on another evening out together, he tells her he had had a nasty crash in his car which has shaken him up. *'He said he wished it had finished him off. I am so very glad it didn't. I know I would have committed suicide if it had. Later on in the evening he began to get over it and later still, he was quite cheerful. I am so glad as I get worried if I think he is unhappy. If only, we could think of something which would enable us to be together. I love him so madly.'*

On Wednesday Keith brings Mary home in his car dinner time and they sit and talk until five to two. She has a terrible afternoon at home just thinking of him and wishing they could be together always and that tomorrow would hurry up and come, so she can see him again. On Thursday, she ventures to the Palace with LH but wishes it was Keith and Friday night stays home where she goes over everything in her head. *'I will never be really happy until he is mine forever. It has been such a long evening this evening. I do wish Keith could have taken me out. It is so heart-breaking to sit at home having to think of him with his wife and family. I do wish we could think of a solution to our awful problem. I know I will never be able to give him up as I am so much in love with him.'*

Saturday 25th '*Very busy day today worst luck, but I have seen a fair amount of Keith today thank goodness. I love him so deeply I just don't think I will be able to stand it much longer. I will either have to beg him to take me away or else commit suicide. I am writing this in LH's house but all the time I am thinking of Keith and I know I will be all day tomorrow when we are at Bournemouth. I just can't get him out of my mind.*'

Sunday 26th '*Jolly good day today except for one thing—Keith wasn't with me. Went to Bournemouth to see Mum and Dad in their caravan. Phew! Was that sun hot. I don't know what I am going to wear tomorrow, I am so sunburnt and it's so sore I can hardly move. If it wasn't for Keith being at work, I would stay at home but I must go in and see him. I am writing this in LH's house as it was too late to go back home, so I will have to get up very early in the morning to go back to Reading on the motor bike by eight o'clock. I hope I wake up in time.*'

Margaret, Kenneth, Auntie V, LH and Mary in Bournemouth 1955

Monday 27th '*Not too good a day today and awful evening. Seen a fair amount of Keith today which has been the only thing to brighten it up a bit. Came back to Reading on the motorbike this morning and phew, I have never been in such agony before in my life. My sunburn is absolutely roar and I could hardly move all day. This evening Auntie made Sarah and I stand for a solid hour while she lectured us about bringing our boyfriends home without asking her first. Oh, it was awful. I nearly went to sleep standing up. She told the boys off as well. It makes my blood boil.'* It is obvious that Auntie had been roped in to look after the girls while their parents went away on holiday.

Mary meets up with Keith on Tuesday evening then on Wednesday 29th *'Not too bad a day I suppose. Went with Auntie and Sarah to Mrs B's in Winnersh this afternoon. It wasn't bad I suppose. Then in the evening I went with Edna to the old school's opening day. Saw a lot of teachers. I do wish I was back there; I was so happy and carefree when I was at school.'*

Thursday 30th *'Not too bad a day again today. I have seen quite a lot of Keith, although not half as much as I would have liked to have done. I wonder why it is that I love him so. There must be a reason. I think it really must have been planned. I do wish things would turn out right for us. I know I will go mad before much longer. I went to the Palace with LH this evening. He is a nice boy, but I just don't love him and that's all there is to it. I can't make myself love him just because I think I ought to. I am in love with Keith, whether I ought to be or not is a different matter. Perhaps things will go right one of these days.'*

JULY

Friday 1st *'Wonderful evening. Went dancing until 6:30 and then went out with darling Keith. Every minute away from him seems like an eternity. I do so wish he was mine for ever. I had to go and fall head over heels in love with him, there must be a reason.'*

Saturday 2nd *'Not too bad a day as I have seen quite a lot of Keith which has made it nice. Mummy and Pop came home this evening, they are lovely and brown. It is nice to see them home again. I had an awful row with Sarah this evening. She seems to fly into a temper at the least little thing. She kept hitting and scratching me and then when Mummy came in to see what was going on, she burst into tears and as usual, Mummy told me off for making her cry. I try so hard not to cry but have an awful job when Mum sticks up for her.'*

Sunday afternoon LH comes round *'not too bad a day I suppose except for the fact it has been raining most of the time and that I haven't seen my darling*

*Keith. I do wish he was mine forever. LH is nice but I just don't love him. I do try because I think that's what I ought to do, but it isn't any good. I am in love with Keith.'*

Monday 4th *'Wonderful evening. Went out with my darling Keith. Oh, I love him so very much. I would give the world for him to be mine forever but at the moment I just don't see how that can be so, even though we have so much in common and I think we must have been made for each other.'*

On Tuesday evening LH takes Mary to Purley *'we were going in the river for a swim but he said as he had got sunburnt during the afternoon so he hadn't better go into cold water. I felt quite annoyed as I would have loved to have gone in and had a swim.'*

Wednesday 6th *'Awful morning. Everything has seemed to go wrong. All my money has gone wrong in the till and in the petty cash. I am sure I will get the sack before much longer. I just can't seem to concentrate on my work just lately. All I think about is Keith. I know I ought not to but I just can't help it. I love him so very much. Perhaps everything will go right for us one day. I do hope so. Stayed in all afternoon and did some washing and ironing, then spent all the evening knitting.'*

Thursday 7th *'Not too good, not too bad a day today. I haven't seen half as much of Keith as I would have liked to today but still, I am going out with him tomorrow and Saturday, thank goodness. Went to the Palace with LH this evening but I even dislike him holding my hand now and all the time I am with him, I am wishing it was Keith. How much longer can I keep this up? I am sure I will be ill before much longer. All I do now is long for him all the time. I wish I had the nerve to kill myself.'*

Friday 8th *'Wonderful evening. Went out with Keith. Oh, he is so wonderful; I am so much in love with him. How could I ever live without him? I am going out with him tomorrow and then of course, it is my holiday, a whole fortnight, I don't know how I will stand it. I do hope he won't forget me during that time. All I hope is that nobody finds out about us going out together. I don't want anyone to get hurt and yet, I know I want Keith for my very own, forever and ever.'*

Saturday 9th '*Not too good a day but lovely early evening. Went up the Warren with my darling Keith for about an hour (much too short a time). I don't know why it is, but I love him so deeply. We are both neglecting our work and I am sure one of us will get the sack before much longer. I just can't seem to concentrate on my work however hard I try. All I think about is Keith and how we could be together forever. Oh, if only we could, I would be so happy.*'

Sunday 10th '*Not too bad a day today except for one thing and that is that I have been thinking of Keith all the time, wondering where he was and what he was doing, wishing he was with me. Oh, if only I could think of some way in which we could be together for always, I know I won't be happy until I do. I went round to LH's for the day today. It is so boring, we played ball in the garden most of the time, breaking my shoe and dirtying my frock in the process. I can never seem to keep clean when I go round there however hard I try, something always goes wrong.*'

Mary now has the next two weeks off from work and has never missed seeing Keith so much. She meets up with him on Monday on his dinner hour in town and they talk for about forty-five minutes. Then in the afternoon '*I went to the pictures with Mummy and Auntie. It wasn't bad then LH came round for tea. Afterwards we went to the Palace but I was rather annoyed as I would rather have gone swimming. Oh well, I will have to go some other time.*'

She meets up with Keith again Tuesday dinner time for about twenty minutes then '*went to Martins Pool this afternoon with Mum and had a glorious swim for about an hour. I am going again tomorrow. I went out with darling Keith this evening. He is so wonderful. I really am in love with him. I always feel so happy and carefree when I am with him. I do wish he was mine. It would make me so very happy. I wonder if he ever will be and how it will come about.*'

Wednesday 13th '*Quite a good day today. Did a bit of shopping this morning then went to the dentist at two o'clock and he said I had a perfect set of teeth thank goodness. Went swimming at Martins Pool with LH this afternoon. It was wonderfully warm and we saw Gerald (W&H) down there and spent all the time with him. I am glad really. It was more fun than it would have been if LH and I*

195

*had been on our own. Thought quite a lot about Keith today, wondering what he was doing and wishing that I was swimming with him.'*

She goes swimming again on Thursday announcing *'wonderful day. Went over to Martins swimming pool again this afternoon. The water was lovely and cool—75 degrees, I could live there. Wonderful evening too, as I went out with my darling Keith. I have never felt like this before. I wonder how it will all end, I do hope it ends the way I want it to. Nothing, not even the whole world could make me happier. I know it would break my heart if I had to part from him. I just wouldn't have anything to live for.'*

On Friday 15th having met up with Keith again on his dinnertime, Mary and LH go to a fair in the evening. *'We won quite a lot of prizes. I felt quite annoyed though, as he wouldn't go on any of the things.'*

Saturday 16th *'Jolly good day today considering I haven't seen my darling Keith. I went to Littlehampton with LH for the day. We went in Smiths coach and it was a lovely ride. When we got there, we went out in a speed boat and then*

*had some dinner. After that, we had a lovely swim and sunbathed. The water was wonderfully warm. Then we went on the scenic railway and on the big wheel and ghost train. We had tea then, and came back home. I am awfully sunburnt. I will be so sore in the morning. I have thought about Keith so much today.'*

Sunday 17th *'Quite a nice day again today. Went to Cheddar and went in the caves. They were wonderfully cool; I could have stayed in there all day. Later on, we went to Western Super Mare. It was so hot I just didn't know what to do with myself. We sat on the beach most of*

Mary at Weston Jul 1955

*the time. We were going in the sea for a swim but the tide was out and we would have had to walk through piles of mud before we could have reached the water.*

*Thought a lot about Keith today, wishing it was him I was with. I wonder what he did today.'*

*Monday 18ᵗʰ 'A nice lazy day today. Stayed in bed until eleven thirty, then got up and met Mummy from the English Leather Co and we went into Lyons for dinner. After she had gone back to work, I went to the pictures by myself. It was a good film but I have never longed for Keith more than I did then. I have been thinking about him nearly all day. I wonder where he has been today and whether he has enjoyed himself.'*

Tuesday 19ᵗʰ is another late start (eleven thirty) then she meets her mother again at dinner time, in this instance going into the Cadena for dinner. *'After that, I came home and made some buns and a sponge. LH came round about four o'clock and we had tea and then went off to the Palace. It wasn't bad, but I have seen better. He wants me to go to his tomorrow but I don't really want to go. I have been thinking of Keith again today. I can't stand it much longer without him.'*

Wednesday 20ᵗʰ *'Not too good a day I'm afraid. Nearly everything has gone wrong. I tried to phone Keith up this morning but there was no reply worst luck. I was so disappointed. I went to LH's this morning, although, of course, he wasn't there. I don't know what I am going to do about phoning Keith tomorrow as I will be with LH's mum all the time. I do hope I will be able to get out to phone him. I don't know how I will last until Monday if I don't. All I do is think of him, wishing he was with me.'*

Thursday 21ˢᵗ *'Not too good a day again today. I have been trying desperately to get to a phone box and phone my darling Keith but I couldn't. Oh, I am so thoroughly disappointed. The day seems absolutely endless. I wonder if he's been thinking of me. I do hope he won't change his mind*

Mary at Cheddar Jul 1955

*about me by now. Haven't done very much today worst luck. If I had had plenty to do, I wouldn't have thought about Keith so much.'*

Friday 22<sup>nd</sup> '*Awful day today. Sat and did nothing all morning but think about Keith. I just haven't been able to go to a phone box. I know I will go mad if I don't speak to him soon. Went to see Billy Graham at the Arsenal Stadium this evening. I have never been so bored in my life. I just couldn't understand what he was talking about. Perhaps that was because I was thinking of my darling Keith all the time. I will try to phone him tomorrow to see if he can come out in the evening.*'

Saturday 23<sup>rd</sup> '*Not too bad a day today, I suppose. I did a bit of shopping up the town this morning with LH, then met Mummy for lunch and after that, we went to the pictures. LH had to go home about six thirty as he has a lot of packing to do—he is going away tomorrow for a fortnight. I know I don't love him because it doesn't worry me a bit to know I won't see him. If I did love him, I would be very unhappy. I managed to phone Keith up this morning while I was out but he was just off out for the day. I have missed him so much.*'

Sunday 24<sup>th</sup> '*Very boring day today. I stayed in bed until twelve fifteen, then had dinner and afterwards read a few papers and did my knitting for the rest of the day. I have been thinking of Keith most of the time. I have not seen him for over a week now. I just don't know how I have lived. Thank goodness I will see him tomorrow. I wonder if he has been thinking about me and if so, what sort of things.*'

It's Monday 25<sup>th</sup> and Mary is back at work and has had quite a good day considering '*I saw my darling Keith thank goodness. It has seemed an eternity since I saw him last. He says he still loves me. Oh, I do hope he really means it as I love him so much.*'

Tuesday 26<sup>th</sup> is another good day with Mary seeing a lot of Keith. She wonders how all this will end and hopes no one will find out about them '*it would cause so many people great unhappiness and that is the last thing I want to do. I am not quite sure what I want at the moment, my brain is so muddled up. I do wish everything would straighten out. I have thought so hard for a solution to this problem but I just can't find a suitable one. I am going out with him on Thursday thank goodness.*'

**Wednesday 27th** *'Not too bad a day. The weather has been beautiful again. I went to the pictures with Mummy this afternoon to see Rory Calhoun. He is lovely. Edna came round this evening and we sat outside on the lawn all the evening and read a book each. I have been thinking of Keith such a lot. I have been wondering if he really does love me or whether he has changed his mind during the holidays. Still, I will know tomorrow as I'm going out with him. I do wish there was a solution to our problem but can't see one at the moment.'*

**Thursday 28th** *'Wonderful evening. Went out with my darling Keith. It is a fortnight ago today that I went out with him last. It has really seemed ages. I wonder why I love him so much. I really think that it all must have been planned, I just don't know. I do so wish he wasn't married. I feel so sorry for his wife and yet I just can't break away from him. Something very strong seems to be holding me back. But still, I don't mind a bit because I don't want to break from him. Life just wouldn't be the same without him.'*

**Friday 29th** *'Not too bad a day today. Seen quite a good bit of Keith today thank goodness. Oh, I love him so much. I keep asking myself time and time again, why? But I just can't find an answer. How I wish we could go away somewhere together where we wouldn't keep getting filthy looks every time, we spoke to one another. It would be so wonderful to be amongst people who would just smile sweetly when they saw two people so very much in love. Oh, what can I do? I can't give him up as it would really break my heart.'*

**Saturday 30th** *'Oh dear, life seems so hopeless. I am desperately in love with Keith and yet I know I can't have him. I have seen quite a lot of him today thank goodness although I didn't get much chance to go down from the office to see him this afternoon. I just don't know what I am going to do. I feel so awful about going out with him and yet I know I can't stop as it would just break my heart. If only people knew, how I am being tormented. If only there was someone, I could really talk to but there isn't. I don't think anyone really knows me. I have to keep all my thoughts to myself.'*

**Sunday 31st** *'Never have I had such an unhappy, long, boring day as today. I have never longed for anyone as I have longed for Keith. I think if he had shown up any time today, I would never have let him go, that is without me. I would* *have gone anywhere with him; in the mood I have been in since this morning. I just don't know how I have managed not to run away today.'*

## AUGUST

Bank holiday Monday *'quite a good day today or should I say a full one which has helped to take my mind off Keith a bit. Went to Weymouth to see LH and his family. Met his Grandparents. Went by coach and the back of it caught fire, twice. Luckily it was put out. Went for a swim in the sea but it was absolutely freezing also pouring with rain. Then we had a float out which I liked very much. I do wish Keith could have been with me. Sitting in the coach I had plenty of time to think about him. I wonder if I will be going out with him tomorrow.'*

Tuesday 2nd *'Not too bad a day I suppose. I have done so much work today and feel so ill and tired out. I have seen Keith quite a few times today thank goodness. I know I will never have him and yet in my heart I am still hoping that perhaps one day I will. I suppose I ought really to leave my job and take something completely different in the hope that I would forget him, but I just couldn't leave. I would make myself really ill, pining for him.'*

On Wednesday after work Mary goes to the pictures with her mother and the film is so wonderful she stays and watches it twice! *'I do wish I had been with Keith. I know I can't go on with all this much longer. How I wish that I was dead, it would make things much easier for everyone. I can't remember when I have felt so lonely. I do wish there was someone I could turn to for sympathy and advice but there isn't. Oh God, why does Keith have to be married? Why am I being tormented like this? I do wish there was someone I could turn to for sympathy and advice, but there isn't.'*

Thursday 4th *'Been very busy today. I haven't had much time to go down from the office and see Keith although I have seen him at various times of the day thank goodness. How I wish I could find a solution to our problem other than finish the whole thing but I just couldn't do that as it would break my heart. How cruel the world is. I do so wish that he wasn't married. I feel so sorry for his wife and yet I feel glad when Keith tells me they have quarrelled. Oh, I must be wicked but I love him'*

Mary and Keith go out together on Friday '*wonderful, wonderful evening. I love him so much I don't know how I stopped myself from, how shall I say—"anticipating marriage". I must have a lot more will power than I thought. I do wish we could get married and be together forever. I would be the happiest girl in the whole world. I wonder if he will ever be mine, or if he will finish with me.*'

On Saturday 6th Mary sees a fair amount of Keith but is contemplating a whole week without him next week as he is going away on holiday '*so I won't see him at work, it really will seem an eternity. He said he may see me one dinner time next week. I do hope he does. I do hope he won't forget me while he's away and still loves me when he comes back. I wonder if he will ever be really mine. I feel so unhappy this evening.*'

Mary stays in bed until 12 o'clock on Sunday pondering how she will survive without seeing Keith next week. '*I don't quite know what today has been. Not too bad I suppose. I stayed in bed until 12 o'clock which helped the day seem shorter thank goodness. I can't quite make myself believe that I won't be seeing Keith at work tomorrow. I will miss him so very much. Why do I have to love him so much?*'

Monday 8th '*it's been such a long day today without my darling Keith. I don't know how I have managed to survive without him. I do hope the rest of the week goes quicker. LH came to meet me from work today. He bought me a very nice needlework box. I feel so sorry for him because I just can't love him. I have tried but just can't. All the time I am thinking of Keith and wishing it was him instead.*'

Tuesday 9th '*It was such a long morning this morning. I just didn't have a thing to do so I just sat and thought about Keith and then at dinner time I saw him. Oh, he is so wonderful. I am just head over heels in love with him. It all seems so hopeless and I do wish I could see into the future to see what God has planned for us. I feel so guilty and awful for going out with him and yet it would break my heart to part with him.*'

Wednesday 10th '*I went to the pictures with LH this evening. Oh dear, I try so hard to love him but it isn't any use, I just can't. I even dislike him kissing me now. All the time I am with him I am thinking of Keith and wishing I was with* him. I do hope Mummy or Daddy won't find out because it would upset them terribly and that's the last thing in the world I want to do. Oh, I do wish I could die and be out of it all.'

Thursday 11<sup>th</sup> 'Been thinking of Keith all day again today! Oh, it is awful this utter loneliness. I have come to the conclusion that nobody really knows me. I have to keep everything to myself. There is just no one who I can talk to. My conscience is tormenting me terribly but I know I can't give Keith up. I am much too in love with him. How I pray to God to help us, as I feel He is the only one who really understands me and how I feel.'

Friday 12<sup>th</sup> 'Went to the Palace with LH this evening. I have such a job to be nice to him and just can't make myself love him. I think he is beginning to know because he keeps telling me I sound fed up. Of course, I have to pretend I'm not but I am really. I am so deeply in love with Keith that I can't think of anything else. I do wish Monday would hurry up and come, I am looking forward so very much to seeing him again.'

Saturday 13<sup>th</sup> 'Not too bad a day today. I bought a radio and a gramophone on hire purchase today and they are lovely. I have been playing my records all evening and dreaming of my darling Keith. I think Mummy is beginning to suspect, that is if she doesn't know already. It would kill me if she ever really truly found out. I love him so much; I just can't give him up. Oh God, please help me. If only he wasn't married.'

Sunday is quite a good day with LH coming over and he and Mary sitting playing her records all morning. 'Then we went on the river in the afternoon. It was lovely. I have felt in a queer mood today. I just couldn't bare LH to kiss me or even put his arm round me and now he's gone (I'm in bed) I realise it is him I really love and not Keith, although I still like Keith. I'm in such a muddle and sure I will have a nervous breakdown before long. I wish I could talk to someone but I suppose I'm just not made that way.'

Monday 15<sup>th</sup> 'Oh God, I have never been so miserable and terribly unhappy in my whole life. I went out with Keith this evening and was quite prepared to finish it. I had had a feeling all day that tonight would be the last, I don't know why and Keith then told me that he only loved me a small bit and that he hadn't missed me a bit while he was on holiday. I don't know why I am upset because it was what I was wanting yesterday. He is coming out again though, although not for three weeks as he has to earn some money in the evenings. Before he went home tonight, he told me he did really love me. Oh, I feel so ill and confused, I wish I could die.'

On Tuesday Keith tells Mary that he regrets what he said to her last night and that he can't wait three weeks before taking her out again! This makes Mary very much in love with him and even more certain that she doesn't love LH. '*I just don't know what I want except, perhaps, to be loved. I am in such a muddle; my conscience is tormenting me and altogether I feel really ill.*'

Wednesday 17th '*Awful day today. I haven't seen very much of my darling Keith worst luck. I am sure I love him and yet I am so unhappy. If this goes on much longer, I will have to put an end to my life. I just can't bare it much longer. LH came round dinner time and then we went on the river during the afternoon and we got drenched. It absolutely poured with rain. I was very annoyed as I had a lot of work to do and didn't do any of it. Oh God, what am I going to do? I just can't bare LH near me now. If only I could die, then everyone would be happy.*'

Thursday 18th '*Awful morning. I hardly saw anything of Keith before work as he didn't come in until about one minute to nine. He wrote me a note when I went to the bank, saying that he loves me more than ever. I wonder if he really means it or whether he is just saying it to please me. He also said he hopes to be able to take me out one day next week. I do hope he can, it seems such a long time since he took me out last although it was only three days ago. I wonder how all this will end. I stayed in all evening and played my records.*'

Friday 19th '*Not too bad a day today. Keith told me he loved me today. He says he regrets what he said last Monday about not loving me. It is queer, because as short as a week ago I would have been thrilled, but today I feel as if I couldn't care less whether he did or not. And yet, in the bottom of my heart I want him to. I just don't know what I want, perhaps I just want to be alone so as not to bother with anyone. If only I could get a little place far away from home, where I could please myself where I went and who I went with. I think then and only then would I be really happy.*'

Saturday 20th '*Stayed in this evening. Been very busy today and have seen quite a lot of Keith. He seems to be eager to make amends for what he said last Monday. I don't know whether he really means it when he says he loves me. I still feel that I don't really want him and yet I do. It is such a queer feeling. He wants me to go out next Wednesday and I expect I will go although I will feel very guilty. I suppose I must love him in a way, I just don't know.*'

Sunday 21st '*Jolly good day today although a very tiring one. Went to LH's for the day and we went to Windlesham Photographic Show. Then we had a picnic. After that, we played ball for a little while then went back to the house. Mrs H gave me a camera and LH had bought me some flowers. I think I am in love with him again. I am not sure. I haven't thought of Keith more than three times today. I don't think I can love him really, probably just infatuation. I am so tired; I don't know what to think at the moment except that I want to go to bed.*'

By the end of the day on Monday having gone to the Palace with LH she writes '*I think I am falling in love with him all over again. I feel sure now that I do not love Keith. He seems to have changed. I don't seem to mind at all whether he is near me or not now and I don't think of him even a quarter of what I used to. There wasn't a minute went by without me thinking of him a little while ago but now, I go for hours at a time without it.*'

Tuesday 23rd '*Awfully hot day today. I don't know how to breathe, it's just too hot for words. Keith told me he still loves me today. Goodness only knows why. I think I still like him very, very much but I don't think I love him. He thinks he may be leaving soon as he suspects that the radio department is closing down.*

*I feel glad in some ways but awfully sorry in others. I will miss him if he goes. I saw LH today during the lunch hour. He said he had a puncture last night and his father had to go and fetch him home.'*

The next couple of days are just as hot. Mary sees quite a lot of Keith who is still expressing his love but her feelings remain unsettled. She goes out with LH to the pictures and states how she is getting *'fonder of him again. I wish I could just go away somewhere perhaps to Spain or Italy where I could forget everything and everybody. I wonder if I ever would forget Keith. I don't think I would but I might. He doesn't seem to thrill me like he used to. I still love him in a way, but not half as much as I did.'*

Friday 26th LH and Mary frequent the pictures again. *'I like him very much indeed but I don't think I really love him. Keith asked me to go out with him this evening but of course I had to say no. I didn't seem to feel disappointed at all, so I suppose that means I don't love him either. I wish I could get away from both of them. I would love to get a job on a ship. But still, you never know, I may one of these days.'*

Writing from LH's house on Saturday night *'quite a good day today again. I am here for the weekend. We are going to Lee on Solent tomorrow. I do like LH. I think I almost love him. His parents are so nice. Coming down on the train there were a couple just off on their honeymoon. I do wish I was the girl, but I just don't think Mr Right has come along yet. Perhaps he will one day. Going out with K on Monday. I don't know whether I want to go or not.'*

Sunday 28th *'Lovely day today. Went to Highcliffe near Bournemouth. We didn't go to Lee on Solent after all. It was scorching hot. I have got all red again and I bet will be sore in the morning. We went in the sea twice, it was very cold at first but after a few minutes it was lovely and warm, I did enjoy it. I would have liked to have stayed in all day but of course I couldn't, I am very tired now and longing to get into bed. I have only thought of Keith about half a dozen times today.'*

Monday 29th *'Horrible day. Everything has gone wrong. My cash has all gone wrong. I have been aching all day with sunburn and I have at last come to my senses and realised that it is LH I really love. I feel at the moment that I would marry him right away if I could. I went out with Keith this evening. I didn't want to. I did everything I could possibly do to put him off but it was no good and I hadn't the courage to tell him I didn't want to go out…so had to go. I do feel awful. I had been feeling quite happy lately but all my unhappiness has come back now, oh dear.'*

Having had a *'queer sort of day'* on Tuesday 30th just thinking about LH and Keith, Mary goes to the pictures with LH in the evening planning to tell him she loves him but having gone out with Keith yesterday doesn't think she does after all.

Wednesday 31st *'W*ent to London with LH this afternoon to see the Radio Show at Earls Court. It was very good but I don't think I have ever been so tired in my whole life. It was absolutely stifling in there and I was pleased to get out. I do wish LH wouldn't try to act so grown-up, it doesn't suit him and it irritates me so. Oh dear.'*

SEPTEMBER

Another difficult and emotional month for Mary regarding her relationships but with work being extremely busy at present and her colleagues and family heightening their suspicions, things finally start to change between her and Keith towards the end of the month.

Thursday 1st '*Seen a fair amount of Keith today, especially dinner time. He came up to the office—I was all alone, thank goodness. I know deep down in my heart that I can't love him and yet on the surface, I am madly in love with him. I just don't know what to do. I will have to go on trusting in God, for I know that whatever happens it will be His will. I bought two more records today and I sat in my bedroom all evening and played them along with all my others. They make me dream of Keith, oh dear. I am so worn out.*'

Friday 2nd '*Awful day. I don't know what stopped me from giving my notice in today. Everything has gone wrong. I feel so ill, tired and fed up. I can't keep going much longer. I have seen quite a lot of Keith today. He came up dinner time again. I like him very much although I am too tired to try and think whether I love him or not. I went to the pictures with LH this evening. It was a very good film (Hit the Deck) so it cheered me up a bit. I do wish I could get right away somewhere so I could think straight.*'

Saturday 3rd '*Another awful day. God, why am I so desperately unhappy. I feel so very ill and think I will have a nervous breakdown before much longer. How I wish I could die, that's the only thing I am wishing for at the moment. Mummy kept moaning this evening, she always sticks up for Sarah just because she cries. She likes her a lot better than me. If only she knew how many times I lock myself in the bathroom and have a good quiet cry to myself. Bought myself a ring today. Seen quite a lot of Keith today. He says he loves me, but I don't think he does really.*'

Sunday 4th '*Oh, how lonely and unhappy I am. How I wish I could die or else go abroad somewhere away from all my troubles. I'm afraid I will be really ill before much longer. If only everyone knew what torture, I am going through. I wish Keith would leave and yet I want him to stay. Oh God, please take my life. I keep praying for strength to give Keith up but it doesn't come. I just can't bring myself to do it, I am much too fond of him. I only hope that no one finds out. I would hate to hurt anybody. Perhaps everything will turn out right one day. I went to Edna's for tea today. She is very nice.*'

Monday 5th *'Bit better day today thank goodness and I expect it was because I didn't feel quite so tired. I have seen quite a lot of Keith today. I do like him very much. I'm not sure whether I love him or not. He wants me to go out with him one day this week. I want to go in some ways and yet I don't in others. Went out with LH this evening, he is very nice but I don't think I really love him either.'*

Tuesday 6th *'About the same sort of day as yesterday. I have seen more of Keith than usual because I stood talking to him for almost half an hour dinner time. He wants me to try and go out with him on Thursday. I don't think I really want to. I'm afraid my conscience has been torturing me far too much lately and I'm afraid I can see exactly how his mind works. He only wants me when he has had a row with his wife. LH came in the shop this morning. He wants me to get engaged to him on my birthday but I don't really want to as I'm much too young.'*

Wednesday 7th *'Not too bad a day I suppose. Haven't seen very much of Keith but funnily enough, I don't seem to mind. I know I don't love him now and yet I still like him very much. He wants me to go out with him tomorrow and I suppose, like a mug, I will go. I don't want to but I just can't help myself. Went to the pictures with LH this evening.'*

Thursday 8th *'A day of ups and downs again today. I have been trying all day to think of an excuse to get out of going out with Keith but it was no use, I just couldn't think of one—so I went out with him. I quite enjoyed it. He is very nice but I am fairly sure I don't love him. He tells me he loves me and I think he does in a way. All this is worrying me to death. I wonder how it will all end. Went out to dinner with LH today.'*

Friday 9th *'I don't think I have ever been so desperately unhappy in all my life. All I want to do is die right now. First of all, Keith came in and said his wife had almost found out about us, she at least had a very good idea that he was going out with someone. Then, this evening LH came round and the talk came round to W&H and Mummy kept on about her not liking that man in the radio department (Keith) and she said she had definitely found out that he was going around with a young girl. She had found out his name too but wouldn't say where she had found out. Anyway, the people who told her are going to inform his wife so they say. How I wish God would help me.'*

Saturday 10<sup>th</sup> *'Never had such a busy day before in my whole life. I have been taking money all day. I am sick and tired of money. I do wish I could get right away from it all. I haven't had much time to talk to Keith today but I did this evening in the yard thank goodness. We were all alone and I suppose we must have stood and talked for about half an hour. I told him about what Mummy had found out and he said if I wanted to pack it up for a while it was up to me as he said that, the last thing he wanted to do was get me into trouble. I just don't know what to do.'*

Feeling miserable on Sunday with a lot to worry about, LH visiting for the day doesn't help. *'Oh dear, I feel so ill. I found I just didn't want LH anywhere near me. He asked me to marry him but I found it difficult to explain so I said I was too young as I know he wouldn't like no for an answer. I just couldn't get engaged to him—I don't love him. Keith is expecting me to go out with him either Monday or Tuesday. I have arranged for tomorrow but I will feel so guilty. Mummy is very suspicious; I hope she won't find out.'*

Monday arrives and Mary sees hardly anything of Keith although still manages to set a date to go out with him on Thursday this week, when he cancels tonight. She knows she will have to think up an excuse to tell LH. She stays in all evening playing her records trying to cheer herself up but all they do is make her think of Keith. *'At the moment, I feel I just don't want either of them. All I want is to go abroad, away from everyone. It would be so wonderful.'*

Tuesday 13<sup>th</sup> *'Bit better day today thank goodness. I have seen a good bit of Keith today. We are going out on Thursday but I do wish he would finish it all as I hate having to keep telling lies. I just go on doing it like a fool. I will be really ill before much longer if it goes on. I went to the pictures with LH this evening. He asked me to marry him. I just didn't know how to answer him. I couldn't say yes because I don't love him enough and I just couldn't say no—I am in such a muddle; I wish I could die.'*

With Mary's Mum getting far too suspicious for her liking, on Wednesday she scolds herself for being such a coward for not being able to just finishing things with Keith. *'I am supposed to be going out with him tomorrow. I don't want to but I just don't know how to put him off. I am such a coward. I just can't tell him I don't love him anymore, partly because that's not altogether true. I do love him in a way but in another, I dislike him very much. I am in such a muddle. Went to Palace with LH this evening. He is very nice but I just can't love him.'*

Thursday 15<sup>th</sup> Mary is supposed to be going out with Keith but, '*I have never felt so alone and desperately unhappy as today. Well today hasn't been too bad but this evening—horrible. Mummy came to meet me from work and she wouldn't leave me so I just couldn't go. I do hope he will still love me as I love him very much. I have never been so near to killing myself as today and if I had a few more aspirins, I would kill myself right now. All I want to do is die. I feel there is nothing left in life for me now. Why, oh why, can't I go abroad away from everyone. I'd like to take Keith with me more than anything.'*

Friday 16<sup>th</sup> '*Not too bad a day, I suppose. I am still desperately unhappy. Thank goodness Keith still loves me, at least he says he does. He said he waited an hour for me last night, I do feel sorry for him and I also feel mad that I couldn't go. I had been looking forward to it all week. Oh, how I pray to God to help me. The office staff are getting a bit off hand with me now. I am sure they talk about me when I am not there. If only there was someone, I could let my heart out to.'*

Saturday is a very busy day with much the same thoughts and worries, then on Sunday '*quite a good day today thank goodness. LH came over for the day and I found myself liking him better than I have for weeks. Perhaps it is him I really love after all, I don't know. I am so mixed up. He wanted to go and buy me a ring tomorrow but I said we would just look. I know I couldn't get engaged to him in my present state of mind, it just wouldn't be fair to him. I am supposed to be going out with Keith tomorrow. I want to go in some ways and not others. I wish I had enough courage to finish it all.'*

Monday 19<sup>th</sup> '*Jolly good evening. I went out with Keith. He is so nice. I wish with all my heart that he wasn't married and I am almost certain he does too. It doesn't seem possible that I have been going out with him for eight months. Wouldn't mind if it was eight years. In fact, I wish it was. I went out to lunch with LH today. We looked at an awful lot of rings. I saw one I really liked. It was an opal, but I just don't want to get engaged yet. I don't want to be tied down. Besides—I don't love LH, not enough for that anyway.'*

Tuesday 20th *'Not too bad a day I suppose. Saw quite a lot of my Keith this morning but have hardly seen anything of him this afternoon. This evening has dragged terribly. I stayed in and listened to my radio and thought about Keith all the time. Oh, he is so nice, I just can't resist him. He wants me to go out with him on Friday. I will have to try and think up an excuse. I like going out with him so much although my conscience is absolutely torturing me.'*

On Wednesday evening Mary goes to the pictures with LH saying she just doesn't feel any love for him whatsoever and can't understand why as *'he is a very nice boy and he loves me very much. He keeps asking me to marry him and I just don't know how to answer him because I can't bring myself to say no and I know I can't say yes. I haven't seen much of Keith today. I do like him so very much. He is everything I have dreamed of. I do wish he was mine.'*

Thursday 22nd *'Another long boring day. I do wish I could get out of this muddle I'm in. I am supposed to be going out with Keith tomorrow. I do hope everything works out alright and that no one finds out or sees us. I am praying to God to help me in this dreadful situation. I have faith in Him that he will. I went to the pictures with LH this evening. I like him very much but I don't love him. I don't even like him kissing me. I know I won't be happy until everything is straightened out. My conscience is torturing me so much.'*

Discreetly going out with Keith on Friday evening they sit and have a serious talk for about an hour and a half. *'He said he was at a crossroads and didn't know which way to turn. I know just how he feels for I am in exactly the same position. How I wish we could run away together somewhere. I wonder how all this will really end and hope to God that He won't make anyone find out about us.'*

Saturday 24th *'Terribly busy day today. I have managed to see Keith quite a lot though thank goodness. Oh, I love him so very much. I just don't know what to do. I know I ought to finish with him but how can I when I love him so very much. Oh, how I have been thinking of him this evening. I stayed in and had my hair washed and had a bath. If only God would make me die that would be the best thing, then Keith could live a normal life again. I do wish I had the nerve to kill myself. Perhaps I will one day. I do wonder how all this will end and hope and pray it will be OK.'*

Mary spends the day at LH's on Sunday 25th and you've guessed it, thinks of Keith all the time. They go to church where she confesses '*I have never prayed so hard in my life that Keith and I could be together. I do hope that happens. LH is a very nice boy, but I am definitely not in love with him. I have tried, but it's no use. I just can't love him.'*

On Monday 26th feeling tired and worn out, she states '*I have done so much work today. I will have a breakdown before much longer, I am sure. I am so terribly unhappy. Nobody realises what I am going through. I suppose it's my own fault but I just can't help it. I love Keith so desperately and have grown up more in the last six months than I have all the rest of my life put together. I went to the pictures with LH this evening. I don't even like him kissing me now.'*

Tuesday 27th having some respite, she comments '*quite a good day today considering. I have had quite a lot of fun. Keith has been in a gay mood and so have I. We have been teasing each other all the time. Oh God, I love him so madly and deeply. If only he wasn't married.'* Sadly, her mood plummets when she gets home staying in all evening and again wishing she could die, saying that's all she is fit for. She sits up in bed listening to the radio all by herself writing that she is no good to anybody.

Wednesday 28th '*Quite a good day again today. I have seen quite a lot of Keith which has brightened it up. If only I could run away with him, but I don't suppose I ever will. I expect he will go back to his wife in the end. People like that usually do and I suppose it would be for the best really. Went to the pictures with LH this evening. He is so sweet and keeps telling me he loves me with all his heart. It makes me feel so guilty but I'm afraid I just can't love him now. I have tried.'*

Thursday 29th '*A queer sort of day today, really half good, half bad. Keith told me today that he had a serious talk with his wife last night, not a row, just a talk. She told him she was thinking of leaving him. Darling Keith said he wished she would. I think he would in a way but I think he would also be sorry in a way which is exactly how I feel. I don't know what I would do if she really did leave him, but still, I will have to wait and see. He was going to have another talk with her tonight. Oh, I wish I was dead. I am in such a muddle.'*

Friday 30th *'Not too bad a day I suppose. I have seen Keith quite a lot but the trouble is he has always had someone with him. I have only been able to catch him on his own once and that was at dinner time. I went to the Palace with LH this evening. He is so kind and thoughtful and is everything a perfect husband should be but try as I might, I just can't fall in love with him, as I love Keith.'*

OCTOBER

A decision by Keith on 5th rocks Mary's world and with LH constantly mentioning about getting engaged, she just wants to run away. We get an insight into Keith's reality and work becomes almost unbearable. Thankfully Mary makes the right decision on a job offer later in the month plus there is a close encounter with a member of the Royal family.

Saturday 1st *'I think today has been the busiest I have ever had; I have not stopped taking money all day. I am sick to death if it. I have seen a fair amount of Keith but not half as much as I would have liked to have done. I do wish with all my heart that we could go away somewhere together, away from everyone we know so that we could start afresh but I don't think that will ever happen, I'm sorry to say.'*

Sunday 2nd *'Not too bad a day today. LH came round for the day. We stayed in during the morning and then went for a walk round the town. We looked in all the furniture shops to see which furniture we would have if we got married. Oh dear, I am in such a muddle, I have liked LH much better today than I have for a long time, but I don't love him enough to marry him. I am supposed to be going out with Keith tomorrow evening. I do hope nobody will see us.'*

Monday 3rd *'A peculiar sort of day today. Keith hasn't been too cheerful all day but I went out with him this evening and wow, he certainly cheered up alright. Oh, I like him so much and yet I dislike him at the same time, at least I have felt like that today. I phoned LH up this evening before going out with Keith and I thought for a moment that I wouldn't go out with Keith. I've liked LH more today than I have for a very long time and yet, now after having been out with Keith again, I find I am still in love with him (Keith, I mean). Life is so cruel.'*

Tuesday 4th *'Mummy's birthday today and I bought her a watch. Not too good a day today. I have felt so ill today. My throat and my left ear have been hurting me terribly. I wonder if it is tonsillitis. The only thing I wouldn't like about that is that I would have to stay away from work and therefore I wouldn't see my darling Keith. Oh, life can be so cruel.'*

Wednesday 5th *'Today has been the unhappiest day in my life. I have never been so desperately unhappy. Keith told me he has given his notice in and that he leaves a week Saturday. I just don't know how I will live without him. I will perhaps pluck up enough courage to kill myself, I don't know what stopped me from doing it today. None of the office staff will speak to me. They think I am terrible for speaking to Keith so much but oh God how can I help it. I love him so madly. LH came round this evening and I had to pretend to be so cheerful when I feel quite the opposite.'*

Thursday is a little better with Mary trying to come to terms that Keith is leaving *'I still can't quite realise that he is really leaving. It just doesn't seem possible. I don't know what I will do without him. He is the only thing that keeps me going. I don't expect I will stay at W&H long after he has gone. I don't know where I would go though. I feel like I will have a breakdown before long, all I know is I can't go on as I am at the moment. I feel so very ill.'*

Friday 7th *'About the same sort of day as yesterday. Oh dear, I feel so ill and desperately unhappy. I wonder how all this will end. I expect Keith will go back to his wife and I will marry LH, even though at the moment this is the last thing I want to happen. I have seen a fair amount of Keith today and it doesn't seem possible that I have only another week to see him in. I will miss him terribly when he has gone. LH came to meet me from work this evening. We were going out but he has a cold so he went home. We had some tea first though, then he caught the seven o'clock train back.'*

Going out with Keith on Saturday and having a wonderful evening, Mary notes, '*I hope he won't forget me as I don't think I could bare it if he really gave me up. He tells me he would even sacrifice his children for me if only his wife would leave him and take them with her. He said he loves me. It makes me feel I can bare anything when I hear that. The office staff hardly talk to me now.*'

Mary visit's LH for the day on Sunday and he is still carrying on about getting engaged on her birthday in November but she can't even focus on that as Keith fills her thoughts constantly.

Monday 10$^{th}$ '*Not too good a day today again. I feel so desperately unhappy. I do wish Keith wasn't leaving. I would give my arm for him to stay. I will miss him terribly. I wish with all my heart that he won't forget me. He has felt fairly miserable today as he has had nothing to do. He tells me he wishes he wasn't leaving now. I love him with all my heart. No one could ever know just how much I love him. If only we could go away together, away from everyone. It's the only way I could be happy. Went to the Palace with LH this evening but I still can't love him.*'

At work on Tuesday Mary sees a fair amount of Keith who says he still loves her but she wonders how long for. '*I wonder if he is leaving in the hopes of forgetting me. I do so hope not. There is so much I wonder and wish for.*'

Wednesday 12$^{th}$ '*I just can't stick this any longer. Every single thing has gone wrong today. LH keeps on at me to get engaged to him and I don't want to for the simple reason that I am not in love with him. I feel so sorry for him because he loves me so much. I do wish I could return his love but I just can't. Mummy and Pop told me off for letting LH into the house looking so dirty. The office staff at W&H don't talk to me at all. It is so awful to just sit and be ignored. I don't know how I stop myself crying. I haven't seen all that much of Keith today worst luck and when I did get a chance to really talk to him, he told me he was taking his wife to the pictures this afternoon. I wanted to go this evening to cheer myself up but there wasn't time so I sat in all evening.*'

Thursday is another unhappy day for Mary with Keith cancelling their evening out last minute. '*I think he must be fed up with me. We have arranged to go out next Saturday now, so I hope nothing goes wrong then. The office staff still don't talk to me. I think they are awful. I don't know how I am going to stick it next week when Keith has gone. I suppose I will just about live through it. I do wish I had the nerve to kill myself then I would be out of everyone's way and wouldn't be a worry to anybody.'*

Friday 14th *'Not too good a day again today although Keith has been in a fairly good mood all day. We are supposed to be going out tomorrow evening but before he went home this evening, he told me he had made up his mind about his wife or me. He said he would be home by about six thirty tomorrow and I am not meeting him until six. That gives me only about quarter of an hour to see him in. I don't know whether he has chosen his wife or me. I think it's his wife but he wrote me a note saying he will always love me. Oh, I do wish I knew one way or the other. He leaves W&H tomorrow for good. I have come to the conclusion that nobody really knows me really, not even Mum or Dad. I do wish I could say what I think instead of bottling it up inside me.'*

Keith's letter is tucked in her diary:

*'Mary darling, you'd better forget about me. I'm willing to give up everything for you but if you don't feel the same way then there seems little point in your continuing with me, for I realise you've your life to live and that you are not going to throw it away, quite rightfully. I hope you'll say…don't be stupid— wait a little while until you're older but I'll try and understand if you feel that with this jealousy and obstacle between us, I'm becoming an embarrassment. I don't want that to happen, for I think too much of you. What I said at lunch was true and honest and so is this—I love you desperately and always will. You can rely on me forever. I am writing this because you looked worried that I'd told my wife—so here's your release darling if that's what you wish.'*

Saturday 15th *'A day of ups and downs today. Keith told me this morning that he was going to finish with me for good this evening. Oh, I was so upset, I don't know how I stopped myself crying. This afternoon, however, he seemed to be changing his mind and this evening after work he told me he could never give me up. He has made me happier than I have been for quite some time. I had a good cry though. It has been such a strain and anxious day.'* They then arrange another date for next Thursday.

Sunday 16<sup>th</sup> *'Not too bad a day today. LH came round for the day, but I have really been thinking of Keith an awful lot today. I noticed in the paper that Currey's (the place where Keith is going) want a cashier. If I see Keith tomorrow, I will ask him if he would like me to work there with him. If he would, I will go and see the manager in my lunch hour and see if I can get the job. I do hope I see Keith tomorrow morning as I don't think I could last the day without seeing him.'*

Monday 17<sup>th</sup> *'Awful day. My mind is in such a whirl. I don't know what I'm doing. I saw Keith this morning but only for a minute worst luck. I applied for a job at Curry's and the manager said the job is mine if I want it. Mum and Dad don't seem too keen. I don't know whether Keith is or not. He seemed quite pleased when I told him. I just can't make up my mind whether to or not. I have missed him today and would love to work with him but everyone at work (W&H) would start talking. I will leave it until I have seen Keith again and then see what happens. Went to the pictures with LH this evening, he is very sweet.'*

Tuesday 18<sup>th</sup> *'Awful day again, at least most of the time. I saw Keith before going to work this morning which cheered me up thank goodness. I phoned up Currey's dinner time and told them I didn't want the job. Then all the afternoon I was regretting it. I felt so terribly miserable and unhappy all the time, so I prayed to God to let me see Keith after work to cheer myself up. I also asked Him if He would make Keith have a note for me. My prayer was answered—I saw Keith and he did have a note for me. I have cheered up a lot since I saw him and he told me he still loves me. I love him so much. I don't know what I would do without God to talk to. I think I would go crazy.'*

Wednesday 19<sup>th</sup> *'Not too good a day again today. It has been raining hard all the time and the bus was full up this morning, so I didn't manage to get to town in time to see Keith, before going to work. I was very disappointed although I did manage to see him when I went to the bank, but not to speak to. It has seemed such a long day. I wanted to see him at one o'clock but I couldn't get out of work until one thirty and of course he had gone by then. I was annoyed. I went to the Palace with LH this evening and he told me he can't come out on Friday. I think God must have planned that as I am going out with Keith tomorrow and it would have looked suspicious if I went out three times running. I did cheer myself up a bit, I bought a coat and a pair of high heel shoes today.'*

Thursday 20th *'Not too good a day again today. I am so desperately unhappy. None of the office staff will talk to me except on business. It is awful. I went out with my darling Keith this evening. I love him so much. He was in a silly sort of mood all the time though—laughing and cracking jokes. He didn't realise it, but some of them hurt terribly. I had a good cry to myself. Thank goodness it was dark. Life is so completely hopeless and I feel that nobody really knows me at all or what terrible mental agony I am suffering. I may only be seventeen but mentally now, I am about twenty-five.'*

Friday 21st *'Saw Keith this morning before going to work but only for a minute. I haven't seen him at all since. It is awful not seeing him more than once a day. I do wish I could think up some jolly good excuse to go to Curry's to work. Sarah is very miserable again today. I don't know what the matter is with her. If she only had half my worries and troubles, she would have something to be miserable about. I have to hide my feelings. Nobody really knows me at all, except God of course.'*

Saturday is a terribly busy day with Mary stating she is sick to death of money and also commenting how the office staff chat and giggle amongst themselves but completely ignore her, only to speak when they want to tell her off about something. She sees Keith only very quickly before work and again after *'I do love him so. I think it would break my heart (that is if it isn't shattered already) if he ever did give me up for good.'*

Sunday 23rd *'Not too bad a day I suppose. Went over to LH's for the day, he is very sweet, but I just don't love him. He keeps kissing me and I really dislike it. I just don't know what's wrong with me. I wore my new coat and all accessories; I did feel grand. I do wish Keith could have seen me. I wonder if I will ever be happy again. I'm sure with enough faith, God will make it alright.'*

Monday 24th *'A very busy day today. I am glad in a way as it helps me take my mind off Keith for a while. Even so, I have thought of him quite a lot today. I saw him this morning before going to work but it was only for a minute worst luck. I also saw him dinner time but not to speak to. Still, I am going out with him tomorrow evening thank goodness. I wonder how much longer I can go on only seeing him once a day. I love him so desperately.'* This evening, she goes to the pictures with LH and once again reiterates that she is not in love with him.

Tuesday 25th *'Another busy day again today but a wonderful evening. I went out with my darling Keith. Oh, I love him so very much. I waited for him for an hour after work and I was just going to give up and go home when he came along. I was so relieved. I had been praying to God so hard to make him come and He worked a miracle and Keith came.'*

Wednesday 26th *'A day of ups and downs today. I had a job offered me in the bank but I don't know whether to take it or not. I saw the Queen Mother this afternoon. She came to open the new technical college. She was beautiful, I could have almost touched her. Went to the pictures with LH this evening and he kept asking why I didn't like kissing him and also why I never told him I loved him. I didn't know what to say. I couldn't say it was because I didn't love him. I am in such a mess. I love Keith so very much. I saw him this morning before going to work but only for a minute.'*

During Thursday and Friday, the atmosphere at work gets progressively worse. *'Awful day today. The office staff won't talk to me yet and it's awful to just sit there and be ignored. Mrs M told me off because she said I was too slow but blimey, if she had all the work I have got, she wouldn't say that.'* Then *'the office staff today are getting worse. They are starting to make sarcastic remarks to each other in front of me and still don't speak to me except on strict business.'* And it doesn't help that she only catches quick glimpses of Keith now, mostly before she gets into work *'it's awful only seeing him once or twice a day. I don't think I can stand it much longer.'*

Saturday 29th *'Another very busy day today. I haven't stopped taking money all day. I am sick to death with it. Keep having rows with the office staff. They still don't talk to me. I saw my darling Keith before going to work this morning, but not to talk to worst luck. He just went by in the Curry's van. He couldn't stop and talk to me because his manager was watching. I couldn't manage to see him dinner time either as Mummy came back on the same bus as me so I had to go straight to work. I saw him this evening though thank God. We stood and talked for quite a time; I do love him so.'*

Sunday 30th *'Not too bad a day today thank goodness. I went over to LH's for the day. His Uncle was there and Brother, he was a worse tease than his father, if that's possible. They were both teasing me all the time. It helped to cheer me up a lot though. We all went to Winchester this afternoon to see Brian in hospital. It was a very nice drive and it was quite nice to see Brian. Then we went back and watched television. It was quite good. I have still been thinking about Keith a lot today though. In fact, I am always thinking of him.'*

Monday 31st *'Not too bad a day I suppose. The office staff have been a little bit better thank goodness. I have been terribly busy today and I will be even busier tomorrow. I didn't see Keith this morning but I went out with him this evening. Oh, we had such a wonderful time. He was in a more serious mood tonight thank goodness and didn't crack any funny jokes as he did last week, when he was in a silly mood. Oh, I do love him so very, very, much and he says he loves me too.'*

## NOVEMBER

Colleagues at work are still up and down, not surprising really as Mary still manages to meet up with Keith for evenings out. On 2nd she struggles into work and to an interview with the bank even though she's full of cold, then quite literally drags herself in work on 17th having been up sick all night. This month her time working at W&H comes to an end and with her 18th birthday at the end of the month we discover whether she actually gets engaged to LH.

Tuesday 1st *'Another terribly busy day again today. The office staff have been quite friendly though, goodness only knows why. It makes me think I don't really want to leave. I go for my interview tomorrow. I didn't see Keith before going into work this morning worst luck but I did see him this evening after work for about ten minutes. I still wish we could be together for always. Perhaps one day we will.'*

Wednesday 2nd '*Oh dear, I feel so ill today. My mind is in such a muddle and I have got such a horrible cold. The only two things that I am really certain of are, that I love Keith with all my heart and that I want to die! I went for my interview with the National Provincial Bank this afternoon. I have got a form to fill in. I am not quite sure if I want the job now or not. I do for some things but not for others. I haven't seen Keith to speak to at all today. I went to the pictures with LH tonight. I still can't love him.*'

Thursday 3rd '*My cold has been terrible today. I can hardly breathe and I do feel so very ill. I took my reference (which I went to Mr W for) to the bank and they seemed very pleased with it, saying it was an excellent reference. I will know next week if I have got the job or not but I don't think I want it now. I saw Keith this morning and at dinner time. Then I saw him this evening and I was so loaded up with parcels that he brought me home. I thought that it was so sweet of him. I love him so desperately.*'

Friday 4th '*I feel awful today. I have been sniffing and coughing all day and my eyes have been running. I didn't see Keith this morning worst luck but I saw him this evening. I had to wait for LH for three quarters of an hour and Keith came and talked to me while I waited. He said he had a free evening this evening. Oh, how I wish I could have gone out with him, especially as he didn't look too happy. I hope he's alright. I went to the pictures with LH but I thought of Keith all the time.*'

Saturday 5th '*I am so desperately unhappy and absolutely fed up with poor LH. I don't know why, but I can't help it. I saw my darling Keith this morning before going to work and at dinner time. He told me to wait for him this evening as he had some thrilling news for me but as it is Sarah's 21st birthday we had a party and LH came to meet me so I couldn't see Keith. I am so disappointed; I just couldn't enjoy the party and I am dying to know what his news is. I hope his wife has left him. I know it's awful of me but I am so madly in love with him.*'

Feeling miserable and full of cold on Sunday Mary stays in all day. She is invited to go with LH to see Brian in hospital but with such a terrible cold doesn't want him to catch it so turns the offer down. '*I am longing to hear what Keith's thrilling news is. I expect he will tell me tomorrow. I do hope so anyway.*'

Monday 7th *'Awful day again today. I had been hoping so much that I would see my darling Keith before going into work this morning so that he could tell me his thrilling news but I waited for just over five minutes in the pouring rain and then he went sailing past in his firm's van. He just waved and smiled and that was all. I haven't seen him since. We are supposed to be going out tomorrow evening and I do hope everything goes off alright. Went to the Palace with LH this evening. I still don't love him.'*

Tuesday 8th *'Queer sort of day today. I told Mrs M and the office staff about the bank job and they told me to take it. I just don't know what to do. I went out with my darling Keith this evening. He was in a very serious mood. He told me he didn't love me, but liked me very much. I was so disappointed, but I managed to persuade him to come out next Monday. I am seriously wondering whether to kill myself tomorrow, I do wish I had the nerve, perhaps I will. I wish Monday would hurry up.'*

Wednesday 9th *'I saw Keith before going into work this morning but he didn't come along until five to nine. I was just going to give up hope and hurry on into work, when he came. I think perhaps he was late on purpose so that he wouldn't see me. I do hope that wasn't so, as I love him deeply with all my heart. I went to the pictures with LH this evening. He keeps telling me he loves me and that he wants to marry me.'*

Her comments on Thursday explain about seeing Keith after work in the evening and how she is relieved that he is getting back to his normal self now. She is still praying to God to let them be together and stating how deeply she loves him. There is more of the same on Friday when she also mentions how she doesn't know how she manages to put up with LH anymore *'poor boy.'*

Saturday is yet another terribly busy day for Mary and it's quite obvious she has been offered the job at the bank because she hands her notice in to W&H today *'boy was I scared. I saw Keith before work but only for a second and also this evening when he gave me a lift home in his car. We sat in it for about half an hour. He told me he loves me and I am so thrilled. Oh, I wish we could be together always.'*

LH comes down for the day on Sunday with Mary admitting she likes him a bit better now. '*He asked me if I would get engaged to him on my birthday. I told him I would let him know for sure on Wednesday. I quite felt I'd like to when he asked me, but I don't think I will by Wednesday, as I'm going out with Keith tomorrow.*'

Monday 14th '*Awful day today but wonderful, heavenly evening. I went out with Keith and he is so wonderful. I love him so much and do so wish we could be together all the time for the rest of our lives. He was in such a lovely mood this evening and now I just can't stop thinking about him. I saw him this morning and I'm not sure if someone saw but the office staff are hardly talking to me again now.*'

Tuesday 15th '*Another awful day which has seemed endless. I saw Keith this morning but he saw someone he knew and had to rush off before hardly saying hello. I saw him several times dinner time as I walked past his shop about seven times but he didn't see me. I went to the pictures with Edna this evening. It was quite a good film but I was thinking of my Keith most of the time. I just can't get him out of my mind at all.*'

Wednesday 16th '*Another terribly long day. I only saw Keith go past in the Currey's van and he smiled and waved. I went to the pictures with LH tonight and he wanted to know if I wanted to get engaged. I said wait until Christmas.*'

Thursday 17th '*Oh dear, I don't think I have ever felt as terribly ill as I have done today. I had to get up four times during last night to be sick. I don't know how I managed to get to work. If it hadn't been that, I wanted to see my darling Keith I wouldn't have gone at all. I saw him just go past in the Currey's van and again felt very disappointed but when I went to the bank later on, I saw him to talk to. I told him I had a free evening tomorrow and he suggested going out, so we are. I do wish tomorrow would hurry up and come.*'

Friday 18th '*Wonderful evening. I went out with my darling Keith again. That is the second time this week. LH had to go to a birthday party so I had a free evening and so had Keith. He is so wonderful; I do love him desperately. We seem to agree on everything. We were talking about if ever he got divorced and we got married, that I could carry on working and then we could do the house work together in the evening. It was so wonderful talking like that. He was quite serious; I am so glad.'*

Saturday 19th *'A queer sort of day today. I have had such mixed feelings. I left Wolfe and Hollanders. They gave me a beautiful dressing table set. I am so sorry I have left but I suppose God arranged that I should, so I will not question His actions. I expect I will get used to the bank after a time. Keith took me home in his firm's van. He only stopped for about five minutes but it will help me get over the weekend.'*

Sunday 20th *'I have had mixed feelings again today. I went to LH's for the day. I like them all there very much but I still can't make myself love LH. I have tried but it is Keith I am in love with and there's nothing I can do about it. I am starting my new job tomorrow at the bank, I wonder if I will like it.'*

Monday 21st *'A long day today. I started my new job at the bank today and I have been thinking of my darling Keith all the time. I saw him before going into the bank but only for one second. I saw him again at dinner time but not to speak to, worst luck. We smiled at each other through Curry's doorway. Oh God, I love him with all my heart and soul. I went to the pictures with LH this evening and he got quite annoyed because I wouldn't let him kiss me. I just can't, I absolutely hate him even touching me now.'* Sadly, being so preoccupied she doesn't mention what she did all day at the bank on her first day or even if she liked it.

Tuesday 22nd *'Not too bad a day I suppose. I just don't realise that I am working in a bank. All my thoughts are for my darling Keith. We were going out this evening, but he only stayed for an hour as he felt terribly ill. He has a headache and sore throat—the lot. I think I must have given him my cold the poor darling. I'm still so desperately unhappy, I love him so much.'*

Wednesday 23rd *'Another terribly long day again today. I saw my darling Keith this morning before going into work but not to speak to. He just went past in the Currey's van. I do wish he had stopped but I suppose he couldn't really as there was an awful lot of traffic about. Oh dear, I don't think I can carry on living much longer. I am under such a terrible strain, what with starting my new* job, thinking about Keith all the time and then going out with LH and absolutely loathing it. I went to the pictures with him this evening. He told me I have changed just lately and I know I have. I don't even like him kissing me now.'

Thursday 24th 'I didn't see my darling Keith at all today. I do so hope he is alright. I have missed him so much and it has seemed such a long day. I have had quite a bit of fun at work today. The girls that have been teaching me—Ruth and Jean, and I have been laughing our heads off. If only I had seen Keith this morning, I would have felt quite happy. I went round Edna's this evening and thought of Keith all the time.'

On Friday, Mary goes out with Keith and has a 'simply wonderful, heavenly evening. He still has his awful cold poor darling; I did feel sorry for him although I soon cheered him up and he was almost back to normal. I wonder if God will ever give him to me. I do hope He will as He has worked so many wonderful miracles before.'

Saturday 26th 'Not too bad a day today thank goodness. I went shopping with LH all the afternoon. He bought me a black bucket bag ready for tomorrow. I feel so tired and I am not a bit excited, not like I usually am when it's my birthday. I managed to see Keith after work having seen LH off on the train. I didn't see him before going to work this morning but I am so glad I saw him this evening. It will make the weekend seem much shorter. I then stayed in all evening and made loads of cakes and stuff for tomorrow.'

Sunday 27th Mary's birthday 'Quite a good day today. I got up quite early and iced my cakes. They do look nice. LH and his parents and Edna all came up this afternoon, well, LH came up this morning. We had quite a good time. I had some lovely presents but I don't know, it hasn't really seemed like a birthday at all. I expect that is because I didn't go out all day to work. It seemed better towards the evening though when we were all in the party spirit. I have thought about my darling Keith today but I have been so busy, I didn't have time to really concentrate. I still love him.'

Monday 28th 'Quite a good day I suppose. I had compliments from work today about my cooking as I took a cake to work. Absolutely wonderful evening.

*I went out with my darling, wonderful Keith. It is funny because all day I have had the feeling that I didn't like him anymore but directly I saw him; I knew that I definitely do love him. He said his biggest and best wish was that we could get married one day and I must admit I am wishing, hoping and praying that it will happen one day too.'*

Tuesday 29th *'Not too good a day where works concerned as Ruth has been bossing me around all day and I have done most of her work for her while she has sat enjoying herself. But where my darling Keith is concerned it has been a wonderful day. I have seen him three times—this morning, at dinner time with Mr V and this evening. Oh, I love him desperately, I do wish we could be together forever.'*

Photograph is of Mary on her eighteenth birthday.

Mary waits to see Keith in the morning on Wednesday but he doesn't come early enough to see her which she blames on the thick fog, so hurries off into work without even catching a glimpse of him. In the evening, she goes to the Palace with LH.

## DECEMBER

Mary is finding work at the bank fairly strict and she gets another harsh reality from Keith on 3rd causing her to take a downward spiral. Unfortunately, she doesn't really help herself when she mentions what she's been doing on 8th. LH gets more insistent on them getting engaged and by the middle of the month things finally turn more positive, if a little more complicated. There are also parties around Christmas and a big announcement Boxing Day.

Thursday 1st *'A busy day today. I don't think I am really going to like it at the bank. You have to stay there so terribly late and everyone is so bossy and strict. I suppose I will have to stick it out but the work is so terribly difficult. I saw Keith this morning before going into work and also after* work this evening. We stopped and *talked for quite a while. I am praying so hard that we might be able to be together all the time.'*

Friday 2nd *'I feel so miserable today as I haven't seen my darling Keith at all and it has seemed such a long day. I have been thinking of him all the time. I went to the pictures with LH this evening. Oh dear, I am so awful to him but I feel I just can't be nice when I'm wishing he was Keith all the time. He kept on at me this evening about getting engaged at Christmas. I just don't know how to answer because that's the very last thing I want to do. All I want is to be with Keith for the rest of my life, it would make me so happy.'*

Saturday 3rd *'Oh dear, I feel so tired and so desperately unhappy. I don't know why, unless it is having to carry such a dreadful secret around with me. I saw my darling Keith this morning and again this evening. He told me he was going to leave Currey's and go and work at Beenham. That means he won't be in Reading so often. I do so hope and pray that he won't go, at least not unless he comes to Reading regularly. I have prayed so hard to God this evening to make either Keith's wife, or myself die. I feel I just can't go on any longer. Went round town today.'*

Sunday she has quite a good day *'considering all the worries I have got'* and spends the day at LH's admitting that she does really like his parents and even LH today. Mary wonders whether Keith will take the Beenham job and whether he will still go out with her. She is so mixed up and concerned that all this deceit is making her ill as she is feeling so tired all the time recently.

Monday 5th *'Oh dear, I do wish God would make me die. I feel so tired and ill and so desperately unhappy. I am so mixed up. I just don't know which way to turn. Keith told me this morning (before going into work) that he was going to give his notice in and go to work at Beenham. I hope he will still come out with me. I am going out with him tomorrow evening, thank goodness. I do wish it would hurry up. I went to the Palace with LH this evening and he will keep on at me to get engaged at Christmas. I just don't know what to do, I'm sure. I took over a machine at work today. I have the afternoon off tomorrow.'*

Tuesday 6th *'Not too bad a day I suppose but awful evening. I went out with my darling Keith and he told me he was going to work at Beenham, so he wouldn't be able to come out with me again. He said he would start going out again next February. Oh God, please help me to change his mind. I will see him Thursday thank goodness so I am praying that he will say he'll come out before that. I think I will commit suicide if he doesn't as I don't think I could live without him. I left my ring in a ladies this evening and after leaving Keith, I went to a policeman for it. The policeman was very nice and asked me to go out with him. I almost wish I had accepted.'* There's no mention of whether she gets her ring back or not.

Mary admits that all she does on Wednesday is think of Keith, worrying about what will happen to them and once again contemplating suicide. Going to the pictures with LH in the evening *'he keeps asking me to get engaged. I said I would tell him on Sunday.'*

Thursday 8th *'A nice surprise today. I waited for my darling Keith after work and he asked me to go out with him so I did. Oh, it was lovely. He said he is weakening and thinks he may come out again. Oh, I do hope he does, I love him so desperately. He told me he had read one of my notes (I write one every day) about a dozen times and he said he had felt so ashamed of himself for upsetting me. He was in a lovely mood this evening and was very loving, so I feel a bit better now, but I still won't feel really well until I know if he is coming out again.'*

Friday Mary exclaims she has never known such a long day and finds herself longing for Keith more than ever. She catches a glimpse of him in the Curry's van with another man. They have planned to meet on Saturday when he will tell her if he will come out again or not. Going to the pictures that evening with LH, Mary echoes that she will let him know on Sunday about getting engaged at Christmas.

Saturday 10th *'I am so glad today as I saw my darling Keith and he told me he will be coming out again. He can't make it until a week Tuesday though, but still, it is better than waiting until February. I know it was God who made him say he would come out again because I have been praying so hard these last three days for Him to send me a miracle and He did! I went to the pictures this afternoon by myself after doing my shopping.'*

Sunday 11<sup>th</sup> *'An awful day today really. LH came over for the day and kept onto me about getting engaged at Christmas. I told him in not many words, that we were much too young and a few other excuses I could think of and the silly boy nearly burst out crying. I just didn't know what to do. I kept thinking of my darling Keith and wishing it was him and not LH asking me to marry him. I told LH I would try and tell him tomorrow. I know it wouldn't really be fair to LH or me to get engaged and yet if I don't, LH will get upset.'*

The next few days pass with Mary being very busy at work, dreaming about Keith and worrying about her situation, hoping things will turn out right. She manages to laugh off any further mention of getting engaged at Christmas to LH and notices *'there is a very nice boy at work called Jeff, but he isn't as nice as my Keith.'*

Wednesday 14<sup>th</sup> *'Another long day today, although a very busy one. I keep making mistakes. I think I will get the sack before much longer. I'm afraid my mind just isn't on my work. Oh, if only I could die and get out of this cruel world. I do wish Tuesday would hurry up and come, it does seem to be taking an age to come round. I don't know how I am lasting out. I wonder if my darling Keith has been thinking of me at all, or if he has been too busy. The nice boy at work—Jeff, is extremely nice, but I don't like him as much as my Keith.'*

Thursday 15<sup>th</sup> *'Keith rang me up at work today about five o'clock and said he was coming to meet me from work. I was so excited. I managed to get out of work early—about 5:30 and he took me home and we sat and talked for about half an hour. I love him very much indeed but I am at last realising how hopeless the situation really is. If I could be sure I would get him in the end I wouldn't mind but it is getting me down all this waiting and wondering.'*

Friday 16<sup>th</sup> *'Quite an enjoyable day today. I have had some fun with Jeff at work. Wonderful evening. I went to LH's firm's dance. Johnny was there (the boy I went out with before LH). I have said I will go out with him on Wednesday. I am glad really. He kissed me in front of LH under the mistletoe. Lots of other people kissed me too including Doug—LH's and Johnny's mate. Wow, is he lovely. I have had about four drinks and goodness only knows how many cigarettes. Its queer, but I feel quite happy at the moment. LH is still on at me to get engaged.'*

Saturday 17th *'A queer sort of day today. I have had such a lot to think about—Keith, Johnny, Doug, the dance, Jeff at work and LH and getting engaged plus piles of other things. LH stayed the night last night and we went shopping, both this morning and this afternoon. We stood outside Wise the jewellers for half an hour waiting for me to make up my mind about getting engaged. In the end, we just walked away. LH is so disappointed but I can't help it. I have felt a little more liking for him since though. I am staying at his place tonight and LH has just gone out of the room after seeing me in my nighty and then in the nude. Boy!'*

Sunday 18th *'Quite a good day today really. I stayed at LH's last night and all day today. I have been to church twice today and have asked God to tell me what I must do. LH and I went for a walk this afternoon and we went behind some haystacks. Cor, it was cold, I don't know what made me but I suppose I just felt like it. I have thought about so many things today. I do wish I could live on my own, it would be lovely.'*

Monday 19th *'A very busy day today although quite an enjoyable one. I have been joking and laughing with Jeff most of the time. I went to the pictures with LH this evening and told him I would get engaged to him at Christmas. I don't know why because I don't really love him but still, we won't get married for three years and if I do discover someone who I really love I can still break it off. He is coming up on Thursday to ask Daddy about it. Saw Johnny this evening while I was out with LH, he is very nice. I am going out with him on Wednesday and Keith tomorrow. I am getting in a muddle.'*

Tuesday evening, she waits an hour for Keith to show up in the rain then decides to go to the pictures by herself when he doesn't show. *'I don't know whether to laugh or cry. I don't know whether I mind seeing Keith or not, but tomorrow I think I will ring him anyway. To my surprise I haven't found myself wishing I hadn't said yes to LH. I had thought perhaps I would regret it, but I haven't done yet. I am going out with Johnny tomorrow evening. I don't know what I will say to him. I do hope he won't turn up either.'*

Wednesday 21st *'I don't think I have ever done so much work before in my whole life as today. I didn't leave off until quarter to seven. I phoned Keith and another man answered and when Keith spoke to me, he had to pretend that I was his wife. I couldn't ask him about yesterday; I feel quite upset. I went to the pictures with Johnny this evening. He told me he loved me and that if I gave LH up, he would marry me. He kept on at me to give him up but I don't think I could if I tried. Johnny is very sweet and he sure has got it bad. He wants me to go to a school dance with him at the Court School on Saturday. I just don't know what to do.'*

LH arrives on Thursday 22nd in the evening to ask her father if they could get engaged at Christmas *'oh it was awful. I felt so silly. I just didn't know where to put my face. Auntie V was here and everyone was thrilled with the idea. Me? Well, I just don't know what to think. They all drank to us to wish us luck. Whew, I'm glad it's over anyway. Saw Edna earlier and we exchanged Christmas presents. I have been thinking a lot about Keith and Johnny today. I just don't know what to do. I will just let God take me upon whichever path He wants me to go. I'm so very tired, too tired to think of it all.'*

On Friday 23rd Mary gets a lovely surprise with two phone calls at work from Keith *'he rang the first time while I was at lunch and then the second time later in the afternoon. He met me from work and he apologised wonderfully for not coming on Tuesday. He gave me a lovely box of chocolates; ever so big it is. He was so sorry about it all. It was lovely because I didn't think I would ever see him again. I do like him very much. I wrote to Johnny today to say that I would go to the dance with him tomorrow, I don't really want to go. Stayed in this evening and wrapped up some of my parcels. I'm getting the ring tomorrow.'*

Saturday 24th Christmas Eve *'Quite a good day today. LH and I went to buy my ring this afternoon. It is a beautiful thing. I am not having it until Monday though. I was supposed to be going out to a dance with Johnny this evening but couldn't get away from LH so Johnny came up for me. Mummy saw him and told him I was engaged now. Oh dear, I wonder what he thought. Sarah and I went to a lovely party with Mike, Rob and their friend Pete. Oh, it was wonderful. Mike got drunk and was sick. I must admit I feel pretty rotten myself. I was kissing Mike all the evening. Both he and Pete said they liked me best. I like them all!'*

Sunday 25<sup>th</sup> Christmas Day '*A wonderful evening. I went to Pete's house with Pete, Mike and Rob. I was sitting hugging and kissing Pete all the evening and I'm afraid I have completely fallen in love with him. Oh, he is wonderful and has big blue eyes. He bought me home in his car. Oh dear, I just don't know what to do. I am absolutely longing for him right now. It's nearly 2am and I have just got home. I just don't know how I can get engaged tomorrow. It is the very last thing I want to do.'*

Monday 26<sup>th</sup> Boxing Day '*I got engaged today. I just can't be completely happy about it as I have been thinking of Pete nearly all the day. We had a party this evening, it was very nice, but it wasn't a patch on yesterdays. It is awful being engaged; I feel so tied down. I have been longing for Pete all the time. I wonder if I will ever find the right one for me. I think Pete could be, I will probably see him on Wednesday. I am, at the moment, in LH's house. I have come back with them this evening until Wednesday morning. I do like them all but I keep thinking of Pete. I would like to break my engagement already.'*

Tuesday 27<sup>th</sup> '*Well, I'm still at LH's house and still thinking of Pete. I wonder who I will land up with in the end. I do hope it is Pete and really hope to see him tomorrow. I have had quite a nice day today and am just getting used to wearing a ring. It is a lovely thing but I do wish Pete had given it to me instead. Oh, LH is very nice but I can't truthfully say I love him, not as much as Pete anyway. Boy, I'm tired out. I have had two nights getting to bed at two am and two at gone midnight and now today it's eleven o'clock. I don't know how I am going to work tomorrow, I'm sure.'*

Wednesday 28<sup>th</sup> '*I've done an awful lot of work today. It does seem awful having to go back to work. I got up at six o'clock this morning and caught the five to seven train back to Reading. I went home to change and then went on to work. I finished about six fifteen. Mike, Rob and Pete came round this evening.*

*Oh, my goodness, I really have fallen for Pete. He has such beautiful eyes. It is his birthday today and he is 19. I went out to the gate with them and Mike kissed me goodnight first then Rob and then Pete. I liked Pete kissing me the best. He does it so nicely. I do wish he was my fiancé/boyfriend.'*

Thursday 29<sup>th</sup> is a really busy day at work too with Mary coming out at almost ten o'clock at night not knowing how to keep awake. She just goes home really tired. *'I have been thinking such a lot about Pete today. I wonder if he will write to me and if so, I wonder what he will put in it. I am looking forward to hearing from him very much. I wonder who I will end up with in the end. At the moment, I hope it will be Pete but I wonder if I will still be thinking the same in about another year's time.'*

Being another very busy day at work on Friday 30<sup>th</sup> Mary gets out of work at seven o'clock absolutely worn out. *'I then had to hang about for an hour as I had to wait until eight o'clock as I was phoning LH and he had said he wouldn't be home until that time. It was so cold waiting. I was on the phone to him for half an hour. There was a lady waiting and she banged on the window and told me to hurry up. I have been thinking of Pete an awful lot today. I do wish he would hurry up and write to me. I am simply longing to hear from him as I think he is wonderful and wish he was mine.'*

Saturday 31<sup>st</sup> *'Jolly good evening this evening. I went to Basingstoke or rather came to Basingstoke as that is where I am now. It is exactly half past one am and we have just been to a dance. Oh dear, my poor feet. I am absolutely worn out. It was a lovely dance though and I did enjoy it. I only wish I could have been there with Pete. I saw him dinner time and he stopped and spoke to me. I do wish he was my boyfriend. Still, I will have to wait and see what the New Year brings. I hope it will be a happier one than this one has been. I wonder when I will see Pete again. Soon I hope.'*

I hope next year will be a happier one for Mary too nor such an exhausting one!

# 1956

A larger diary now called the Collins Royal Two Day Diary with all the usual information you'd expect to find within its first few pages—festivals and anniversaries for the year, a calendar showing the leap year, bank holidays and one page for memoranda from 1955. It also includes a month per page for Cash Accounting at the rear. At approximately 20cm high and 13cm wide and having two days to a page, it means she can write considerably more every day. Inside the cover are small folded random personal notes, various handwritten letters and old photographs.

With apparently no lessons learnt last year, during 1956 she unfortunately falls for and juggles, two married men. Thankfully later this year she meets John, which fortunately over time causes her to cease all other love interests including with the long-suffering LH. She writes and circles inside the cover of her diary—Thursday 31st July first saw John and 23rd August first went out with John. Two of her biggest dreams come true this year when she is asked to sing in a band and starts having horse riding lessons. There's also a shocking announcement regarding her sister in April. Plus, Mary embarks on her first foreign holiday with friends this summer.

*NB. Something to remember, when Mary talks about 'making love'; she means kissing and cuddling and whispering sweet nothings, not the way we interpret it these days.*

## JANUARY

Settling into life at the bank Mary starts to relax and have fun again. Realising she is still very young she feels the enormous weight of being tied down now that she is engaged to LH and craves more than ever to be fancy free again. Being eighteen she is now able to attend more parties and Do's and can't resist the allure of planning a foreign holiday or the excitement of being able to sing in a band as she absolutely loves music. Unexpectedly her sister is also contemplating marriage but her parents don't seem to approve.

Sunday 1st Mary gets up early at LH's house and goes to church with his family. They then pile into the van and head off to see his Grandparents near Portsmouth. It is a sunny day and she comments, '*it wasn't a bad ride as the sun was shining brilliantly and it was just like a lovely spring morning instead of winter. I do wish the summer would hurry up. We had a very nice time at LH's grandparents, going for a long walk in the afternoon. It poured with rain then and was such a pity. It did seem funny today when people congratulated me on our engagement because I haven't got my ring. It has gone back to the factory as one of the diamonds was split, but still, Mr H is going to get it back for me tomorrow thank goodness. I have thought quite a lot about Pete today. I wish I had never met him, then I wouldn't have liked him so much as I do now. I am muddled lately. One minute I think I like LH, another I think it is Pete, another Keith and yet still another Johnny. I expect I will end up with LH and I dare say I couldn't find anyone much better. I am praying all the time to God to help me to stop my emotions when I see other boys, but up till now, I still like nine out of ten I see, I just can't help it. But I know God will help me to straighten out in the end alright.*'

Monday 2nd '*An awful day at work today. I don't think I have ever felt quite so fed up with my work as I have done today. I have been so completely worn out. I had to get up at six o'clock this morning because I stayed at LH's. It nearly killed me at that unearthly hour. I don't know when I have ever longed for LH quite so much as I have today. I have been thinking of him most of the time. I just don't know what came over me. He came up this evening along with his mother and father. I am very disappointed though as my ring hadn't come in. I do wish it would hurry up. I am longing for it to come back. I guess I must like LH after all.*'

With Tuesday being better at work she comments, '*I think it's mostly because I haven't been so tired today. I really was dead beat yesterday. I have been thinking of LH again most of today. I just can't make out why. I think it must be him I like best of all. I have thought about Pete, Keith and Johnny as well, but not as much as LH. I found myself longing for my ring to come back. I think God must have brought about this mysterious change in me or else I am beginning to grow up at last and realise how silly and wrong I have been behaving. With God with me, I will try to walk in the right way. I have been feeling happier than I have for ages.'*

Wednesday 4<sup>th</sup> *'Quite a good day at work today. Had some fun with two of the men there—Max and Jeff. They are both very nice indeed. I am afraid I have gone back to my normal self today and haven't been thinking about LH at all. I have been thinking about Pete and Keith most of the time. I went out with Mummy and Nadine dinner time and bought a wonderful dress. It is for me to wear at Nancy's 21<sup>st</sup> birthday party on 23<sup>rd</sup>. I don't want LH to come with me as Pete will be there and I want to be free to be with him. I hope I can pull it off. I don't really want him to come to the bank's dance either. It's been terribly foggy today.'*

On Thursday 5<sup>th</sup> Mary doesn't have so much work to do and also doesn't feel so tired. *'I saw LH this morning when I went out to coffee and arranged to go out to dinner with him and Nadine, as he had got the day off from work. Went to the Cadena Cafe and Nadine talked all the time. It was very nice though. I still haven't been thinking of LH again today, although I think I like him a lot better than I have done during the past few months. I don't know if it would please me or not to land up with him.'* In the evening, she catches up with Edna over coffee *'she told me she is going dancing at the Oxford on Saturday with a fellow. I am pleased.'*

Friday 6<sup>th</sup> *'Another good day at work again today. I have had some fun with Jeff and Max. I think Max is after me as he keeps coming up to talk to me. I like Jeff a lot better and I wish he would talk more often. I have thought quite a lot about Pete and Keith today. I wonder how they are both getting on. I still love them both in different ways.'* She sees LH at coffee time in the morning and invites him to stay the weekend, which he accepts and as he has the day off today, goes straight home to pack a bag. LH also picks up her ring, *'he brought my ring back. I like it but I don't like LH enough to marry him.'*

Feeling quite tired on Saturday 7<sup>th</sup> and not having seen much of Jeff or Max today, she writes '*LH, Mummy and I all went to the Palace this afternoon to see the pantomime "Dick Whittington and His Cat". It was very good, I quite enjoyed it. I have come to the conclusion that I don't really know my own mind yet or else it is because I haven't found the right man yet. I know I don't love LH, at least not enough to marry him. There are so many things about him that irritate me. I expect I will really meet the right one, one day but I do feel sorry for LH though.'*

Having got up early and cooked breakfast for LH on Sunday they spend the morning talking and reading the papers. After dinner '*Auntie V was in a miserable mood and because I asked if we could have the wireless on, she said she would go home and then I could have it on as much as I liked. So up she got and went home. I do wish she wouldn't say things to embarrass people because that certainly embarrassed me. Anyway, we had the wireless on and sat listening to that the rest of the afternoon until Daddy asked if we could go down the General to post a letter. So, we went on our way to church but LH said he didn't feel like going to church this evening so we came back home. I was glad really as I haven't felt too good today at all. LH left this evening and I went with him to the station. My goodness, I was frozen. I didn't know how to walk as my feet were like lumps of ice. I am really getting tired of LH. I like him alright; he is a very nice boy but I am quite sure I don't love him. I am so glad I have God to talk to. He has become such a big part in my life and helps me all the time. I had a good cry last night and He comforted me at once.'*

Mary wakes up to snow on Monday morning and its bitterly cold. '*Not too bad a day today thank goodness. I have had some fun with Max and Jeff. I do like Jeff very much. Been very busy today and I had an awful lot of work to do. I have thought about Keith, Pete and Johnny today. I do wish I could have them all. I think the thing I wish for most of all is to go abroad, the hotter the better, away from everyone and everybody, so that I could meet new people. That would make me so very happy. Sarah and Mummy keep having rows lately because Sarah says she is getting married in March and Mummy doesn't want her to. I do wish I wasn't engaged; I feel so tied.'*

Tuesday 10<sup>th</sup> is an average sort of day but a very, very busy one. '*I do wish there wasn't quite so much to do. I have had some fun with Max and Jeff again today but I felt so jealous this afternoon as Jeff came back from lunch with lipstick on his shirt. I wonder why it is I want nearly every boy I see. I do wish I could control my emotions better. I don't know why I should have been jealous because I don't really love him. I will have to try and concentrate more on work. There is also another nice fellow at the bank—Richard. I walked to the Post Office with him yesterday and this evening. He is very nice. I went round to Edna's this evening and she wants me to go to the Oxford with her on Saturday evening.*'

Wednesday 11<sup>th</sup> '*Quite a good day today I suppose. I was very pleased this morning as I found out that it was red ink on Jeff's shirt yesterday and not lipstick. I just don't know why I was pleased but I certainly was. Went out to dinner with Mary and Doris and we went to Cooks Travel agency and got some booklets about all the different countries. I want to go to Italy this year. I think Mummy would let me go if I went with Edna and I think Daddy could be persuaded. I will ask Edna when I phone her on Friday. I do hope we can go as I'm excited already. I am praying to God to let me go. Jeff is going to Italy too. I wonder if I would see him there. Went to the pictures with LH this evening.*'

Thursday 12<sup>th</sup> '*Another good day today. I have had quite a lot of fun with Max and Jeff. I do like Jeff very much indeed. I have been doing such a lot of thinking this evening. I had a bath and sat in it just dreaming for two solid hours. I was thinking about singing in a dance band. I will find out which band it is that is playing for the bank dance and, if I have the nerve, I will write and ask if they would engage me. I have also been thinking of going to Italy for my summer holidays this year. I do hope Edna will come with me. I have come to the conclusion that I need some excitement soon or else I will have a nervous breakdown. I do wish LH was livelier but he's so serious and I do wish I hadn't got engaged because I know for sure I don't love him.*'

During Friday 13<sup>th</sup> Mary finds out that the name of the band playing for the bank dance is the PM Quartet but doesn't know who could give her their address. '*I just don't know how to find out. I would love so much to sing with the band. I wonder if I ever will. I decided this evening to go in for the Miss Reading contest again this year. I don't really know if I shall have the nerve but do hope so. I think Joan will win but I think I stand a fair chance. I had LH up this evening. Oh dear, I do wish I could fall in love with him.'*

Saturday 14th *'Not too bad a morning. Ruth had the morning off so I had quite a good time with Jeff and Max. I really do like Jeff. I wish I could go to Italy with him. Boy, would we have a good time. Oh dear, I'm not really happy at all. Everybody says how lucky I am to be so happy but if only they knew just how unhappy I am. I am staying at LH's for the weekend. I should have caught the five ten train but I stopped to fill in an entry form for Miss Reading contest and missed it so I caught one at five forty-five. Sat watching television all evening. I do wish something exciting would happen. I really must try and find out the address of The PM Quartet as I would love to sing with them.'*

Sunday 15th *'I don't quite know what today has been. I have been at LH's and we have been watching television most of the time. I have had quite a lot of time to think and I have had so many things to think about such as: Miss Reading contest, singing lessons, The PM Quartet, Jeff, Keith, Pete, Johnny, work, Nancy's 21st birthday party next week, the bank dance, LH's birthday next Sunday, and lots of other things. I have come to the definite conclusion that I want to sing with a band and not have a special boyfriend at all, just go out with anyone I fancy. I have asked God to help me in all my worries and I have great faith in Him. I feel safe when I think of Him and it comforts me to know that He is always with me. Mummy, Daddy and everyone who knows me think I am a happy person. I know they would get a great shock if only they knew what I have been through this last year. If they only knew what God knew, I'm afraid they wouldn't think so much of me as they do now. I'm afraid I can't help the way I was made but I am trusting in God to help me. I have grown up a lot mentally in this last year but I still feel I am too young to be tied to LH and do wish I hadn't accepted his proposal. I do love him, but I don't love him half enough to marry him.'*

Monday 16th *'A good day today. I have had some fun with Jeff and Max today. I wonder if Jeff will ever get round to liking me enough to ask me out? I don't know what I would say if he did though.'* During the day Mary tries to think up excuses to keep LH away from the bank dance as she would much prefer to

239

go on her own. She visits Barnes and Avis (record shop) and gets the names of two singing teachers but when she phones them, they apparently, both only teach classical music so she goes to Norman Hackett's Music Shop and he is actually talking to a man who owns a dance band. *'He gave me his card and told me to go and see him for a sort of audition. I asked him about the PM Quartet too and he gave me their card also. I will phone them up tomorrow.'*

Tuesday 17th *'Jolly good day today. I believe (only believe) that Jeff is beginning to like me a bit more now. I have looked up a few times today to see him sitting staring at me. I do like him very much. I phoned up The PM Quartet dinner time but he was out so I phoned up again this evening and he was in. He said he didn't think they wanted a singer but he would ask the other boys in the band at the weekend and drop me a line to let me know. I do so wish he would take me on. I so very much want to sing at the bank dance. I want Jeff to hear me. If I don't go in that band, I will try the other one—The A Band (the man that gave me their card yesterday). I suppose it will do but I would much rather go in The PM Quartet.'*

Wednesday 18th *'Not too bad a day I suppose but just an ordinary one. I have had an awful lot of work to do today and I've had such a lot to think about. I have been hoping and praying that The PM Quartet will say they will have me and that if they do, I have been hoping that I will be good enough for them to keep me on. I have definitely decided that LH must not come to the bank dance. I don't want him to as I won't be able to have any fun at all. He is so serious and miserable all the time. I feel so embarrassed when I am with him. He came up this evening, but bores me so much that I hate him even holding my hand. Oh dear, I wish I could give him up.'*

Thursday 19th *'Quite a good day today. I have had more work to do than usual but, there again, I have had more fun with Jeff and Max. I went to the pictures with LH this evening and funnily enough I sat next to Paddy (W&H). He is very nice. I'm afraid every time I go out with LH, I dislike him more. He is so boring and I do wish I had the nerve to give him up. It is his birthday on Sunday. I was going to give him a signet ring but two things stopped me. The first is simply that I can't afford it and the second is that it would tie me to him more* than ever. How I wish I had never met him and I am praying to God to help me find a solution to all my problems.'

Friday 20th 'Quite a good day again today, apart from loads of work. I have had some fun with Jeff and Max again today. Jeff has been exceptionally nice to me. I do like him very much. I do wish I could go to Italy with him, he is so very nice. I haven't got into the Miss Reading contest this year. I think I must have been too late. I am fairly disappointed but, in another way, I am quite relieved as I don't think I could have beaten Joan, she is lovely. If I don't hear from The PM Quartet within the next week, I will go to the other man and see if he will have me. I do hope so.'

Saturday 21st 'Nothing really exciting has happened today. I do wish the Quartet would write to me, even though I wonder if I would have the nerve to do it. If I don't hear by Wednesday, I think I will try The A's Band. I have had a fair amount of fun with Max and Jeff today. I do wonder if Jeff likes me at all—I don't expect so. I am at LH's now. I came here this afternoon and we have all been to a play this evening in Basingstoke. It wasn't bad but I keep thinking about giving LH up, even though I don't think I have the nerve. I definitely can't marry him because I am not in love with him.'

Sunday 22nd 'Quite an enjoyable day today on the whole. Mummy and Daddy came to LH's house, (myself already being here) for about two o'clock and then they caught the half past nine bus back again. We all went round to Mr H's brother's bungalow. It is really beautiful, the bathroom especially. It is a beautiful pastel shade of pink. The bath was in a small alcove and it had sweet little curtains to draw across while having a bath. I do wish it was all mine. I think I would like to live there. LH has been a bit livelier today, I expect it's because of his birthday. I do wish I could fall in love with him but however hard I try, the harder it gets. I seem to notice every single fault and it irritates me, I don't know why, but I just can't help myself. He is a very sweet boy; in fact, an almost perfect boy and I like him very much indeed but that is as far as it goes. We are going to Nancy's party tomorrow and I will see Pete again. I do wish I hadn't got engaged. I am much too young to be tied completely. I want to get out and enjoy life.'

Monday 23rd *'Jolly good day really. Got up at six this morning and caught the train back to Reading. Had some fun with Jeff today, he is so nice, I do like him very much. A lovely evening this evening. Sarah, Jerry, LH and I all went to Nancy's twenty first birthday party at the Grosvenor Hotel. Pete was there, oh he is so nice. Mike came and said Pete was going to write to me. I got Mike outside and told him I wasn't happy about my engagement and he said he would do what he could about Pete. At the moment, I am still a bit tipsy I think and I reek terribly. I have had about four Gin and O's and a glass of champagne.'*

Tuesday 24th *'Oh my poor head today. I had intended to get up and see LH off this morning as he stayed with us last night, but when Mummy woke me up, he had been gone an hour. I just don't know how I have been able to work today. I have hardly been able to keep my eyes open and my head feels as heavy as a cart load of lead. I have had so much work to do but I'm afraid I am all behind in it, as I just couldn't get on with it properly. I will really have to try harder tomorrow to catch up a bit. I still haven't heard from The PM Quartet yet.'*

Wednesday 25th *'I feel a lot better today thank goodness, although I am still very tired. I managed to get all my work done by three fifteen today. I just don't know how I managed it, but I am very pleased about it. I had some more fun with Jeff at work again today. He is very nice.'* She wonders if Pete will ever write to her and is still wishing she had the nerve to give LH up but attends the pictures with him tonight nonetheless.

Thursday 26<sup>th</sup> *'Jolly good day really. I have had quite a lot of fun with Max and Jeff today. I walked from work all up Broad Street with them both after work this evening. They are both very nice indeed. I think Jeff is best though. I went to the Friars Tea Bar with Edna this evening and arranged to go dancing at the Oxford on Saturday. I don't know whether I want to go or not. We were discussing how we could raise enough money to be able to go to Italy for our summer holidays this year. I do wish I could get a job in a dance band. I will just have to try harder that's all. Haven't heard from The PM Quartet Band nor Pete. I just wish they would hurry up and write.'*

Friday 27<sup>th</sup> *'A good fun day today with Jeff and Max. I had a letter from Pete this morning. He wanted me to go out with him this evening but I had already made arrangements to go out with LH so I couldn't go. I was quite disappointed because I really would have liked to have gone.'* This is one of the letters Mary kept in her diary all these years. It states within its pages that in answer to her almost desperate request for him to drop her a line, which he finds so touching, he couldn't do anything else but write. Pete proceeds to invite Mary to go out this Friday and enquires after her present love life not knowing her current situation but mentioning that he doesn't want to put his foot in any works. *'I wrote back to him this evening and told him I was sorry I couldn't come tonight and that if he could, to meet me on Tuesday. I hope he comes. He is very nice. I'm going dancing with Edna at the Oxford tomorrow evening.'*

Saturday 28<sup>th</sup> *'Jolly good day today, had more fun with Jeff. I really do like him very much. I went to the Oxford this evening. Oh, I did enjoy myself and I did almost every dance. Whew, do my poor feet ache. I saw Jerry do his drum solo. Boy, he's terrific, I wish I was Sarah. There was a nice base player and a smashing trumpet player. Oh, how I wish I could sing with a band. Oh, I really do wish I wasn't engaged. I would love to forget all about LH for a while and have the time of my life. I just want to be free. Got home this evening about eleven forty and I am tired but still, it was certainly worth it.'*

Getting up at ten o'clock Mary is really tired on Sunday 29<sup>th</sup> when LH comes round and states in her diary that it's been a boring day. They sit reading the papers and talk until dinner time then in the afternoon play records on her gramophone on the kitchen table that is, after listening to "Educating Archie" and "Life with the Lions" on the wireless.

*'I still can't fall in love with LH, the harder I try the more faults I find with him. I just can't bear him to even put his arm around me now and when he tries to kiss me, I just have to turn my face away. I feel so sorry for him and so ashamed for treating him the way I do but I just can't help myself. I keep telling myself that I must be nice to him and show a little affection but every time I am with him, I feel so fed up and miserable, I just can't bring myself to be affectionate. I went to church with him this evening and I am praying that God will help me.'*

Monday 30<sup>th</sup> *'not too bad a day today really. I had an awful lot of work to do but I have had some fun with Max and Jeff thank goodness. I phoned up the pianist of The A's Dance Band dinner time to find out where they were playing. He said at All Saints Hall on Friday. I have asked LH if he will come with me and he said he will. I will find out on Friday if they want a singer. I wonder if I would have enough nerve to sing. I do hope so as I would feel so silly if I blundered. I went to the pictures with LH this evening.'*

Tuesday 31<sup>st</sup> *'lovely day and wonderful evening. Been busy but have had some fun at work today. I went out with Pete this evening. Boy oh boy, he is wonderful. I think I am falling in love again. I will have to control my emotions or else I will fall head over heels in love with him. We went for a drive in his wonderful new car and stopped in some woods. Oh, he is lovely and has got such heavenly blue eyes. How I am praying to God to give me the courage to give LH up. I can't go on pretending to love him when I don't feel anything for him. I feel sorry for him but I can't help it.'*

## FEBRUARY

Being successful in joining a band this month Mary's parents fiercely do not approve and forbid her to go, sparking rows at home. Mary and her friends set a destination for their summer holiday and she has to let Edna down causing a bit of annoyance.

Wednesday 1st *'A terribly busy day today. We have had all the end of month balances to do, so I didn't get out of work until seven ten. It has been absolutely freezing today, my feet and hands have been so cold I could have cried with them. I haven't felt at all well today with a stomach ache and feeling sick all the time, probably because I came on. I have been thinking of Pete most of today. I am wondering what he will put in his letter which he said I would receive tomorrow. I do like him very much and do wish I wasn't engaged to LH. I would love to be absolutely free. LH came up this evening. I'm afraid I just can't love him.'*

Thursday 2nd *'Not quite so busy today thank goodness but it's still freezing today and I have been frozen all the time. Had some fun with Jeff today. I came home dinner time because I wanted to see if I had received a letter from Pete but I was disappointed I didn't get one. I have been hoping all the afternoon that I would get one by second post but when I got in this evening, I still hadn't had one. I do hope I get one tomorrow. I will be so terribly disappointed if I don't. I went to coffee with Edna after work this evening. She has written to some hotels in Jersey about us going there for our holiday.'*

Friday 3rd *'wonderful day or really, I should say wonderful evening. I went with LH to All Saints Hall to a dance where the band was The A's and they have asked me to go to Woodley on Sunday and sing with them. We had a long talk about it. I went on stage and they introduced all the band to me. I am so thrilled and yet I am scared stiff. I do so hope I will be able to sing alright. I don't want them to have to turn me down. I would feel so silly. I do wish Sunday would hurry up and come. I didn't hear from Pete again today. I do wish he would write to me.'*

Saturday 4th *'Jolly good morning this morning. Had a lot of fun with Jeff, Mary and Doris. We were mucking about most of the time. I had a letter from Pete this morning thank goodness. Nobody knew I had because Sarah and Mummy were in the kitchen and didn't hear it, so I just picked it up and no one is any the wiser. In his letter Pete asked me to go and meet him at eleven this morning, or if I can't make that, then eight tonight. He also told me not to worry if I can't find my headscarf and necktie because he found them in his car. I managed to get out of work at eleven and saw him. He had Rob with him worst luck but I was able to tell him I couldn't go tonight. Went to the pictures with LH today. Got my singing to do tomorrow.'*

Sunday 5th '*Wonderful evening this evening. I was going to say a wonderful day but it hasn't been very wonderful. LH has developed a bit of a cold and, my, doesn't he make a fuss of it. He kept moaning all the time. He said he didn't really want to go this evening but he supposed he had better. Anyway, we went— to Woodley. We had to wait about twenty minutes when we got to the hall and oh my goodness, I think they were the longest minutes in my whole life. I was absolutely scared stiff. I was shaking all the time. The band came in the end and we just had time to find out the right key for me to sing it to before everybody came in, so I had to sing straight away without them even hearing me. I forgot the words of the first verse but I was alright after that. The microphone was queer. I thought it had gone off but apparently you can't hear yourself but everyone else can. Anyway, the band thought I was very good, thanks to God. They want me to stay with them. They are going to try to get a mic all the time. I do hope they do as I love singing very much. I was most surprised with myself as I didn't blush at all, I was so thrilled. I have thought about Pete an awful lot today.'*

Monday 6th '*Quite a good day really. I've had some fun with Jeff but apart from that, nothing exciting has happened at all. I have been thinking about my singing most of the time and when I haven't been thinking about singing, I have been dreaming about Pete. I am supposed to be going out with him tomorrow and I do wish it would hurry up and come. I do wish the next time for me to sing would hurry up too as I really do love doing it. I know I won't be so nervous next time.'*

Tuesday 7th '*A queer mixture of ups and downs today. Mummy told me she had found out about me going out with Pete last week. Oh, we had an awful row. I came home dinner time to try and straighten things out. We had another row but she was alright after that. Anyway, I went out with Pete and, boy, he is so wonderful. I really do like him very much indeed. We stopped at the same place as Keith and I used to. It brought back memories. I wish I could have a nice flat all to myself so I could do just what I liked. I don't know how to go about giving LH up. I wish I could think of a way especially as I don't want to hurt him.'*

Wednesday 8th '*Quite a normal day really. I have had some fun with Jeff, but I don't think I would really like him as a boyfriend. I have thought quite a lot about Pete today and wish he would hurry up and write to me, as he told me he would before the weekend. I went to the pictures with LH this evening and I'm afraid I neglect him terribly. I keep telling myself I will have to be kinder to him as he is the perfect boy (much too perfect for my liking) but every time I am with him, I just feel so fed up and just can't be nice to him. After seeing him off on the train, a soldier came up and asked if he could see me again. He wasn't my type.*'

Thursday 9th '*Another quite ordinary day really. Had some fun with Jeff again with him calling me his favourite machinist. I do wish he was serious, still, you never know, he may be. Johnny met me from work at dinner time. He keeps asking me to give LH up and go back to him. Well, I would like to give LH up but if I did, I wouldn't want any one special boyfriend as I would want to be free to be able to go out with anyone I liked. I wonder if I will ever pluck the courage up to give LH up. I will either have to do that or else fall in love with him. I am going crazy with worry.*'

Friday 10th '*Oh dear, I am so desperately unhappy. At the moment, I am crying my eyes out. I went to see The A's Dance Band and they asked me to sing for them next Tuesday. They said they would pick me up in their car. I was absolutely thrilled as I have always wanted the chance to be a singer but when I got home Daddy told me I wasn't to go. I just don't know what to do. I am thinking about getting lodging elsewhere so that I wouldn't be tied to such old-fashioned parents. Oh God, please help me. I have not much strength left what with worrying about LH, Pete, Johnny, Jeff and the soldier. I am just about all in. I wish I was dead.*'

Saturday 11th '*Quite a good day I suppose. Had some fun with Jeff this morning. Daddy and Mummy were extra nice to me today. I don't know whether it was because of yesterday or not. Had my hair permed this afternoon. Oh my goodness, it is absolutely terrible. I could have cried when I saw it. After having it done, I caught the train to LH's and in the evening LH, Brian and I went to a Valentine's dance in Basingstoke. We were with two of LH's friends most of the time—Jim and Norman. Boy, they are both smashing, especially Norman. I wish he was my boyfriend, oh if only I was free.*'

247

Sunday 12th *'Quite an ordinary sort of day really. I have been at LH's all day and I am still at his, as I am going back home early tomorrow morning. We went to church this morning and then after dinner listened to the wireless for about an hour and a half, then played "Sorry" for about a couple of hours. After tea, we watched television for the* rest *of the evening. LH keeps kissing me and I'm afraid I hate it. I do wish I could fall in love with him because he is such a nice boy and I do like him very, very much but I just can't seem to fall in love with him. I do wish I could go abroad and start all over again, although I suppose in time, I would get into exactly the same muddle. Oh dear, I do wish I wasn't interested in boys (like Edna) but I can't help it. I flirt like mad even in front of LH. I know it's an awful thing to do but I suppose it is the way I am made. God is helping me I know. I wonder who I will end up with.'*

Monday 13th *'An awful day really. Got up at six and caught the 6:55 train back to Reading. Directly I got home, had an awful row with Mummy and Sarah about all my singing. I told Mummy I would find lodgings elsewhere. I do wish I could really because then I wouldn't be a burden to anyone. I do so hate all these horrible rows. When I got in this evening, Daddy didn't speak to me at all. I am so desperately unhappy and wish I could either drop dead or else go abroad as far away as possible. Sent half a dozen Valentine cards today.'*

Tuesday 14th *'Quite a good day really apart from the fact that I was a little disappointed as I didn't receive any Valentine cards. God worked a wonderful miracle for me today. He made the microphone from the band go wrong. Anyway, their secretary—phoned me up to tell me that I wouldn't be able to sing. I am so glad as Mummy and Daddy had almost forbidden me to go and I have been so worried as to whether I should or not. Oh God is so wonderful; I knew He would help me if I had enough faith in Him. Saw Edna this evening. Looked at some books on hotels. We are going to Jersey for the holidays.'*

Wednesday 15th *'Quite a good day again really. Had some fun with Jeff, he is very nice. He looked pleased this morning. I expect it was because of his Valentine. Went round to Grandma's and Grandad's this evening with LH. I went round there to try on a pair of Auntie O's jodhpurs. They are quite a lot too big worst luck but I will get them altered. I will love to go riding and wish it would hurry up. I also wish my holiday would hurry up too. Edna and I are definitely going to Jersey now. I am thrilled but I do wish we could have afforded to go to Italy.'*

Thursday 16<sup>th</sup> *'Not too bad a day really. I got all behind in my work this morning but I finished first even then. I do wish Pete would hurry up and get in touch with me. I like him very much. Edna came round this evening and we sat and discussed our holiday all evening. We have worked out the cost of it and we find we will have enough and fifteen pounds over. I do hope it works out the way we have calculated it. We will have a smashing time. I am looking forward to it immensely. Going to Oxford on Saturday. It does seem a long way off.'*

Friday 17<sup>th</sup> *'Not too bad a day but not too good an evening. Went to the Palace with LH this evening, then into the Oxford Café afterwards. I asked him if he would come with me on Sunday to sing with the band. At first, he said no as it was against his principles but after a time, he must have realised it would make me unhappy so he said he would come with me this time. I don't know what I will do if they ask me about going next week. I do wish I could live on my own and have no ties so that I could do as I liked.'*

Saturday 18<sup>th</sup> *'Quite a good day all around, I think. Not too bad at work. Walked all up Broad Street with Jeff—wow, I do like him very much. Wonderful evening this evening. Went dancing at the Oxford with Edna. It was very good especially the last part. I do like dancing and am going with Edna next Saturday to the Rag dance at the town hall. I don't know what I will wear. I do wish I had lots and lots of clothes. I am supposed to be going to Woodley tomorrow to sing with the band. I do hope Mummy and Daddy will let me go.'*

Sunday 19<sup>th</sup> *'Not too good a day I'm afraid but wonderful evening. LH came this morning about eleven and after dinner we sat and read the paper most of the time. It was so boring. Then I asked him if he would come singing with me this evening—well, that started it. He sulked, he moaned, he groaned. Oh dear, what a to-do and all the time he was moaning he kept telling me he loved me. I felt sorry for him really. I do wish I didn't like singing so much. I'm afraid I am terribly selfish but as I have always wanted to sing in a dance band, I don't want to let this chance go by. Anyway, after a very long afternoon he said he supposed he would have to come with me. It was wonderful there. I sang two songs—*

"Love and Marriage" and "I'll Come When You Call". I do wish I had a better voice. LH looked miserable most of the evening. I do wish he was like other young boys. Perhaps the forces will alter him when he goes in. The band wants me to sing in The Olympia Wednesday week and not far from Basingstoke next Saturday. I hope to go in the car with the band this time.'

Monday 20th 'About an average day really. Made quite a lot mistakes at work and got all behind but still I managed to catch up thank goodness. Wrote to Auntie O dinner time about the jodhpurs and also rang Edna up to ask her not to get me a ticket for the Rag Dance on Saturday, but she was at lunch. I waited for her this evening and she had got the tickets so I didn't like to tell her I couldn't come. I will have to tell her on Thursday. Stayed in this evening and sat by the fire. Mummy and Daddy were in a very good mood and have been laughing and joking most of the time. I am so pleased.'

Tuesday 21st 'Not too bad a day really. Nothing at all exciting has happened. Finished work at four thirty today. Stayed in all evening and sat and started making a rug. It is one I have had for well over a year. Saw Edna today at dinner time and I asked her if she could come to London with me on Thursday evening to get an evening dress but she can't come as she is taking Margaret to see "Snow White and the Seven Dwarfs" at the Palace. I do wish I had a lot of money; I need so many things. I do hope I will be able to save enough for our holiday.'

Wednesday 22nd 'An awfully busy day at work today. I don't know how I managed to get through it all, but even then, I managed to get out at four forty-five. It was much too early for me to meet LH, so I went round to the High Café and had something to eat. I stayed in there until half past five and then came out in time to meet LH. Then we went to the Gaumont. It wasn't bad. After I had seen him off on the train, I phoned Stan up (from the band) but he was out so I told his wife to tell him I would see him in Rotherwick on Saturday. I wish it would hurry up.'

Thursday 23rd 'Not too bad a day today I suppose. Had quite a bit of fun with Jeff. He is very nice. Saw Edna dinner time and again this evening for coffee. I told her I wouldn't be able to go to the Rag Dance on Saturday as I would be *singing and she was very upset about it. I think she was rather annoyed too. She was thinking up all kinds of excuses for me and even dragged me round to find out the times of the trains back from Basingstoke so that perhaps I could go later on in the evening. I would like to go but I think I like singing better.'*

Friday Mary sees Edna again at dinner time and thinks she is still quite annoyed at her for choosing to go singing rather than accompany her to the Rag dance at the town hall on Saturday. *'I must admit I am quite disappointed myself really as I had been looking forward to going very much. It would have been fun but I think I would rather sing with the band. I will be glad when they start to pay me. Went to the pictures with LH this evening. I am so terribly muddled up.'*

Saturday 25$^{th}$ *'Not too bad a day again really. Work seemed fairly dull this morning as Jeff was away. I have missed him. Went to LH's this afternoon and then this evening Brian, LH and I went to Rotherwick to a dance there. I sang with the band again. Oh, I do like it so much. They were very nice to me and gave me a cup of coffee during the interval. They want me to sing at the Olympia on Wednesday and said they would pay me. Poor Brian was as miserable as sin all the evening. He just won't dance with anyone. I think I have a cold coming. I do hope not.'*

Sunday, whilst still at LH's, she feels absolutely rotten having gotten into bed at 2am. *'I am tired out and I was right about having a cold on the way. I have got an absolute stinker. I have been sniffing and coughing all day long. LH has been dosing me up with different kinds of tablets all day long and just before I came to bed, he gave me a glass of quinine. I took one sip and it made me feel sick so after he had gone off to bed, I crept into the bathroom and tipped it down the toilet. It's already eleven fifteen pm and I have yet to get undressed and ready for bed and I have got to get up about six o'clock tomorrow in time to catch the train back to Reading. I have been thinking a lot about Keith today as it is exactly a year ago today that we first went out together. I think I will phone him up tomorrow and wish him a happy anniversary.'*

Monday 27$^{th}$ *'A day of ups and downs today really. I have felt absolutely awful all the time. My head seems to be splitting open all the time and I just can't stop sniffing. I feel just awful. I have had some fun with Jeff today and think he likes me a little more now, although I don't know what I would do if he did really get to like me enough to ask me out. I do wish I hadn't got engaged. I went round town dinner time looking for an evening dress to wear on Wednesday, but they are all so terribly expensive. I do wish I was rich.'*

Tuesday 28th *'An awful lot of work today worst luck and I still haven't been feeling at all good all the time. I have had some fun with Jeff though. He keeps coming up to me and telling me not to let the work get me down. He certainly is very nice. Oh, I do wish I had never met LH. I wonder if I will marry him in the end or not. At the moment, I should hate to marry anyone. I would like to travel all over the world just singing. Talking of singing, I will be singing at the Olympia tomorrow. I hope my cold will be better by then. I wonder if I will ever be a famous singer?'*

Wednesday 29th *'Wonderful, heavenly evening. I went to the Olympia and sang with the band. LH couldn't come as he had a cold so I went by myself. Danced quite a lot with Norman, the trumpet player before singing. Sang three songs. We were on for two and a half hours. I sat on the stage all that time. Oh, it was lovely. After we had finished (12 o'clock), we had coffee and then Stan and Norman and the drummer were all arguing as to who should dance with me and also who should take me home afterwards. I danced most with Norman including the last waltz (2 o'clock) and he took me home in the end and kissed me goodnight. Oh, I like it all so very much. Got into bed 3-15.'*

MARCH

Although singing with a band is wonderful to Mary, her parents are unsurprisingly very disapproving sparking arguments which lead to her stating she wants to move out. But on the plus side she has a memorable night at the bank dance on the 23rd and LH turns up the romance.

Thursday 1<sup>st</sup> '*Oh dear, what a day. I just haven't known how to keep my eyes open. I have had an awful lot of work today worst luck as it is the end of the month and I haven't had time to breathe all day. I have been dreaming about the fellows in the band and me singing, all the time I have been banging away on my machine at the bank. I do hope I won't have too many mistakes tomorrow. Had an awful row with Daddy this evening about my singing. He won't speak to me now. It is poor little Mummy I worry about. All these arguments worry her and I don't want anything to happen to her, as I love her better than anyone in the world. Phoned LH up today and he has to stay in bed with the flu.*'

Friday 2<sup>nd</sup> '*Wonderful, wonderful evening. Went singing with the band by myself. Oh, I do love it so much. We were laughing and joking most of the time. Stan managed to leave his sax so that he could dance with me. Came home in Norman's car. He took Dick and Frankie home first and then we sat talking until one thirty. He kissed me lots of times and made love to me. I do like him very much. In fact, I like them all and would like to go singing with them every night. I am going with them to Rotherwick tomorrow and am looking forward to it so very much.*'

Saturday 3<sup>rd</sup> *'Quite a good day and another absolutely wonderful evening. Went to Rotherwick with the band. Oh, I did have some fun. They took me in their car or rather Norman's car. He was holding my hand most of the way. We stopped at a public house and had a drink on the way. I did enjoy it. We were mucking about most of the evening, laughing and joking. I do love it all so very much. Came home in the car with Norman, Freddie and Ted. It was wonderful. Norman took them home first then we stopped before we got home and he made love to me again. I have arranged to meet him on Wednesday.'*

Sunday 4<sup>th</sup> *'Not at all a good day today I'm afraid. Had an awful row with Daddy and Mummy about me singing. Daddy told me I wasn't to go again so I told him I would find lodgings elsewhere and he said I could please myself. Oh, I am so unhappy about it. I love being with the band and singing so much. I know I couldn't give it up now. I don't think I could afford lodgings and I know I wouldn't really like leaving Mummy. I am trusting in God to help me like He has done so much in the past. I know He is with me and loves me. I have been dreaming about the band all day long especially Norman and Freddie as I like them best. I came to LH's today. It is awful having to be cheerful and letting LH kiss me when I am so desperately worried. Spent all afternoon and evening watching television but I couldn't really concentrate. I do wish Mummy and Daddy could see my point of view because I can see theirs. It is only natural for them to be worried about me but I wish they would understand that I love singing so much. Perhaps then, they wouldn't try to stop me.'*

Monday 5<sup>th</sup> *'Not too bad a day I suppose. Stayed in all morning and helped LH to learn his play. He made love to me. I didn't want him to but I couldn't stop him. Went to Winchester this afternoon. It wasn't bad. Sat and watched television this evening. After everyone had gone to bed, LH again made love to me. Now I am sitting all by myself on my bed thinking deeply. I am dreaming about the band mostly and about Mum and Dad. I am praying to God to make them realise that I love singing with the band so much that I couldn't possibly give it up now. I am so desperately worried. I do wish I could live on my own although I love Mum and Dad.'*

Tuesday 6<sup>th</sup> *'Apart from the fact that I have still been worrying about my singing—today hasn't been too bad really. We watched television most of this* morning, all this afternoon and all evening. LH went to the doctors this evening, who said he wasn't to go back to work until next week. I have to go back to work tomorrow. I am quite glad really, as it will be nice to see Jeff. I am wondering how Mummy and Daddy will act towards me. I am supposed to be singing in the band on Friday. I do hope I will be able to go. Going out with Norman tomorrow.'

Wednesday 7th *'Jolly good evening. In fact, wonderful day altogether really. Had some fun with Jeff at work. He is so very nice. Went out with Norman this evening. We went into a public house and had a drink first and then we drove all through Sonning and Woodley then stopped in a very dark lane. Wow! We sat in the back seat. It was wonderful. He certainly is very nice but I am not in love with him, but I like him an awful lot. I will see him again Friday as I will be going singing. Came back from LH's this morning alone as he has to stay in until next week. Saw Edna at dinnertime and will see her again tomorrow.'*

Thursday 8th *'Just an ordinary day really. Nothing exciting has happened apart from having fun with Jeff. Been very busy though. There certainly is a lot of work to do in the bank. Saw Edna this evening. We went to the Friars Tea Bar after work and discussed our holiday, dances, money and nearly everything else under the sun. I don't know how I am going to save up enough money for everything I need. I do wish I had lots of money. Perhaps I will one day. Sarah and I have decided to try and get a flat for us to live in. Oh, I do hope we can. I would be able to go out every night without being told off afterwards.'*

Friday 9th *'Wonderful day altogether. Had an awful lot of fun at work today with Graham (one of the fellows). We had a lovely fight dinner time. He put me across his knee and spanked me, then he locked me in the girl's cloakroom. I did enjoy it all. Went singing this evening or rather went with the band. They hadn't got a mic so I couldn't sing. Met Norman outside the place and then went and had a drink. The rest of the boys were there. Oh, it was lovely. Had some fun during the evening, laughing and joking most of the time. Norman took me home. He is nice.'*

Saturday 10th *'Heavenly, wonderful evening. Lots better than yesterday and that's saying something. Went with the band again. I did sing this time thank goodness. We went to Sherfield on Loddon. Went in the car with Norman, Frankie and Dick. Stopped on the way at a pub and had a couple of drinks. During the evening the boys kept drinking beer and I had a little drop too. It wasn't at all bad. During the interval had some fun and more beer. After it had finished, we stood and laughed and joked and then had more beer. Frankie got a bit tight; he really is a scream. I like him very much indeed. In fact, I like them all. After having got all the instruments into Norman's car, I got in with Norman and the rest piled into Stan's car. Stan got out of his car came up to me and kissed me in front of all the others. I did enjoy that. Well, on our way home, Norman wanted to stop out in the country but Stan kept stopping so that we had to go on ahead. We kept dodging them and they kept finding us. Oh, we had a proper game. It was wonderful. When we had really dodged them, Norman told me he loved me. Got in at 2-15am. Wonderful!'*

Sunday 11th *'An awfully long day today. I just feel as if it has been wasted. Got myself up this morning about eight and came to LHs, leaving Mummy and Daddy in bed. They were quite nice to me this morning; I was most surprised as I didn't say goodnight to them last night. I had prayed hard to God for us not to have any more rows and He must have answered me again as I was quite expecting Daddy to go up the wall. Went to some friends of LH's today—Alison and Graham. They aren't bad but I have been dreaming about the boys in the band all day long. I do wish I could have gone with them tonight to Woodley. I love being with them so much as they are so wonderful.'*

Monday 12th *'Lovely evening, in fact jolly good day altogether really. Went out with Norman this evening to a small public house in Sonning and had a drink. It was lovely, I did like it. I like Norman very much too. He is so nice. We went for a ride round after coming out of the pub and then stopped in a quiet lane and we had a serious talk. He told me he loved me and that he wished it was possible for him to marry me. I like him very much indeed but I don't think I love him although it wouldn't take very much to me to do so. Going out with him again on Wednesday.'*

Tuesday 13th *'Just an ordinary day really today. Nothing at all exciting has happened. Had quite a lot of work to do worst luck. Had a bit of fun with Jeff and Max. I do like them both very much. Been thinking about Norman and the rest of the band most of today. I don't think I will be going with them again until Saturday. It does seem a long time off, but still, I will be seeing Norman tomorrow. Phoned LH up this evening. He is going back to work on Thursday so that means I will be going out with him again worst luck. Gave Edna £2 for my deposit for our hotel in Jersey. I'm broke.'*

Wednesday 14<sup>th</sup> *'Jolly good evening this evening, in fact a jolly good day altogether. Had some fun with Jeff and Dave. They are both so nice. Went out with Norman this evening. We went to Sonning and stopped in a quiet lane. It was wonderful. He told me he loved me again. He said he would really like to make love to me but was frightened to. Oh, I do like him very much and it wouldn't take very much for me to fall in love with him. He is going to pick me up on Saturday, as I am going singing with him and the rest of the band. It seems such a long way off, I do wish it would hurry up and come. I want to see the others.'*

Thursday 15<sup>th</sup> *'Not a very exciting day really. Nothing at all outstanding has happened. Had some fun with Jeff and Dave and been thinking about Norman and the rest of the fellows in the band all day today. I have been worrying about how my money is going to make out. I have such a lot of expenses during the next fortnight. I will have to go up to London next Thursday and get an evening dress and then there's Mum and Dad's silver wedding anniversary and also Pam's (Edna's sister) wedding.'*

Friday 16<sup>th</sup> *'Had quite a lot of fun at work today in the dinner hour with Jeff, Max and KN, especially Ken. He held my hand and said I distracted him. I like him very much indeed. In fact, they are all lovely. Went to the pictures with LH this evening. Oh dear, oh dear, everything he says and does seems to annoy me I don't know why. I think it is because he is so serious all the time, he never jokes about at all. All he does, is tell me he loves me. I know it's nice to hear that but when you hear nothing else, it gets boring. I do hope he will change when he goes in the forces next year.'*

Saturday 17<sup>th</sup> *'Wonderful, wonderful evening. Norman picked me up in Downshire Square and we went to Woodley where we met the rest of the band. We all went and had a few drinks first and I believe Norman, Frankie and Stan were a bit happy. Anyway, we had lots of fun all through the evening. I only sang one song, worst luck, but I did lots of the dances. Afterwards Frankie kissed me goodnight (wow, can he kiss) and then Stan came up and said it was his turn so he kissed me (he did pretty well too). Norman took me home and we stopped on the way. He told me he was hurt because of the kisses and kept telling me he loved me. I had an awful job to get him to take me home. I think he had had a lot too much to drink.'*

Sunday 18<sup>th</sup> *'I can't remember a day in my whole life which was as boring and miserable as today has been. I am really fed up. Got up quite early this morning. Mummy and Daddy were a bit sulky at first but after about quarter of an hour of being out in the kitchen with me, they chatted away quite happily. I am so glad as I do hate having rows with them. I went to LH's later on in the morning. After dinner, we went for a long walk. It wasn't bad but LH would insist on me helping him learn his play that he's in. It was such lovely weather. The sun was shining without a cloud in the sky and it was really quite warm that I certainly didn't feel like going along reading a play. I felt like just running off across the fields. Watched television for a while after we got back and had tea. Then went to church. After that, went with LH to a play rehearsal. I have never been so bored and fed up before in my life. I had to be prompter and I just couldn't concentrate on the play. I kept thinking about Norman, Stan and Frankie and lots of other things. I could have gone out with Norman this evening and do wish I could have thought of an excuse so that I could have done. I would have liked that.'*

Monday 19<sup>th</sup> *'Wonderful evening again in fact jolly good day really. Had some fun with Jeff and Dave at work, then went out with Norman this evening. Oh, he is so very nice. We went to Woodley and then stopped in a nice dark lane. He made love to me it was lovely and he told me he loved me. I think I love him in a special sort of way but not really deep love. He wanted me to go out with him every day this week but of course, I couldn't worst luck, but as I'm not seeing LH this week, I will be going out with him again on Wednesday—lovely!'*

Tuesday 20<sup>th</sup> *'Jolly good day again today really although nothing really exciting has happened. Have had some fun with Jeff and Dave again and I had a fight with Graham dinner time—it was lovely. Oh, I do like working at the bank* so much, I have got properly into it now and I can do it thank goodness. I have been thinking of Norman, Stan and Frankie and my singing all day today, also about the bank dance on Friday. Mr W says they have arranged for me to sing but I just couldn't, not in front of the entire bank. I would go so red. I do hope they won't make me. Stayed in this evening and having an early night. It certainly makes a change. Going up to London on Thursday evening.'

Wednesday 21st *'Wonderful day and evening. I have had some fun with Jeff, Dave and Ken today. They are all nice but I like Jeff best for sure. Went out with Norman this evening. It was wonderful. He is so nice. We went to Woodley again and stopped in the same dark lane. Oh, I do like him. He kept telling me he loved me all the time and said he didn't go to sleep on Monday night through thinking about me so much. He wanted me to go out with him again tomorrow, Friday, Saturday and Sunday. I do wish I was able to. I do so wish I had a flat of my own so that I could go out every night. I wish I could give LH up too. Phoned him up this evening. He is coming on Saturday worst luck.'*

Thursday 22nd *'Jolly good day and evening again. Had some fun with the fellows at work. Went to London about four o'clock this afternoon by myself. It was wonderful. I didn't know where I was but I managed to get to C and A's alright. I had a jolly good look round there then I went to Selfridges and into several other shops. In the end, I went back to C and A's and bought an evening dress. It isn't bad, but it isn't quite what I wanted. Anyway, it will have to do as it is the bank dance tomorrow. My poor feet ache terribly so I hope I will be able to dance. Norman said he may come but I don't know if I want him to or not.'*

Friday 23rd *'Wonderful, heavenly evening. Went to the bank dance, oh it was wonderful. Sat with Max for a while but that was boring so I went and stood with Ken, Margaret, Jean, Sam and a few others. Sam kept asking me to dance, so I became his partner for the rest of the evening, including the last waltz. Afterwards, he took me home. Badgie and Dave took us in their car and departed after having kissed me goodnight. Sam and I stood and made love to each other until half past two. Boy! Can he kiss. I'm afraid I was a bit tight. He wants to take me out one evening. He certainly is wonderful. Wore my new frock, I did feel grand thank goodness.'*

Mary at her Bank Dance 1956

Saturday 24<sup>th</sup> '*Oh dear, what a morning. I have had my leg pulled unmercifully for going home with three fellows last night. Hardly done any work this morning. Quite a good evening really, I suppose. Went singing with the band in Rotherwick this evening. Norman picked me up and when we got to Rotherwick we all went in a pub and had a couple of drinks. LH was at the dance as I am staying the night at his house. Oh, he makes me sick and spoilt all our fun. Stan, Frankie and Norman couldn't even kiss me goodnight. I hardly spoke to LH all the evening. I know I will have to give him up before much longer. I just can't stand him. I love being with the band so much and wish I could go with them every single time.*'

Sunday 25<sup>th</sup> '*A most boring and worrying day today. I have been at LH's and got up early this morning and went to church and then had dinner. After that, went for a short walk with LH and I hardly spoke to him at all. Every single thing he does or says annoys me; I don't know why. Watched television for a while before tea and then went to church again. LH stayed there for a rehearsal of his play and I went back and watched television for the rest of the evening. I have been worrying so much about Norman all day today. He was going to meet the* train this evening in case I could get back but I just couldn't find an excuse for going back home so I just had to sit and worry. I do hope he didn't wait long. I won't see him now until Tuesday. I have also been worrying about how to get enough money for Mummy and Daddy's silver wedding present. I do wish I had lots of money. I am so pleased I have got God to talk to. He always comforts me and helps me. I am praying that He will help me with my singing and that He will let Mum and Dad see my point of view about going. I do so hope I will be a great star one day. I wonder if I ever will be. I would love to get Mummy all the things she needs and wants. Perhaps I will one of these days. I do wish Tuesday would hurry up as I want to see how Norman got on last night as he had had a row with his wife.'

Monday 26th 'Jolly good day today. Saw Sam, he is wonderful but not as nice as Jeff. I had fun with all the men today. They have all been teasing me about going home with Sam on Friday. Oh, I do like them all so much. Saw the photographs of the dance today. They have come out jolly good. I do like it at work, all the men are so jolly nice. Came back from LH's this morning. I am really fed up with him but I can't help it, he just irritates me so much. I will not see him until Friday thank goodness as he has got rehearsals for his play. I have thought a lot of Norman today and do hope he got on alright.'

Mary is subjected to more teasing on Tuesday and sees quite a lot of Sam, especially after work in the cycle shed with his friend Alec. 'I do like him very much. I went out with Norman this evening, it was lovely. We went to Woodley. He is so nice, although I don't think I am in love with him. I am going out with him again on Thursday. It is awkward having to make excuses to Mummy though. I don't like telling lies but there is no other way. Perhaps I won't have to one of these days. Saw Edna for coffee this evening. She is nice.'

Wednesday 28th 'Not too bad a day again today. I've had some fun with all the men again today. They are all so nice. I just don't know which I like the best (after Jeff). Nothing really out of the ordinary has happened today. Bought Mummy and Daddy eighteen green tulips as it is their silver wedding day today. LH came round early this morning to bring them a present and nearly let the cat out of the bag. He said he had had a rehearsal last night and I had told Mum and Dad I had been out with him, but I managed to give him the tip and he corrected himself. Saw Edna dinner time and gave her a salad set for Pam's wedding present. I will be going out with Norman tomorrow evening—goody!'

Thursday 29th 'Wonderful day today. Had some fun with all the men again today, they are all so nice. Wonderful evening—I went out with Norman. Went to Woodley on the bus to meet him and I got off at the wrong stop and was wondering around for forty-five minutes in the dark roads trying to find him. In the end, he found me so everything was alright, thanks to God. I had prayed so hard to help me find Norman and He answered me. It's so wonderful to know that He is with me all the time and that He loves me. LH is coming over tomorrow, I have got to try and make an excuse not to have to go with them to Weymouth for the weekend. I do hope I will think of one.'

Friday 30th Good Friday 'Not too bad, not too good a day today. LH came over for the day and I told him I have got to all day work tomorrow (I haven't really) so I wouldn't be able to go to Weymouth. Oh my, oh my, the fuss he made. He nearly burst into tears and kept on and on about it. I do wish he wasn't so awfully serious about everything. You can't have a joke at anything like that with him. It's just not normal for a fellow of his age. I would so much like to love him but I'm afraid he just bores me terribly. We all went down to Grandmas and Grandad's this evening. Aunty O was there. I do like her. She is fun. Going to Pam's wedding tomorrow. I am a bit scared as I have never been to a wedding before.'

Saturday 31st 'Jolly good day really but absolutely horrible evening. Had some fun with the men at work this morning, they are so very nice. Went to Pam's wedding this afternoon. She did look lovely. I do wish I could find someone to love as much as she loves Danny. After the reception, Edna and I went to see her sister-in-law in hospital. She does look ill. We took her the bouquets. I was going singing tonight with the fellows in the band but on phoning LH up, his father almost forced me to go with them to Weymouth which is where I am now. LH came to pick me up and I made him wait to see Norman who was picking me up. We were both so disappointed that I couldn't go. I have hardly spoken to LH at all.'

<u>APRIL</u>

Mary's social life really ramps up a gear this month and I don't know just how she fits so much in! But that's nothing compared to the shock announcement her mother makes on 3rd regarding her sister.

Sunday 1st Easter Day *'Not too bad a day I suppose really, considering. Slept in the same caravan as LH's grandparents last night. I did feel a bit scared. Got up about eight this morning, then went across to the other caravan to have breakfast with LH's parents and Brian. After breakfast, Mr H, LH and I all went for a long walk across hills and meadows. Oh, it was cold right by the sea. When we got back, we had dinner with his grandparents and then went to the town and had a walk around. My poor feet! Had tea and cakes in a little place called Burt's Café. The cakes were wonderful. After that we went to church, then back to the caravan, playing cards until it was time for bed. My bed was lovely and comfortable. It was a double one and I had such a lovely lot of room. I have been thinking about Norman and the rest of the band most of today. I do wish I could have gone with them yesterday and yet; I am enjoying myself fairly well here I suppose. Anyway, I am going singing with them tomorrow evening and do wish it would hurry up. I am not looking forward to work on Tuesday as I don't know how I will get through it all.'*

On Easter Monday after another walk around the town, Mary comes back from Weymouth with everyone arriving at LH's house in Basingstoke about 6 o'clock. They then have tea and she changes to catch the train home to Reading. She then gets a bus to Woodley where she arrives about 9.30pm *'Oh, I did have a lovely time. The band are so nice. There was a new sax player who is very young. Norman took me home about 2am and I found the door locked so had to ring until Daddy got out of bed. He was so annoyed and said they didn't know I was coming home this evening. If I'd known, I could have stayed out all night with Norman. I don't think I would have really liked to do that. I bet I will be told off tomorrow.'*

Tuesday 3rd *'Mummy woke me up this morning and told me Sarah had got married. I was so shocked. We thought she must have got married on Saturday but Mummy went to the registry office this afternoon and found out that she actually got married on February 8th. I am absolutely shocked and it hasn't sunk in yet. Apparently, Jerry came round yesterday and told Mum and Dad that they were married. I just don't know what to think. Worked until 10:30 this evening. I have had some fun with the men there, especially Graham. He came into the girl's cloakroom and kissed me and then lots of times after work in the cycle shed. He is very nice. Saw Stan dinner time and he gave me my ring back which I had given him last night and Norman rang me this morning.'*

Wednesday 4th *'Saw Sarah dinner time. Went to Maurice's to book an appointment for my hair. Sarah looked very upset. I did feel sorry for her. She has got a lovely ring. She was ever so nice but I do wish she had got married properly. I would have loved to have been a bridesmaid. It still hasn't quite sunk in that she is married. It does seem queer at home without her. I have been so tired today. I had arranged to go out with Norman this evening but had to work late again, so slipped out at 8 o'clock and told him to meet me at 9:45. Well, I saw him at 9:45 and we went up the Warren. He was a bit tipsy; I do wish he hadn't have had so much to drink. I am quite worried about Mummy. She isn't well at all. Phoned LH up today and saw Edna dinner time.'*

Thursday 5th *'Jolly good day really. Had some fun with all the men especially Graham. He kissed me lots of times after work in the cycle shed. I think Jeff is beginning to like me a bit better now. I am so glad. I have still felt tired today. Went out with Norman this evening. We went up the Warren again. He is very nice but I do not love him. I think I could if I tried hard enough. It does seem queer at home without Sarah and I do miss her. I feel quite lonely and I do wish she hadn't just gone off like that and got married. I hadn't realised before just how much I loved her and do wish she would come back to live but of course, she can't now. Oh dear, I do feel lost. Saw Edna dinner time and again this evening for coffee. She is terribly shocked at Sarah.'*

Friday 6th *'Not too bad a day I suppose. Had some fun with the men at work again especially Graham. Had a lovely fight with him dinner time. He is very, very nice. Had hair done after work, it does look a sight. I went out this evening with the band. It was in the hall opposite the Oxford. There wasn't a microphone there so I couldn't sing, I was so disappointed. I also had an awful disappointment after the dance. I had been looking forward to going to*

*Rotherwick tomorrow with them but Stan told me he just couldn't take me as there wasn't enough room in either of the cars. I felt like crying my eyes out. I would love to have gone so much. I had some fun with Frankie and Stan and also the new sax player (he is very nice). Norman took me home.'*

Saturday 7th '*Quite a good morning at work this morning. Had some fun with Graham. He kissed me after work in the cycle shed after having walked up to Woolworths together. He came up to me in work this morning and said he adored me. He is so nice. Boring afternoon and evening. LH came and I dislike him more every time I see him. I was annoyed because if he hadn't come, I would have been able to go with the band to Rotherwick this evening but with him here, there wasn't room in the car. I do wish I could give him up. I even hate him near me. We went with Mummy and Daddy to the pictures this afternoon. I was thinking of the band and Sarah all the time. I do wish I lived alone. It would be lovely to be so free.'*

Sunday 8th '*A terribly boring day today. Done absolutely nothing all day but sit and dream and worry about everything such as Sarah and Jerry. I do miss her so much and wish she was still living here. I am glad she has married Jerry as I like him very much but I still miss her an awful lot. I have also been worrying about Mummy as she is really ill. I hope nothing happens to her. I have been dreaming about the band and wish I had more chances to sing and really knew if they wanted me, as I feel sort of in the way when I do go, although we have an awful lot of fun. I expect it is just my imagination really. I wonder if I will ever be a famous vocalist like Doris Day or someone like that. It is the thing I wish for most in the whole world, I think. I am going out with Norman tomorrow and I have also been worrying about that in case Mummy did find out about it, as it would break her heart and that is the last thing I would want to do as I love her more that I can say. I am going out with Graham on Tuesday which is another thing I have been worrying about. Oh, I have such a job to hide my troubles. God is the only one who knows what I am going through and I know he understands. I do wish I had enough courage to give LH up, as I detest him even coming near me now. I don't know why as he is such a nice boy. I do wish I could live on my own somewhere.'*

Monday 9th 'Not a good day really today. My temper got the better of me at work as Joyce, the new girl, made me a whole days' worth of work behind. But I soon cooled down. I don't know why I am so moody lately. I expect it is having so much to worry about. Went out with Norman this evening up the Warren, and we were both a bit fed up. He told me either Stan or Frankie had said that I had been saying nasty things about him. I think it must have been Stan as Frankie is too nice for that. It did upset me as I know I haven't said nasty things about Norman. I do hope he didn't believe him. Going out with him again on Wednesday. Saw Sarah dinner time, I do miss her terribly.'

Tuesday 10th 'Jolly good day all round really and wonderful evening. Had some fun at work with all the men. Max caught me kissing Graham in the cycle shed dinner time. Phew we didn't know what to do. Went out with Graham this evening to a field at the back of his house. He really is a nice man and behaved like a gentleman, I was surprised really, although very pleased. He does kiss wonderfully. I know I could easily fall in love with him, in fact, I do love him in a special sort of way. Oh, why is it all the nice ones are already married? I seem to have been born much too late. I wonder if I will ever find someone whom I can really love. Saw Edna this evening after work and we had coffee in Friars.'

Wednesday 11th 'Terrible morning. Everything went wrong. Mummy told me this morning that she had found out that I didn't go out with Edna yesterday. I had never felt so awful because she was almost in tears. She told me not to do anything to hurt her as she loves me so much. It was the first time she had talked to me like that. Oh, I feel so mean and I absolutely despise myself as that is the last thing I want to do and I love her with all my heart. I have been praying to God for forgiveness and understanding. Went out with Norman this evening but was worried all the time I was with him in case Mummy found out about it. May be going with LH to see Sarah's room tomorrow, I wonder what it's like.'

Thursday 12th 'Quite a good day really. Graham told me he is in love with me today. I really do like him so much, but he is married though. We have been passing notes to each other all day. I believe I am falling in love with him. Went with LH this evening to Sarah's new home. Oh, how I wish I was her. She and Jerry are so happy and so much in love and here's me absolutely longing and praying to God to give me courage to give LH up. I am so unhappy. I wonder if

*I will ever find someone who loves me the same way as Jerry loves Sarah. If only LH was more like Jerry, instead of being so terribly serious and boring. He is no fun at all and is so serious all the time, I feel so angry at myself but I just can't help it.'*

Friday 13th '*I think today has been one of the unhappiest days of my life. I went with the band this evening and afterwards Stan told me that Ted didn't want me to go again. Oh, I just didn't know how to stop myself crying. Anyway, on the way home Norman took me home first, so I told him to take Frankie and Dick home first. I thought perhaps he didn't want to see me again. Anyway, he took them home and then stopped in a quiet lane and I had a good cry. Norman said he loved me and that he was going to take me home first because he didn't think I wanted to see him anymore as Frankie had told him I had said horrible things about him. That made me feel even worse and I had another cry. I felt like killing myself there and then. We had a long talk and sorted things out a bit and he told me he didn't believe what Frankie had told him. He did at first but after having this talk he was convinced I hadn't said anything, which I hadn't. I don't know why Frankie should have said that. It was nasty of him. I am very upset about the band as I loved singing with them so much. I will phone Ted up tomorrow. I suppose I will look around for another band. I did get into trouble when I got in as I was an hour and a half late. I am dreading tomorrow and at the moment I am crying my eyes out.'*

Saturday 14th '*Not too good, not too bad a day really. I had a bit of fun with Graham this morning but he went home long before I did so I don't know when I will see him. I will try and see him Monday morning. I have felt so unhappy today mainly about the band. I tried to phone Ted up but he was out. I will try again on Monday. I really am upset as I did love singing with them so much. I cried myself to sleep last night and the way I feel now I think I will again tonight. LH came today and we went to the Palace this evening. Got home and then had a row with Mummy and LH. Oh, I do wish I could kill myself. Anyway, it blew over and they were as nice as anything to me. Oh, I do love Mum and Dad so much but they are so old-fashioned.'*

Sunday 16<sup>th</sup> '*A queer sort of day really. One minute I have felt like laughing and forgetting all my troubles and the next I remember them and feel like crying my eyes out. Went for a walk this afternoon and then to the pictures this evening. We had to queue for over an hour and while we were waiting, I saw Stan's car go by with them in it and Frankie's drums strapped on the top. I don't know what stopped me from running out into the road and calling to them. I am so desperately unhappy and disappointed. I did so love singing with them and will try and speak to Ted tomorrow. I don't know why he changed his mind about me. He used to be so friendly. How I am praying to God to make them have me back.*'

Monday 16<sup>th</sup> '*Saw Graham this morning before going to work. Stood talking for about ten minutes then he had to go to Mortimer branch. It did seem queer at work without him. I have felt quite lonely but I did go out with him this evening. Boy, oh boy, he is wonderful. I feel almost as strongly about him as I did Keith last year. He got hold of my diary and only when I threatened not to talk to him again, did he give it back to me. Whew, it was a narrow squeak and I won't take it with me again. Oh dear, I won't see him tomorrow, not unless I see him after work. I am going to phone him up anyway so I will be able to talk to him. Going out with Norman tomorrow.*'

Tuesday 17<sup>th</sup> '*I don't quite know what today has been really. I feel so terribly lonely at work without Graham and so terribly lonely at home without Sarah. Phoned Graham up this afternoon. He is really sweet. Went to see him this evening before he went to night school. Stood talking for about ten minutes and he told me he loves me. I am so pleased, as I love him too in a sort of way. Hurried back into town to meet Norman whom I was going out with this evening. I met him but he told me he had to go to a dance. I felt like crying my eyes out but he told me he loved me which cheered me up a bit. Oh, I feel so ill and feel like killing myself.*'

Wednesday 18<sup>th</sup> '*Not too bad a day really. Had a bit of a row with Jeff and Dave but it soon blew over. Phoned up Graham this afternoon and then saw him this evening after work in the cycle shed. We were just enjoying ourselves when Edna came along so I had to say goodbye to Graham so I could go and have a coffee with Edna. Saw Johnny and he asked me to go back to him, I told him to phone me sometime. After I got rid of him, I phoned LH up, then met Norman.*

*We went for a walk up the Warren. He is so nice; I really do like him. I love both him and Graham in their different ways. It's a shame they are both married. I feel I will have a nervous breakdown before much longer as I hate having to tell so many lies to Mummy, but I suppose I am just made that way.'*

Thursday 19<sup>th</sup> *'Wonderful evening this evening. Waited for Graham after work and we went to the new college and had some tea, then I waited while he did his lessons after which we went to Palmer Park. Oh, he is so nice, he is such fun, teases me terribly and told me he loves me, I enjoy his company so much. After we came out of the park, we cycled right past his house. He collected his lovely big dog and we cycled to the end of the road and then said goodnight. Oh, he kisses so wonderfully. I wonder if I will ever find a single man like him whom I could really give my heart to. I am praying to God to help me.'*

Friday 20<sup>th</sup> *'A dreadfully boring evening after yesterday and the rest of the week. Went to the pictures with LH. Oh dear, I really do dislike him. I feel so sorry for him but I just can't alter my feelings towards him. I don't even let him hold my hand now and he looks so terribly hurt. I feel horrid but I just don't like him near me. I wonder if I will ever pluck up enough courage to give him up and I wonder if I would regret it at all. Saw Graham after work before meeting LH. He is so nice. I really do like him so much. Oh, why is it I always fall for the married men? Why can't I fall for a nice single one? If only God would help me find one.'*

Saturday 21<sup>st</sup> *'Had some fun at work this morning. Sam and two other chaps put my bike upstairs in the storeroom and I had to make them get it down again. I had a lovely big fight with them all. I did enjoy it. I was in the shed with all three and they were all teasing me. After I got my bike back, I met Graham. He told me he loved me again. Norman phoned me up today too, I was so pleased. I seem to be very popular today, it makes me so happy. Had hair done this afternoon then met LH. We were going to London but couldn't get tickets for show so went to the Palace then back to Basingstoke, where I am now. I do wish Monday would hurry up and come.'*

Sunday 22<sup>nd</sup> *'Not too bad a day really, I suppose. Got up fairly early and went to church with LH and his parents, then after dinner, LH and I went on his motorbike to some woods where he took some photographs of me in the nude. We had arranged beforehand to do this as we both thought it was a good idea. LH was a perfect gentleman thank goodness. I do hope they come out alright. He has eight more to take yet so I expect he will take those, next weekend. I am longing to see what they come out like. After tea, we sat and watched television for the rest of the evening. I have been doing such a lot of thinking today about Graham, Norman, Sam, Alex, Jeff, the band and lots of other things. I am praying to God to help me out of all my troubles. It is so wonderful to know He is with me and I don't know what I would do without Him to talk to. I do wish I could have gone singing with the band over the weekend. I did love it so much. I wonder when I will sing again.'*

Monday 23rd *'I feel so tired today and just can't concentrate on my work. Wonderful evening. Went out with Norman and he really is wonderful. I love him in a sort of way and I also love Graham too in a way too. I have had some fun with him today. We have kept giving each other little notes all the time and went into the High together after work for a cup of tea (before I met Norman). Graham had got to take an exam on Law this evening poor man, I did feel sorry for him as he was so nervous. I wonder if he'll pass. Norman told me this evening that Stan wanted me to go singing on Saturday!'*

Tuesday 24th *'Not too bad a day again today. Thought quite a lot about Norman today. He really is nice. I had some fun with Graham today. Went to the High again with him and then into Friars with Edna where we met some very nice boys. Went up to hospital with Edna to see her sister-in-law. After that, met Graham as he had been having another exam. We went into the bicycle shed and locked the door. Oh, he is wonderful, I really do like him so much. The only thing wrong was that he had to go home so early. We only had about half an hour together. Cycled right past his house afterwards with him where he collected his dog and we carried on up the road where we said goodnight. Going again tomorrow.'*

Wednesday 25th *'Another fairly good day, although I keep having rows with Dave about all the work. Had some fun with Graham again. He doesn't think he has passed his exams. We went to the High again and Doris and Jean came in and saw us. Went round to Friars with Edna and saw those nice boys again.*

After that, sat in the station waiting room until nine o'clock then went and met Graham. We went into the cycle shed again but the poor thing didn't feel at all well. He was suffering from the exams I think but still they are all over now. Graham said he will have to think up some good excuses for getting out now that night school is finished for another year. I do wish he could have stayed out longer.'

Thursday 26th 'Not too good a day today. Graham has been at Basingstoke Road branch today so I haven't seen much of him worst luck. I don't quite know when I have longed for him so much as today. I have felt so ill, I really am ill. I have had an awful row with Dave but still, we made up. Wonderful evening. Went out with Norman to Peppard Common and sat in the back of his car. Stan phoned me up yesterday and asked me if I would like to go with them on Saturday. I phoned him up this evening and told him I would love to. I phoned LH up yesterday and today. He can't manage to get a mic for under £3 so I don't think there will be one. I do hope Ted won't mind. It will be so nice to be with them all once again.'

Friday 27th 'Not too bad a day today but I'm afraid I have felt really ill most of the time. I have seen Graham quite a lot today but I think he is cooling off a bit because every time I give him a note or talk to him, he keeps laughing at me. I do hope he is not tired of me already as I love him very much in a special sort of way. He hasn't written to me once and it has made me so unhappy. I don't want to start chasing him as that is what I did to Keith and he was something like Graham. I feel so alone. I keep praying to God to help me but I don't expect He thinks I deserve help, but I still have great faith in Him and I know that one day He will make everything turn out alright. Went to the pictures with LH. He does bore me.'

Saturday 28th 'A day of ups and downs today. Didn't see much of Graham this morning but saw him dinner time and he said he was scared as some of the girls at work had found out about us. He said we must try and be very cool to each other for about a month until they have forgotten it but I don't know how I can, I really do love him and I'm so upset. I had a nice evening though which cheered me up a bit. I went singing with the band in Basing. They are all so nice especially Arnie, the new sax player. Ted was ever so nice to me; I am so glad.

*Went into the Allied Arms before singing and had a drink with Frankie and Norman. I do like them both very much. I do wish I could go with them every night. I love singing so much as it takes my mind off of all my worries and unhappiness.'*

Sunday 29th '*I don't quite know what today has been really. I have had such a lot to think and worry about and I have felt really ill and thoroughly worn out. I haven't known how to keep my eyes open. Stayed in all the morning and threaded pearls which had broken last night. After dinner, went for a walk (I stayed at LHs last night) with LH and he took some more photographs of me in the nude. I am wondering what they will come out like. Went to church this evening and then watched television for the rest of the evening. I have thought such a lot about Graham today and do wish he wasn't married. I don't know how I am going to manage to be cool to him for the next week, as I love him very much (in a special way) so it is going to be so very hard. I do hope he will be able to find a good excuse very soon so that we shall be able to go out together again. I have also been thinking an awful lot about Norman and the band. It was so nice to be able to sing with them again yesterday. I hope there will be many more times to come. I am going out with Norman tomorrow and I'm so glad, as I love him too (in a different sort of way). I think he is more sincere than Graham. Oh, why do I have to fall only for married men? I feel like I'm being tortured and despise myself for it, my conscience is unbearable. I am almost dying with worry. I do wish I could die.'*

Monday 30th '*A lot better day today thank goodness. Got up at 6 o'clock and came back to Reading from Basingstoke. Saw Graham quite a lot today. I was thrilled because he told me he still loved me and that it was a great temptation to keep coming over to speak to me. I am so glad he still loves me as I really do love him in a sort of way, although it's not quite deep enough as the way I would like to love a man. Went out with Norman this evening. He really is so very nice. We went to Peppard Common for a short walk and then sat in the back of his car for the remainder of the evening. I do love being with him as he makes me feel quite happy.'*

## MAY

With people starting to talk at work about Mary and Graham, this potentially could be the reason he gets a temporary transfer for 4 months. Norman's 'no-shows' are becoming more frequent but even so she's still willing to climb out her bedroom window for him, and there's also an incident with a muddy ditch. Sibling jealousy rears its ugly head again and an old flame begrudgingly reignites. And Mary is adamant this month not to break a promise she's made.

Tuesday 1st *'Not too bad a day really, I suppose. I have seen Graham quite a lot although only once or twice to speak to. I do love him very much in a queer sort of way and I do wish we could hurry up and go out together again. I have been thinking about Norman an awful lot today, he is so nice. I worked until 8 o'clock this evening and am now really tired out. I feel I want about a fortnight in bed.'*

Wednesday 2nd *'Quite a good day really. I have seen quite a lot of Graham today and a lot to talk to. He has been in a wonderful mood today, very loving. He kept coming up to me and telling me he loved me and adored me. I do love him so much in this kind of mood. I am disappointed though as he is being sent to Pangbourne on Tuesday for FOUR MONTHS. I just don't know how I will be able to stand it at work without him being there. I'm going to miss him terribly. Still, I may see him some evenings. I do hope so. Lovely evening. Worked until seven then went to Peppard Common with Norman again and sat and talked all evening. I did enjoy it and would like to see him more often. He makes me so happy.'*

Thursday 3rd *'Jolly good day today really, I suppose. I have seen a nice lot of Graham today and he has told me a lot of times that he loves me and I am so pleased. LH met me from work and I told him I was going to meet the band and tell them I couldn't go with them, but instead I cycled up to Graham's as his wife was going out. We stood and chatted and I got back to LH at 6:45. He was absolutely fuming as he had bought tickets for the palace, and had to go and change them for tomorrow now. I felt very mean but I felt a bit happier as I knew Graham loved me. Norman is expecting me to meet him tomorrow night at 11:30. It would mean getting out of my bedroom window. I don't think I will.'*

Friday 4th *'Quite a good day really. I've had some fun with Graham today especially at dinner time. He came and emptied the hole making machine all over me. I was covered in small pieces of paper. It was such a mess. He is really so nice. I have been worried all day today as to whether I should get out tonight to see Norman. Anyway, went to the Palace with LH this evening then after I got in, got ready for bed and then plucked all my courage up into both hands and got out of my window and went round to Downshire Square and waited for half an hour for Norman, but he didn't turn up. So, I lost my nerve and ran back to the flats and had an awful job getting back into my bedroom. The window was so high. I managed it but I never want to go through that again, phew!'*

Saturday 5th *'Norman said he would phone me up this morning, but he didn't. I don't know what went wrong and have been wondering all day. I do hope he will ring on Monday. I would hate it not to see him again. Had some fun with Graham today. We had a little talk just before going home and he said he was really serious when he said he was in love with me and I think he means it. It made me so happy as I love him very much in a special kind of way. He is going to find out the times of the swimming baths so that we can go swimming together. Oh dear, I will miss him when he goes next week to Pangbourne. LH came this afternoon and I think we had disagreed about everything. I am sick to death of him. Oh dear.'*

Sunday 6th *'A boring day really, although not too bad an afternoon. Didn't get up too early but when I did, I helped Mummy to get the dinner ready while LH sat and read the paper. After dinner, Daddy lent LH his bicycle and we rode to Sonning and sat down by the river most of the afternoon, then cycled back home, had something to eat, then went to the pictures. Been out without a coat all day today as it has been wonderfully hot. I do hope it keeps like this for the rest of the summer months ahead. I have been thinking about Norman and Graham such a lot today. I wonder if Norman will ring me up tomorrow at all. I do hope he does as I don't know what I will do if he doesn't. I am much too fond of him to finish with him now. I wonder why he wasn't able to phone me up yesterday and I would also like to know why he didn't turn up on Friday night, but still, perhaps I will know tomorrow.'*

Monday 7<sup>th</sup> '*Not too bad a day today really, although I am a bit disappointed as Norman hasn't phoned me up. I wonder what has happened to him. I will phone him up tomorrow, I think. I have had some fun with Graham today, he is wonderful. He waited for me after work and we cycled to some woods and lay down on his coat and whispered sweet nothings to each other. He keeps telling me how much he loves me. I am so pleased as I love him very much in a special kind of way. We are going swimming tomorrow evening. I do wish it would hurry up. I am going to miss him terribly from now on as he goes to Pangbourne tomorrow. I don't know what I will do.*'

Tuesday 8<sup>th</sup> '*Not too bad a day really and absolutely wonderful evening. I have missed Graham terribly all day but went swimming with him this evening. Oh, it was wonderful and he is such fun. Cycled home with him afterwards and then went with him to take his dog for a walk. He told me he loves me and I told him I love him which I do very much. Oh dear, I wonder what it is about married men that I like. I phoned Norman up dinner time and arranged to go out with him tomorrow evening. He didn't sound too pleased but still I will know just what has happened tomorrow, I am still very, very fond of him. I phoned LH up to tell him I couldn't go out tomorrow.*'

During the day on Wednesday 9<sup>th</sup> Mary misses seeing Graham although she does sees him quickly before and after work. '*Went out with Norman this evening. It has seemed absolutely ages since I last went out with him. It was wonderful. We went to Peppard Common and sat in the back of his car and he told me he loves me. I have told myself firmly that I mustn't get too serious with Graham or Norman as I will probably get hurt again, as I did with Keith and I don't want to go through all that again. Went into the Friars with Edna this evening. I feel so old beside her. It is all this worry that I have got.*'

Thursday 10<sup>th</sup> '*I have missed Graham more than ever today as I haven't seen him at all. I got down to the station to find that his bus had just gone and I could have cried. I had my hair done after work then cycled up Graham's road in the hope of seeing him, then looked for him in Palmer Park but was disappointed. Went out with Norman this evening for an hour. He really is so very nice. I am so terribly worried though as he wants me to get out of my window again tomorrow night to see him but I have promised God I would never do it again. I would love to go so much but I don't think I can break my promise to God.'*

Friday 11th *'Not too bad a day today as I managed to see Graham before going into work and again this afternoon after he had finished. He was with all the other men though so I didn't have a chance to speak to him. By the time, I got out of work he had gone. Went round to Grandmas and Grandads this evening with LH which was very thrilling I don't think. I suppose it wasn't bad though, at least it kept me from being alone with LH for too long. I didn't go out to meet Norman tonight as I had promised God, I wouldn't do that again. My ears have been terrible today, I can hardly hear. I think it must be the swimming.'*

Saturday 12th *'Saw Graham before work this morning and then again after work. We went into some woods and we had to get over a very muddy ditch and muggings had to go and slip and fall in it. My feet were absolutely covered in thick mud. Graham had to go and leave me to it, as he had to get home. I was a bit annoyed about that. He really is an awful cad but there is something about him that attracts me. LH came this afternoon for the weekend. I am so fed up. I really am absolutely sick of him. I've been thinking an awful lot about Norman today and do hope he didn't wait too long last night. I won't see him until Tuesday now.'*

Sunday 13th *'Absolutely horrible day. Got up fairly early and helped Mummy get the dinner ready while LH read the paper. Then after dinner, was getting myself ready to go out for a cycle ride when Sarah came with her puppy. Oh, she is such a sweet little pup. I played with her for ages and then LH and I went for a cycle ride to Prospect Park. We sat and watched some cricket. I was bored to tears almost and LH kept putting his arms round me. He nearly drove me crackers as I just can't bear him touching me. He kept asking me why I have changed and I just couldn't answer him and he got quite annoyed in the end. Anyway, we went back home for tea then walked halfway back with Sarah. I carried the little puppy. Sarah is so lucky, she always was. She has got everything she wants and I am really pleased for her but I am so terribly jealous. I don't suppose I really deserve to have anything. I feel so wicked and yet I know I'm not really, not at heart. I am just so terribly unhappy. I wish I had the nerve to commit suicide. I have been thinking such a lot about Graham and Norman today. I don't know why I bother with them really as I don't suppose either of them are very good and yet both of them have got something that attracts me and I love both of them in their different ways. I wonder if God will ever forgive me.'*

Monday 14th *'Quite a good day really, I suppose. Had a bit of fun at work as all the men tease me. I have missed Graham, even though I saw him this morning before work, but not to talk to, and this evening after work. I do wish I wasn't so easily attracted to him because he's an awful rotter really but I just feel I need him so much. Perhaps I will come to my senses one day. I have also been thinking of Norman today. I like him but not as much as I used to. I suppose that proves I am not grown up yet, and yet, I feel so old and ill. I wonder if I will ever be completely happy. I know I don't deserve to be. Went to the Palace with LH tonight. I will have to be a lot nicer to him.'*

Tuesday 15th *'Not too bad, not too good a day today really. I didn't see Graham before work today and I have been worried about him all day but I saw him after work and he told me he cycled to Woodley yesterday and found out I wasn't singing there. I had an awful job to get out of that. Met him at 7:30 and went into some woods. He told me he still loves me and I don't know whether I am pleased or not. Saw Norman after leaving Graham and we went into some woods. Oh, I am so muddled up. Phoned LH up this evening and I realised that I really have been treating him terribly. I will have to try and mend my ways.'*

Wednesday 16th *'Not too good a day at all as I didn't see Graham before work this morning but phoned him up when I got into work. He told me he still loves me and I am pleased about that as I would not like to lose him now. Been very busy at work today. Went to the pictures with LH this evening. He is very nice and he really does love me sincerely, for which I am very pleased. I know I can really trust him. I am still not really in love with him but I certainly like him a lot better now. When I got in, I had a row with Mum and Dad, about me keep going out. I feel so ill. I am getting spots all over me and I am losing weight fast. I feel I will pass out before much longer. I feel so old. I have such a lot to worry about and do wish God would let me die.'*

Thursday 17th *'Not too good a day but lovely evening. Saw Graham this morning before work and he said people at work were talking about us so he said we had better be very careful. Saw him again this evening and he said he would try to find out tomorrow, just what was being said about us. He really is scared and I felt quite sorry for him. I don't know when I will see him again. I went out with Norman this evening. He is very nice but I want him just as a friend, not anything else. We sat on Burghfield Common and just talked about anything and everything. He really does love his boys as he is always talking about them. I would love to meet them. He wants me to get out and see him tomorrow night but I don't think I will go as I promised God I wouldn't.'*

Friday 18<sup>th</sup> *'Not too bad a day I suppose. Saw Graham this morning before work and he said we would have to be extra careful. He said he would try and find out today just how bad the rumours were about us. He came in the bank, this evening, but I didn't dare speak to him. I think I am losing my attraction for him, although I still like him very much. I bought a new bag today and some new gloves ready for Maureen's wedding tomorrow. I don't really want to go. Been thinking a lot about Norman today. He wanted me to go out and see him this evening, I would have loved to but will not break my promise.'*

Saturday 19<sup>th</sup> *'Not too good, not too bad a day today. I haven't seen Graham to talk to at all today. I saw him on the bus this morning but he didn't see me. I was quite disappointed as I was all dressed up ready for Maureen's wedding and I wanted him to see me looking nice. I won't see him until Tuesday now. Went to Maureen's wedding this morning. She really looked lovely. I felt very envious of her, not because she was getting married but because she was really and truly in love. I wonder if I will ever be. I know I won't be happy until I am. After the reception, I went and looked at her presents then went home and got ready to come to LH's, where I am at the moment. I feel so unhappy.'*

Sunday 20<sup>th</sup> *'Got up fairly early and after breakfast went off to church with LH, Brian and Mr H. Mrs H has a nasty cold so she didn't go. After dinner, we all went to Winchester in the van. We had intended having our tea out as we took sandwiches, cake and tea with us, but it turned out very cold so we walked all around the town and looked in all the shops. They had some wonderful clothes there. After that, we went all over Winchester Cathedral. It took us just over an hour. It is a beautiful place. Just the sort of place I would like to get married in. Lovely drive back. We stopped at some woods and picked dozens of bluebells.*

*There were absolutely hundreds of them, you couldn't tread anywhere without treading on some. After we got home, we had tea and then watched television for the rest of the evening. I feel so tired now. I have thought such a lot about Graham today. I have been wondering if he has finished with me or whether he still wants to go out with me. I do hope I see him on Tuesday to talk to so that I can ask him. I hope he still wants me. I have also though a great deal about Norman. I feel so jealous at the thought of him at his dances and knowing I can't go. I do wish they would hurry up and ask me to sing with them again. I do love singing so very much and wonder if I will ever be a famous star. I do hope so.'*

On Whit Monday Mary gets up fairly early and drives in to Basingstoke with LH and Mr H to watch as they erect some speakers, which turns out to be a big job and lasts all morning. After lunch they go to a horse show to watch the show jumping. *'Oh, there were some wonderful horses there. I do wish I could ride. I really will have to start going to lessons. Stayed there until seven thirty, then went back for tea and watched television for the rest of the evening.'*

Tuesday 22nd *'Not too bad a day I suppose as far as they go. Saw Graham on the bus this morning but not to speak to and again this evening outside the cycle shed, but he walked straight past me so I couldn't talk to him then. I am so fed up and will really have to try to talk to him tomorrow. I was most surprised today as Keith phoned me up. I nearly fell through the floor. I told him I would go out with him on Friday. I am so desperately worried as three married men on the go at once is enough to make anyone commit suicide and I think I will have to before much longer. I feel so ill and unhappy and completely worn out. Phoned Norman today and arranged to go out with him on Thursday. Phoned LH and arranged to go out with him tomorrow. Thankfully, I am liking him a lot better lately. Went for coffee with Edna today.'*

Wednesday 23rd 'Not too bad a day again today. I haven't seen Graham at all today. I was a bit disappointed but not really sorry. I think that is all over now. It was very short and very sweet and I still like him very much indeed. I went to the pictures with LH this evening and I find I am falling in love with him again. I don't love him half enough to marry him, but I expect I will before very much longer. I am so pleased, as he really is so very good and kind and he really

279

*does love me. I've been thinking about Keith today. I am wishing he hadn't phoned me up as I was getting on alright without him, but now I am going out with him on Friday. I do hope I won't fall in love with him again. I've been praying to God to make me good. I do want to be so much, but I am so easily led. I know if I have faith in Him, He will make me better.'*

Thursday 24th *'Not too bad a day again today. I saw Graham this morning and was just going to speak to him when his bus came along, so there wasn't time. I haven't seen him since and hope I see him tomorrow. I walked round town dinnertime, with Ken, one of the fellows at work. I did yesterday too. He is very nice and I do like him, but must try hard not to fall in love with him, as I have enough worries already. I had an examination today by a lady doctor, Dr C. She is very, very nice, I do like her. She passed me as very fit. Went out with Norman this evening. He is very nice but my conscience is absolute torture to live with. I want to be good so very much and yet I still continue to be wicked. I just can't understand myself. I phoned LH up this evening and he says he won't be able to come on Saturday.'*

Friday 25th *'Oh dear, what a day! I am so terribly muddled and just don't know what to do. I walked round town with Ken dinnertime. He is very nice. Saw Graham this evening but couldn't speak to him as he was with Dave. I was annoyed. A lovely, but muddling evening. I went out with Keith. He is very nice and just the same handsome man I was madly in love with last year. And just the same bundle of mischief. I could easily let myself go and fall for him madly again but I have grown a little wiser since he gave me up. I was so terribly hurt last time, that I am letting him do the running. We sat in the back of his car and talked and talked and talked. I did enjoy it. We are going out again next Wednesday. After I left him, I had to go and bump into Johnny. We walked all up Broad Street together and up through the market place. He kept begging me to go out with him again and kept telling me to give LH up. I like Johnny very much but I can't just give LH up just like that. After all, I am engaged to him. I do wish I wasn't as I would like to be free to be able to go out with other boys as well, without having to do it behind everyone's backs. I do so hate telling lies. LH may not be coming until Sunday, so I may go out with Johnny in the evening. Oh, what a life!'*

Saturday 26<sup>th</sup> '*Quite a good day today really. Saw Graham to speak to, although he was with several other people so he couldn't say much. Walked to the station with Ken. We stood talking for a whole hour. He proposed to me! He is very nice and I would like to go out with him but I just can't cope with anymore. Went for a short walk with Norman this afternoon, he really is nice and I do like him. After he had gone, I saw Leslie who asked me to go out with him. I said I would see him at the Oxford later. When I had got rid of him, I rang LH who is coming tomorrow. After that, I went home for tea then got ready and went and called for Edna and we went to the Oxford. It wasn't bad except a Scot kept hanging onto me, but I managed to get rid of him eventually, then met one of Edna's friends who was very nice but not my type. He brought me home in a taxi. Am I tired!*'

Sunday 27<sup>th</sup> Mary has an absolutely horrible day with LH being round all day. They read the papers until dinner time then go to the pictures in the afternoon and all Mary wants to do is get rid of him. '*When we got back, Sarah was at home. She had brought all her new clothes to show us. She had some wonderful things. Oh, why is it she has all the luck. She always has been the lucky one. Mum and Daddy have always liked her best I know and even now after she has hurt them like she did, they treat her as if she was a heroine. They pet and fuss over her and all they say to me is—do the washing up or get your things out of the way. Well, I have felt like killing myself before now but I don't think I have ever come as close to it as I feel right now. I am so desperately unhappy, but I suppose I deserve to be really.*'

Monday 28<sup>th</sup> '*Not too bad a day I suppose. Saw Graham this morning on the bus, but I couldn't talk to him because Jeff was with him. Saw him this evening, in the cycle shed though and it seems as if he wants to go out with me again. I don't know if I want to or not. I have had some fun with Ken at work today. I think he wants to take me out and has written me several little notes. I would like to go, but I just haven't got any spare evenings. I do wish I lived on my own, then, I could go out when I liked. I went to the pictures with LH and his mother after having tea in the Oxford Café. His father had to go to a meeting then they took me home in the van with my bike stuck in the back. Going out with Keith on Wednesday and then Norman on Thursday.*'

Tuesday 29<sup>th</sup> '*Saw Graham this morning to talk to, although didn't have very much time as his bus came. He said he hadn't changed his mind about me and I don't know if I'm pleased or not. When I saw him, he told me I hadn't any make up on. I had been in such a hurry to get out and see him, I had forgotten to put any on! Keith phoned me up today, I was most surprised, as it makes such a change for him to run after me instead of the other way about. I am going out with him tomorrow—he is nice, but I had been trying so hard to forget him, as I know nothing can ever come of it. I went into Sally's Café dinner time with Ken. He is also very nice. Then, I went into Friars Tea Bar with Edna this evening. Afterwards, I phoned LH, then stayed in all evening.*'

Wednesday 30<sup>th</sup> '*Quite a good day really, I suppose. Saw Graham this evening and cycled halfway to his home with him. He said he'd waited for me for the last few evenings. I am going to see him tomorrow evening for a short time. Went into Sally's Café again dinner time with Ken. He certainly is nice and I wouldn't mind him for a permanent boyfriend. Wonderful evening, as I went out with Keith. We went into a field with terribly long grass and lay down under the blazing sun. It was wonderful, so lovely and hot. I could easily fall madly in love with him again like before Christmas, but I am trying to keep my emotions under control as I was hurt so badly last time. I don't think I could stand it again. I do wonder who I will eventually end up with.*'

Thursday 31<sup>st</sup> Mary notes it as '*a queer sort of day really.*' She goes to Sally's Café at dinner time again with Ken '*he is really very nice. I would like to elope with him to a desert island.*' In the evening, she sees Graham for about 10 minutes after work then cycles to his house where they go into a field and lay down in more long grass. '*I have realised that I don't like him at all. I know he only comes out with me for one thing. After having got back to town, I dashed round to the town hall where I was supposed to be meeting Norman, but he wasn't there. I waited a solid two hours, from 8–10. I was so disappointed and don't know what can have happened to him? I will phone him tomorrow. While I was waiting, I spoke to three soldiers for about a quarter of an hour. Went into Friars after work with Edna.*

JUNE

Mary has fun at work partaking in a few pranks and embarks on a couple of trips to Weymouth with LH. Another of her dreams comes true in June along with trying out roller skating for the first time. With her relationships getting ever more complicated and admitting she is in a dreadful muddle where men are concerned, she yearns for her holiday. Disappointingly this brings upset of its own on 25$^{th}$.

Friday 1$^{st}$ *'A queer sort of day today. It's been so terribly busy at work; I just haven't known what to do first. I had some fun with Ken though. We went into Sally's again at dinner time and sat holding hands, then walked all the way back to the bank still holding hands. Oh, I do like him very much and wish I was engaged to him instead of LH. I also like Sam very much. I put his bike upstairs yesterday in the storeroom as a joke and he said he would have his revenge. I do hope it's something nice. Haven't seen Graham at all today, but not at all worried. Phoned Norman this afternoon but he couldn't talk as he had someone in the same room. I told him I would phone again on Monday. Went to the pictures with LH this evening. We are going to Weymouth with his people tomorrow.'*

Saturday 2$^{nd}$ *'Quite a good day today. I had some fun with Ken at work, he really is very nice. I lent him my bike this morning to go to the doctors and arranged to meet him on the train to Basingstoke this afternoon. I just managed to catch it. We had a compartment to ourselves. He had bought me a large bar of chocolate and asked me if I would go dancing with him in Rotherwick this evening. He said he had asked his parents if I could stay with them over the weekend. Oh, I do wish I could have done. I think I am falling in love with him. I would like to give up everyone and just have him as a boyfriend. We sat holding hands all the way, I could have stayed there forever. He is going to phone me up next week. Went to Weymouth with LH and his parents to their caravan this evening. It was a lovely ride but I was thinking of Ken the whole way. I do wish I hadn't got engaged. I just don't know what to do.'*

Sunday 3$^{rd}$ *'Phew! I don't think I have ever spent such an uncomfortable night as last night. I slept in the caravan and had the single bed and there was hardly enough room to stay on let alone turn over. I woke up this morning to find all the bed clothes on the floor and I was freezing. I don't want to go through another night like that again.'* After breakfast, they go along the sea front and sit on the sand. *Then after a lot of persuasion from Mr and Mrs H, LH and I changed into our costumes and ventured into the sea. Burr! I just don't know when I have ever been in such cold water before. My fingers and legs went absolutely numb straight away, which is a thing they've never done before. We didn't stay in the water for five minutes and came out quick, had a brisk rub down and got dressed straight away. We felt warmer after that. We went back to the caravan for dinner then LH and I went for a walk round the cliffs at the back of the caravans. I had a nice climb, I quite enjoyed it especially as I kept imagining I was with Ken. After we got back from the walk, we had some tea and then winded our way back home in the van. It took three and a quarter hours and I was almost asleep by the time we reached home. I feel so tired now and am longing to see Ken again. I do hope he phones me tomorrow. It will seem awful at work without him and I'm going to miss him terribly.'*

Monday 4th *'I feel very, very tired today. Got up at six and caught the train back to Reading. Had loads of work to do all day. Phoned Norman up lunch time and he wants me to go out and meet him tomorrow after a dance, but I am still remembering my promise to God, so I will not go even though I would like to very much. I was expecting Ken to phone me today but he didn't. I don't suppose he had time. I wonder how he got on at his new job today. I am longing to see him again as it seems so long since I saw him last, even though it was only Saturday. Stayed in all evening by myself. Mummy and Daddy have gone to Auntie S's to watch TV. I am sitting in bed wishing with all my heart that I could be a famous singer.'*

Tuesday 5th *'Keith phoned me up dinner time and we've arranged to go out on Thursday. I like him I suppose, but I'm certainly not in love with him like I was before Christmas. I have been disappointed again today because Ken hasn't phoned me. I do hope he hurries and gets in touch with me. I like him so very much. Stayed in all evening and wondered who I will eventually end up with. I don't really deserve anyone as I feel so wicked, but I just can't help the things I do. I seem to have been made that way. Going out with LH tomorrow. I do wish I really could fall in love with him.'*

Wednesday 6th 'Quite a good day I suppose. Ken hasn't phoned me up yet. I do wish he would hurry up and do so, as I am longing to see him again. Saw Graham today and he said he thought I had finished with him, as I hadn't waited for him in the mornings lately. He was quite upset about it. I am certainly not in love with him as he only goes out with me for one thing only, and I definitely do not like that. Went to the pictures with LH this evening. He really is very sweet and I think I do love him in a way and yet I don't love him enough to marry him. I wonder if I ever will. Oh, how I wish I could go abroad and start all over again. Perhaps I will one day.'

Thursday 7th 'A day of ups and downs really. Dave didn't speak to me all morning as we had a row yesterday. But he was alright again this afternoon. Graham phoned me up twice today. He really has changed. I was so surprised. I don't want to go out with him again, although I expect I will, goodness only knows why. I went out with Keith this evening. He is alright I suppose, but he is a dreadful liar. He tells me he keeps having rows with his wife and I don't believe a word of it. I don't know why I go out with him. I know I shouldn't and yet I feel unable to stop myself somehow. I wonder if I will ever find perfect happiness. I know I don't deserve it and the way I am going on; I don't think I ever will. Going riding on Saturday.'

Friday 8th 'Not too bad a day I suppose. Graham phoned me up dinner time. He is really upset as he said he thought I had cooled off towards him. I certainly have cooled off him a lot, although I still like him in some ways. I have been wondering why Ken hasn't phoned me up. I do wish he would as I like him very much. I went to the Palace with LH this evening, then had a meal in the Oxford Café. I do wish I could fall in love with him. After seeing him off on the train, I walked up Russell Street and saw Norman's car, so I quickly wrote a little note and put it in the window frame. I do hope he found it as I said I would phone him Tuesday and I didn't. Going riding tomorrow with Doris.'

Saturday 9th 'A jolly good afternoon today. Went with Doris for my first riding lesson. Oh, it was wonderful. Had a nice big brown horse called Judy. I learnt how to trot and to turn properly. I was absolutely thrilled. Doris went with all the other people through the woods galloping and I went with just a boy instructor all along the roads. I really enjoyed it. I would love to go all day, every *day. After our lesson, we walked all up Broad Street in our jodhpurs. I did feel grand. Doris came to dinner and tea. LH came round this afternoon and we stayed in all evening.'*

Mary gets up about ten o'clock on Sunday and after breakfast sits at the table reading the paper with LH. After dinner they make some cookies together, '*got into a bit of a mess but they turned out very nicely in the end. After clearing up, we had a game of consequences with Mummy and Auntie V. It was quite funny really. Then we had tea. After that, Mummy and Auntie V went to the chapel and Daddy stayed in the kitchen to press some trousers, so LH and I went into my bedroom and played nearly all of my records. I quite enjoyed it. I have been thinking about so many different things today. I have been dreaming of horse riding and am longing for the next time. I have also been thinking about Norman. I wonder if he got my note and what he thought if he did. I have been thinking of Graham. I am most surprised he is upset. I thought it was all over. He seems to want to out with me as soon as possible again. I have also been thinking about Keith. He is a little devil really, but I like him just the same. Ken has also gone through my thoughts today. I wonder if he still thinks of me.'*

Monday 11th '*Not too bad a day. Doris and I have been giggling most of the time. Phoned Norman up this morning at coffee time and he said he could probably come out tomorrow. He said all the band saw my note, but apparently nobody guessed who sent it. Graham phoned me up dinner time. He told me he loves me and was so upset again as he thought I had finished with him. Saw him this evening after coming out of the hairdressers. He kissed me in the cycle shed and told me he loves me. He really has got it bad. I don't really want to go out with him again but I suppose I will. I went to the pictures with LH this evening.'*

Tuesday 12th '*Busy day today. Had an awful lot of work to do. Saw Graham this morning and again this evening. He had written me a long letter (three full pages) telling me how much he absolutely loves me etc. It was the sort of letter you read in books. I have never before read such a love letter. He said he wanted me for life and he didn't care who knew. He has scared me rather as I am certainly not in love with him and I don't want to break up his marriage. I hope it will all turn out alright. Went out with Norman this evening. He told me he loves me lots of times. I am in such a muddle. Keith phoned me up dinner time* and also told me he loves me. Phew! I wish my holiday would hurry up and come. I certainly need it.'

On Wednesday evening, having turned down going out with Graham, Mary goes to the pictures with LH and sees him off on the train. Afterwards she bumps into Ken on the platform and he walks home with her. They stop at a pub on the way for a drink then stand on the corner of Brunswick Street. *'He certainly was shy. He kept asking me to demonstrate how lipstick got on to men's faces. I didn't know what to do. Anyway, he kept on so when he was standing extra close, I just kissed him. He was alright after that. Got in at 11:15. Mum was terribly worried. I do like Ken.'*

Thursday 14th *'Phew! What a day. Saw Graham this morning before going to work who told me he still loves me. Saw Ken dinner time outside the bank and we stood and held hands for a quarter of an hour. He invited me to a party over the weekend. Oh, how I would love to go. May see him tomorrow. Went out with Keith this evening from 6 until 7:45 and I'm falling in love with him all over again, before taking Dad home some chips as Mummy was out at the Oxford. Then went out to meet Norman and spent the rest of the evening with him. He had been drinking and was a bit tipsy. I don't like him when he is like that, as he scares me. I am in such a dreadful muddle.'*

Friday 15th *'Oh dear, I have felt fairly happy all day today but now (11:15pm) I am feeling unhappy. Saw Graham this morning and again this evening before seeing LH. After I left him, I met LH and we walked all along the river. We were going to take some photos, but couldn't find anywhere so sat and read a book. After seeing him off on the train, I saw Ken. He cycled home with me. He read me a letter from his girlfriend giving him up which was a coincidence as he had written giving her up the same day. We stood and talked until 10:30 and were both so sad. He wants me to give LH up and I also want to but I somehow feel I may regret it later on. Oh dear, I am even more muddled now because Keith, Graham and Norman are unobtainable, but Ken is completely free which makes such a big difference. I know I can never have the other three but with Ken it is different. I don't like LH enough to get married and yet there is something that stops me from giving him up. I think it is pity as I don't want to hurt him. I know Mummy and Daddy and also LH's parents would be upset if we didn't get married now, but the way I feel now I know we can never marry. I am relying on God to help me out but right now feel like killing myself as I don't want to hurt anyone.'*

Saturday 16<sup>th</sup> *'Horribly wet day today and far too wet to ride my bike to work. Didn't see Graham before work but saw him after for a few minutes. Went horse riding this afternoon all by myself as Doris couldn't come. It was quite nice really but I got very wet. We went all through the woods and I had to almost lie on the horse to dodge the branches of the very wet trees. I do love the horses very much. I would love to work with them. After the lesson, I rushed home, changed, packed my case and dashed to the station to catch a train to Basingstoke. I am going to Weymouth tomorrow with LH and family.'*

Sunday 17<sup>th</sup> *'Got up at 6 o'clock and went with LH and family to Weymouth, arriving at 10:30. We went over on the ferry and climbed some lovely hills on the other side. After dinner, LH and I went for a walk and went into some thick gorse bushes where he took the final photographs of me in the nude. I am wondering what they will turn out like. We then went back to the caravan, had tea and watched LH's Grandparents cut their cake together. It was their golden wedding anniversary yesterday. We then started the long journey back. Just getting into bed now at 11:15 and dreading having to get up at 6 tomorrow.'*

Monday 18<sup>th</sup> Mary catches the train back to Reading having got up at six and is really tired. She sees Graham who has written her another love letter *'I don't really know where he gets his art of writing romantic letters from but he certainly can write them.'* She also sees Ken at dinner time who is apparently going out with his ex-girlfriend on Wednesday. Mary is a little jealous but has made up her mind not to chase him as she can't really expect him to give her up.

On Tuesday 19<sup>th</sup> *'I am so desperately unhappy. I feel so ill and tired out and have such a lot to worry about.'* She prays to God to help her with her worries stating *'I am not really bad, not deep down, it's just the surface of me that needs cleaning up a bit. Mum and Dad keep talking of Sarah all the time. I'm afraid I am terribly jealous. She is so beautiful and she has everything she wants—lovely clothes, a husband whom she loves, a mother and father who adore her best of* all, even after what she did to them. She always has been the lucky one. I had a good cry this evening.'

Wednesday 20<sup>th</sup> *'I feel so ill today. My throat is so sore and I have been sneezing all the time. I don't know how I have got through my work today. Saw Graham this morning and he told me he still loves me. I phoned him up dinner time and he told me again. Norman phoned me up this afternoon and I have arranged to meet him tomorrow after seeing Keith, but after seeing LH off on the train this evening (we had been to see Jane at the Palace) I met Ken and arranged to go roller skating with him tomorrow. Altogether, I have arranged to see all three tomorrow. Well, I will definitely see Keith, but I don't know what to say to put Norman off. I am in such a muddle and really don't know how I managed to get myself into this muddle, but I am up to my neck in it.'*

Thursday 21<sup>st</sup> *'Saw Sarah dinner time, I really wish I was her. Wonderful evening this evening altogether, also not too bad a day. Saw Graham this morning before work and he gave me some more pages of letter. Whew, he certainly can write letters. I went out with Keith this evening. He really is wonderful. I really like him very much. He really can make love wonderfully. Left him about 8:30 and met Ken outside the Majestic and went roller skating. I really did enjoy it very much. It was a bit difficult at first but got easier after a few times. I think I like Ken better than any of the others. He brought me home and we chatted outside until 10:45. He really can kiss. I do wish I was engaged to him instead of LH. I have great faith in God that He will help me.'*

Friday 22<sup>nd</sup> *'Quite a good day really. I have had some fun with Jeff, Dave and Alec today. They all tease me terribly. I do like them all so very much. Saw Graham before work this morning and again after work. He gave me another instalment of his letter. He sure has got it bad. Met Ken dinner time and again this evening after seeing LH off on the train. Ken cycled home with me and kissed me lots of times. I think I will be going skating with him again next Thursday. I do like him very much indeed but I still haven't fallen in love with anyone.'*

Mary works Saturday morning where nobody is really in the mood for work. She has more fun with the fellas who tease her about Ken. Attending a riding lesson in the afternoon she states how much she loves the horses. Sarah comes round after she finishes work '*but Francis came and took her out for the evening. Oh, why couldn't I have been Sarah? She is so lucky. I can't remember a more boring evening than this evening. LH came about eight thirty and we just sat all evening doing absolutely nothing. Oh, this is driving me mad and I can't go on like this much longer. I will either have to kill myself or run away from it all.*'

Sunday is a busy day. Mary gets up around 10:30. '*After dinner, LH and I cycled down to the river and took a boat out. We went almost all the way to Tilehurst. Saw Jean's house boat. It is lovely, I would like to live in one. We were about an hour and a half on the river and then we cycled back to town and left our bikes in St Mary's churchyard and went and had a cup of tea and a cake in Lions. After that, we went to the Gaumont. It was a wonderful film (The Toy Tiger) better than I have seen for ages. We arrived back home about ten thirty. I have done such a lot of thinking today. I know I will never be happy until I cease to be so wicked. I am in such a dreadful muddle. I just feel I'm going crazy. After all, when one is going out with three married men and two single ones (one of whom you are engaged to) all at the same time, it's enough to make you go out of your mind. How I pray to God to help me. I used to be such a nice girl. I would hate to hurt Mummy and Daddy. They are so good and kind and I love them both very much indeed. Why can't I die? I think even Hell would be better than this. It is so terrible to have a conscience.*'

Monday 25th '*Just another day. One seems so much like the rest lately. After seeing Graham after work, I met up with Norman and we went to see a man about a trailer for the back of his car. I sat in the car for over an hour and it was too late to do anything after that so he just took me back home. Saw Edna dinner time. She has written to the Miranda Hotel to see if her friend Carol can come with us. I am so upset. I don't think I will go if Carol does. I am surprised at Edna as she didn't even ask me if I minded. She and Carol always giggle at the least little thing. I know I would be left out of everything.*'

Tuesday 26th '*Not too bad a day I suppose really. Had an awful lot of work to do as it is balance time. I went out with Keith this evening. Oh, he is really so very nice. I do like him so very much. Won't see him now for three weeks as he is going on holiday next week. After seeing him off, I cycled up to Graham's place and met him. We went for a walk. He isn't bad I suppose but I am certainly not in love with him. I wonder if I will ever be completely happy. I will probably see Ken tomorrow. He is also very nice. Going swimming with Doris after work tomorrow. I am so tired.'*

Wednesday 27th *'Quite a good day really, I suppose, although I was terribly disappointed as Ken didn't phone me up like he said he would. I don't know when I will see him now. Saw Graham this morning before work and again this evening. I went swimming with Doris and he came later on in the evening. We had some fun and he threw me in lots of times. I did enjoy it. It was a bit cold but once you got in, it didn't seem so bad. Afterwards, we all went into the Jack of Both Sides and had a drink. I had a Babycham. It was jolly good. Then I cycled down to the station and waited for Ken but he wasn't there. I do wonder if he will phone me tomorrow. I also wonder if Carol can come with us on holiday.'*

Thursday 28th *'Another jolly good day really, although Ken hasn't phoned me up and I am very disappointed. Saw Graham this morning before work. Worked late this evening until ten past ten. Alec had to climb up to close some windows, so I took the ladder away and when he eventually got down, he locked me in the ladies room. I did enjoy it. Jean, Doris and I went in to the Oasis for our tea. It was jolly good. I quite like working late as we have such fun. I am most annoyed with Edna today. I saw Carol dinner time and she said the hotel in Jersey can put her up, so it looks as if she is all set. I am so upset. I don't want her to come.'*

Friday 29th *'I don't quite know how I have got through today. I have felt so ill. I am simply aching all over and even went to sleep in my dinner hour. I don't think I have ever felt quite so ill before as I really thought I was going to pass out any moment. Worked until about seven thirty*

Mary at a dance in 1956.

*and on my way home I bumped into Stan, Frankie and Arnie. Stood and talked, then Stan and Frankie left and Arnie and I cycled to Prospect Park after him having given me a kiss lasting FIVE whole minutes in the main Cranbury Road. Laid down on the grass and he kissed me loads of times. Oh, it was heavenly. I could have stayed there all night. Got home about 10:45. He was supposed to have gone playing.'*

Saturday 30th *'Jolly good day all around really. I worked all day today but had some fun. Went over to LH's this evening and we went to a dance where the band was playing. I was dreading going as I didn't want Arnie to see me with LH, but luckily Arnie didn't come. They want me to go singing with them next Saturday in Simmonds's Grounds. I am looking forward to it immensely. Ted said he would try to fit me in a lot more often as he liked me coming. I am so glad as I love singing so much. Norman was a bit upset as he heard about me seeing the rest of the band yesterday. I think they all guessed I went out with Arnie. I certainly like him a lot.'*

JULY

Not a great start to this month but singing with the band again soon lifts her spirits. Changing sections at work proves challenging causing rows and spiking tears. And attending a party on 31st which she states as horrible is where she, unbeknown to her, gets noticed by a certain boy who is set to become the most important one in her life. She does note in her diary at a later stage that this is when she first met John.

Sunday 1st *'Not too bad a day today I suppose. I got up fairly early and went to church. I was so tired I nearly went to sleep. After dinner, we just sat all afternoon as it was raining and we couldn't go out. If it had been fine, LH and Brian were going to have a game of tennis while Mr and Mrs H and I watched. I would have hated that. It came out nicer later and we all, except Brian who had gone to bed, went out into the garden and played ball for about half an hour. Then LH seemed to get a bit daring and got me up on his shoulders and Mr H got out his camera and took a photo, so we both got a bit boisterous. LH picked me up and held my head in the water, but then took my shoes off and tickled my toes and all sorts of different attitudes. Mr H took photos of all of it. I am looking* forward to seeing them. I have been doing a lot of thinking today about my "boyfriends". I do wish I was completely free then I could go out with whom I like without feeling guilty. I do wish I was good. I know I am deep down but I am so wicked on top. Perhaps I will be good one day.'

Monday 2nd 'I just can't remember a worst day. Every single thing has gone wrong. The moment I got to work, Alec came and told me Ken had got engaged over the weekend. I don't really love him but I feel jealous all the same. I am awful and have felt miserable all day. Saw Graham before work and waited for him for an hour after but he didn't come. That sank my spirits down even lower. When I got home, Sarah came round and Mum and Dad fussed over her so much. She said she has been asked to become a model. Oh, I am stupidly jealous. I think it is because I am so tired and all this secret worry is wearing me out. I am desperately unhappy and think God is punishing me for being so wicked. I feel like crying my eyes out and killing myself. I feel so ashamed.'

Tuesday 3rd 'Thank goodness today has been a lot better than yesterday. If it had been even half as bad, I think I would have killed myself. Saw Graham before work then found Keith waiting outside the bank for me. He was going to get a haircut. He is very nice but I'm afraid my conscience is beginning to get too much for me. I went out with Norman this evening. He isn't bad either but I am not in love with anyone really and right now I am wondering if I ever will be.'

Wednesday 4th 'Just an ordinary sort of day today really. Nothing at all exciting has happened. Been very busy at work and I'm glad, as it doesn't leave me much time to think and worry about everything. Stan phoned me up dinner time and said they would like me to go dancing on Friday so as to get used to the new songs ready for Saturday. We are going to Simmonds's dance and it is in a tent. I am looking forward to it very much. Stan said Ted had told him he thought I was very good. I am glad as I love singing so much. Went to the pictures with LH this evening.'

Thursday 5th 'Saw Graham before work this morning and again after work. Went into some woods with his dog. He told me he loved me. He was talking about his wife very intimately. It was quite embarrassing. We had quite a long serious talk. After I got rid of him, I phoned LH up to say I couldn't come out *any more this week. After that, I went and waited for Norman but I waited in vain because he didn't come. I waited just over an hour and a half. On the way back home, I saw his car up Russell Street so I wrote him a little note and stuck it to his window. I wonder what could have happened to him.'*

With Friday's arrival Mary had been looking forward to the dance with the band but when they get to the hall there is another girl there that Stan had said could sing as well! *'Oh, I am madly jealous and can see Stan likes her a lot. Well, she certainly hasn't got much. I know if she does sing with the band, I will see Ted about it. I am absolutely furious. Norman took me home and we talked for ages. He told me he still loves me.'*

Saturday 7th *'Not too bad a day really. Quite a good evening, at least the first half. I went to Simmonds's dance this evening. Oh, it was lovely. There was Stan, Frankie, Ted, Norman, Dick, Arnie and the double bass player Roy. I do like Frankie and Arnie very much. Sang about seven different songs. Came home in the back of Norman's car and had to sit on Frankie's lap. Phew, he sure is nice. I think this upset Norman though.'*

Sunday 8th *'It has been a wonderfully hot day today. I am very red and hope it won't be sore in the morning. Came to LH's at eleven forty-five and shortly after, we had lunch, then a short game of ball. We then all trooped down to a park in Basingstoke where Mr H had to fix up a microphone for a band. LH and I went for a walk round the park and then sat and listened to the band. It was an open-air service. Later on, we had an ice lolly. I did enjoy it. When we got home, we had tea then played some ball in the garden for the rest of the evening. It is so terribly hot. At the moment, I am sitting on my bed thinking about the band. They will be playing in Woodley at this minute and that girl will be there. I bet the boys will take her home. I am absolutely mad with jealousy and I'm praying to God not to let her get a job of singing with the band. I am so upset. Stan said he was going to pay me for last night so I expect he will be in touch with me tomorrow. I do wish I had had the chance to talk to Arnie yesterday. I think I am in love with him.'*

Monday 9th *'What a day! Changed over sections at work and I've been doing Ruth's work. Phew, what a mess I got into. There is such a lot to learn and at the* moment, I just don't know how I am going to cope with it all. I went out with Norman this evening. He really is so very sweet. He told me that girl went on Sunday, but didn't sing because Stan didn't go. I am thrilled that Stan didn't, as it is him, I want to like me. I do not usually feel catty towards any girl but I feel like killing this one. I hope Stan won't let her sing and I am praying to God not to make him.'

Tuesday 10$^{th}$ Mary sees Graham after getting out of work at seven o'clock and they go for a short walk where once again he expresses his love for her. Mary is disappointed today though as Stan still hasn't rung her up regarding paying her for Saturday, but then cheers herself up by seriously contemplating taking up singing professionally, *'I would love to, but I wouldn't know how to go about it.'*

Wednesday 11$^{th}$ *'Not too bad a day really, I suppose. Had such a lot of work. I am a whole day behind everyone else. I do wish I could catch up. Saw Graham before going to work this morning and he told me he loves me. He is fairly nice but I don't think I would like him for a husband. I wonder if I will ever find someone whom I can really love, someone who I won't mind anyone else knowing about. I do so hate all these lies I have to keep telling. I only hope God can forgive me.'* This evening, she goes to the Palace with LH then they go for a meal at the Oxford Café, where she wishes she could fall in love with him'

Thursday 12$^{th}$ *'Quite a good day on the whole really. Still had an awful lot of work but I think I have caught up a good deal thank goodness. I went for a short walk with Graham and his dog after work then cycled back to town and met Norman. We went out into the country in his car and he played his trumpet to me. I was itching to have a go but I didn't like to ask. I would love to learn to play. Norman is so very nice. I love him in a way, not the way a wife loves a husband, but I just feel I love him. It is difficult to explain, but I just know.'*

Friday 13$^{th}$ *'Jolly good day all around. Didn't see Graham this morning as I got up terribly late. I was supposed to have met him this evening but it was raining so I didn't bother. When I got home, Mum and Dad weren't there so I went back down town to see if I could see any of the band. I went back and forth so many times and eventually I saw Stan and he paid me for last Saturday. I went*

*into the dance for just over an hour and left about ten fifteen and hurried home wondering what to say to Mum and Dad for being late but they still had not arrived home. Eventually they came at 12:30, I was so glad.'*

Saturday 14<sup>th</sup> *'Quite a good day on the whole really. I saw Stan this morning before going to work then after I had left him, I saw Graham just getting onto the bus. Saw him again after work but not to talk to. Went to LH's this afternoon. Phew! My poor feet. We went to a carnival and walked around all afternoon then went to a dance in the evening. Mrs H went and left me on my own there and a boy came and danced with me. We then walked round the park and he kissed me loads of times. His name was Dave. I said I would meet him tomorrow but of course I can't. Roy walked home with me last night. He wants me to go out with him. Oh dear.'*

Sunday 15<sup>th</sup> *'Felt absolutely tired out today. Got up about nine o'clock (after having got into bed about 2:45 this morning) and had breakfast then went out into the garden with Mrs H and picked loads of raspberries. LH and Brian didn't get up until about one fifteen. After dinner, LH and I sat upstairs in the living room and I almost went to sleep but he kept kissing me. I just couldn't get any peace at all. Anyway tea time came round and then after all that was over LH, Brian, Mrs H and myself all got in the van and off we went to church. When we got back LH and Brian had a game of tennis in the back garden while Mr and Mrs H and myself had a game of boomerang tennis. We did get into some muddles but all had a jolly good laugh. When we were thoroughly worn out, we had supper and came to bed. I have thought such a lot about the band today. We are going to make a record. I am thrilled and am longing to know what it will sound like. I have also been thinking about Keith, Ken, Norman and Graham. I am going out with Norman tomorrow and Keith on Thursday. I am still in such a muddle.'*

On Monday, a sort of average day, Mary sees Frankie before work which makes her too late to see Graham beforehand. But she goes for a short walk with him and his dog after work then rushes back to town to meet Norman who doesn't turn up. Mary waits from eight to nine thirty-five and then decides to go home. '*I am so upset as I love going out with him. I will phone him up tomorrow. Going out with Keith tomorrow. Had some fun with Jeff today at work. I do like him.*'

Tuesday 17th '*Quite a good day again today. Had some more fun with Jeff dinner time. He seems to like me a lot more than he did. I am so glad. Saw Frankie before work this morning. Went to the back of his shop and he kissed me lots of times and told me he loved me. I certainly do like him but I don't think I am really in love with anyone at the moment. Didn't see Graham before work but saw him afterwards although, not to speak to. I went out with Keith this evening. He is very nice too although I can't believe a word he says. I wonder why it is I seem to like all the bad ones. I pray so hard to God to make me good.*'

Wednesday 18th '*Not too bad a day really, I suppose. I saw Frankie before work again this morning. Went into his shop and we were all alone. He is so nice but even so, I do not really love him, not in a way I would like to love a husband. Didn't see Graham this morning and I expect he is wondering what has happened. He too is very nice. Oh, why is it I like all the ones I can't have and dislike all the ones I could have. I am trusting in God to help me and have great faith that He will. I went to the Palace with LH this evening. I do wish I could be nicer to him. I feel so awful.*'

Thursday 19th '*Saw Frankie again before work this morning but didn't have time to see Graham though. I really will have to see him tomorrow. Phoned Norman up dinner time and he said he could come out this evening, so I waited for him but he didn't turn up, so I prayed really hard and he came. I was so thrilled because it was a miracle. Norman is very sweet but I feel I just want to look after him.*'

Friday 20th '*Not too bad a day again today. Saw Graham this morning. He said he still loves me and I feel quite glad. I don't know why as I am not in love with him. Keith phoned me up dinner time and we have arranged to go out next*

*Thursday. I do wish he hadn't contacted me again as I was just beginning to get over him. I think I really did love him before but now after having been hurt so bad, I find it a bit difficult to love him quite so much. I went to the pictures with LH this evening. On my way home, I put a note on Norman's car which was parked in Russell Street.'*

Saturday 21st *'Quite a good day on the whole although much too much work. Ruth is on holiday now so we have got hers to do as well. Saw Graham again this morning. He says he still loves me. LH came this afternoon and we didn't do very much but then in the evening we decided to go dancing at the Oxford. We both enjoyed it very much. There were two boys who kept excusing LH and were both very nice. They both danced with me at once in one dance. I did enjoy that. Don't know how I walked home as my feet were absolutely killing me. I don't know when they have hurt quite so much before. I do wish I could fall in love with LH.'*

Sunday 22nd *'An average sort of day really, I suppose. I got up about ten o'clock and cycled down to Lyons for some rolls. When I got back, I found I hadn't brought enough so I had to go all the way back for more. LH got up about eleven thirty and after dinner we packed a picnic tea and cycled to Burghfield Common (a place where I go often with Norman and Keith). We sat and read the paper then I wanted to try and get some sleep but LH kept wanting to kiss me which annoys me as I hate him kissing me or even holding my hand. I don't know why; I can't explain it. I do wish I could. I am absolutely horrid to him. After all, we are engaged and poor LH expects to kiss me which is only natural. He keeps telling me how I've changed and I know I have, from a very nice girl into a horrible adulteress. Oh, how I long to be a good girl again. I should hate to do anything in any way to hurt Mummy and Daddy. In every way, I love them so very much and they are so fond of LH, they would be so disappointed if I didn't marry him.'*

Work is very busy again on Monday but Jeff is supervising so Mary doesn't mind so much. During the day she sees Graham and arranges to go out tonight with Norman, who doesn't show up, even though she waits until 9:15. *'A horrible man stopped to talk to me, I had a job to get rid of him.'*

Tuesday 24<sup>th</sup> *'A terrible day today with every single thing going wrong. Frankie had someone in with him and I was too late to see Graham this morning. This afternoon, I had a terrible row with Mr B, Doris and Jean and am so far behind with the work. I had a job to stop crying. A few tears did come and I think Jeff saw. He was so nice to me and told me not to worry about them. I think I would have broken down if he hadn't been there. I do like him so much. When I was in the pictures this evening, someone broke my 3 speed on my bike. I am so desperately unhappy. Saw Stan this evening. He said he will phone me when they make the record. I am looking forward to it.'*

Wednesday 25<sup>th</sup> *'A lot better day thank goodness. Saw Frankie this morning, went into his shop and he kissed me lots of times. He is so nice. Also, managed to see Graham. He isn't bad. Phoned Norman up dinner time and he is going to try to come out on Saturday. Going out with Keith tomorrow but I don't think I really want to. Went to the pictures with LH this evening. I do wish I really loved him. It would make things so much easier. Jeff has been so nice to me today. He has stood up for me all the time. I do wish I was engaged to him. I really am fond of him.'*

Thursday 26<sup>th</sup> *'Another terrible day today. I've rowed with all the girls again and they hardly speak to me at all. I don't know how I stopped myself from crying. I think I would have done if Jeff hadn't been there. He really is wonderful. Didn't see Graham this morning as I went to see Frankie. He is nice too. Went out with Keith this evening, it was wonderful, the sun was burning down. We lay together on a rug and I felt so peaceful but my conscience is absolute torture.'*

Friday 27<sup>th</sup> *'One of the worst days of my life I think today has been. Had a terribly big row with the girls again. They went to Mr B and he had me over. We stood talking for half an hour and he said he didn't think I was doing my best. Oh, I had to blink to keep back the tears. I had an awful job to stop crying. I don't know how I managed it. Dear Jeff stuck up for me all the time and I love him for it. The girls haven't spoken to me at all and I feel I want to sit down and just cry my eyes out. Went to the Palace with LH this evening. He goes on holiday on Sunday so I won't see him for a fortnight.'*

Saturday 28th '*Another horrible morning, although not half as bad as yesterday. I went out to coffee with Margaret this morning as I couldn't have stood going out with the girls. They have been strangely polite though. Lovely evening. I went to tea with Edna and we made some omelettes. Afterwards, we went in town and looked in all the shops and then we went into the Palomino. Mike and Rob were in there and we sat at a table with two girls they knew. They have invited Edna and I to a party on Tuesday. It will be good and really cheered me up no end. I am looking forward to it.*'

Sunday 29th '*Wonderful day today. Stayed in all day. It is the first Sunday I haven't seen LH since long before Christmas. Oh, it was such a relief. I didn't bother to put on any make up or stockings on nor do my hair. I got up about ten fifteen and slowly dressed then got the sewing machine out and did some of the dress I'm making. It is a lovely frock—white organizer. After dinner and washing up, I went back to my frock all afternoon listening to the wireless. I have thoroughly enjoyed today. It was so peaceful after all the rows of the week. I do hope next week will be better as I hate arguments. I have been doing a lot of thinking today. I wish I could see into the future to see what God has planned for me. I would so much like to be a professional singer and I would also love to travel all over the world. I wonder if I ever will. Above all, I would like to buy Mummy and Daddy everything they wanted.*'

Monday 30th '*Not too bad a day today really. Saw Grahm this morning before work. He is rather sweet really although I am not in love with him. I am glad to say the girls at work are speaking to me again. I am so glad because I do hate rows of any kind. I have almost caught up with my work now so I don't suppose there will be any more rows at all. Went out with Keith this evening. He really is so very nice and I do wish he wasn't quite so handsome. I don't think I would like him so much if he wasn't. Phoned Norman dinner time. Going to a party tomorrow.*'

Tuesday 31st '*Horrible evening. Went to party with Edna, Mike and Rob. It started off alright I suppose. We had a game of postman's knock and I went out several times. After that though, we played Murder but I was left out of it completely. Edna went off with some boy and Mike and Rob didn't appear to want anything to do with me, so I sat all the rest of the evening stroking the dog.*

*I know it is only because I am engaged that Mike and Rob have cooled off me. Oh, how I hate my engagement. I don't think I have ever felt such desperate unhappiness. I feel like killing myself. It must be all the drink I've had.'*

## AUGUST

Quoting about the unbearable amount of work in her section at the bank on top of all her other worries, it's no wonder rows spark with her parents at home. Cheering herself up Mary engages in a little retail therapy for her holiday. Find out how her first date goes with John on 23rd and what happens shortly after to LH.

Wednesday 1st *'Another completely horrible day. I don't know how I have managed to bear it today. Had a row with all the girls again and Mr B. Told him I was sick to death of the lot of them and so I am. I have had such a headache all day and when the girls kept telling me off, I just lost my temper I'm afraid. I am so unhappy and I feel as if nobody wants me at all. Went out with Norman in the evening. That cheered me up a bit.'*

Thursday 2nd *'Not quite such a bad day today really. The girls have been a little bit kinder although not until this afternoon. Mr B doesn't speak to me at all but that doesn't really worry me. Went up to London this evening with Edna. That was rather fun. We went to C&A's and I bought two summer frocks. I had intended to get lots more things but there just wasn't time. After coming out of there, we walked to Piccadilly and went into one of Lyons Corner Houses and had a lovely meal. We met two boys on the way home. One of them took me home in a taxi.'*

Mary manages to see Graham before work on Friday and when she gets out of work finds a box of chocolates left on her bike from him. She wishes he hadn't left them because she is not in love with him. That evening Mary meets up with Keith. *'I don't know why I go out with him really as he keeps shooting the old line about lots of rows with his wife, which of course I don't believe a word of. I bought an evening top and a stole today. I really am looking forward to my holiday.'*

**Saturday 4th** '*Not too bad a day I suppose really. Saw Graham after work this morning. He is on his holidays now for a fortnight. It will be quite a relief not to have to see him in the mornings. Met Edna this afternoon and I bought a bright red bikini. It is beautiful. This evening, we went into the Palomino and met a couple of Italians. One was lovely. They tried to teach me Italian and were so interesting. I would love a foreign boyfriend. Saw Norman this evening. He is also on holiday next week. I will miss him I know. I expect I will see him on Tuesday. Saw Johnny this evening. He has turned into a proper teddy boy!*'

**Sunday 5th** '*A wonderfully peaceful day. Did absolutely nothing all day. I do wish every day could be like this. Got up about ten thirty then gave Auntie V a display of all my dresses and other things I have ready for my holiday. She didn't really seem very keen on any of them. After dinner, I read the paper and then started to adjust my frock I've been making. The back is all baggy so I made a strap to go on it. I think it will look quite nice when it's finished. I am looking forward to my holiday. I do hope the weather will be nice. I will be so disappointed if it isn't. Going round to Edna's tomorrow. I don't know what we will do though. I am having all my hair cut off on Wednesday. I do hope it won't look too bad. I am dreading it and hope Sarah won't cut it too short.*'

**Bank holiday Monday 6th** '*No work today, thank goodness. Stayed in bed until 9:30/10. Got up and helped Mummy. After dinner Mummy, Daddy and Auntie V went to the pictures and I got ready and went down to Edna's. Later on, after tea, we went to the pictures then into the Palomino. Saw Mike, Nancy, Sarah and two other fellows. Later on, Pete came in. Oh, did my heart miss a beat. He is wonderful. One of the other fellows took me home—Ray.*'

**Tuesday 7th** '*Jolly good at work today really. Jean is on holiday and it is so peaceful. Ruth is back now, thank goodness. I have caught up with my work already. Ray came to meet me dinner time. We went into the Forbury. He isn't bad but I would rather have Jeff at work. Ray wanted me to go out with him this evening so I told him to meet me from work. Well, he did and he invited me home for tea. Well, I didn't know what to do as I don't want to get entangled with him, but he kept on at me so I went. I met his mother and twin sisters. They are very nice. After that, I waited for Norman but he didn't come so I will phone him tomorrow.*'

Wednesday 8th *'Another peaceful day really at work. It certainly is a lot better without Jean there. Phoned Norman up dinner time and he said he hadn't managed to get out last night but he would try tonight. Edna met me from work or rather waited at Friars Tea Bar for me. Pat at work gave me a lift on his motorbike today. He wanted to take me home on it but I had to see Edna. I was rather disappointed as I like Pat very much indeed and hope he will ask me again. Edna said she would meet me later in the evening so I went to pictures for one and a half hours. Went to Palomino with Edna. Waited for Norman, but he didn't come.'*

Thursday 9th *'Not too good a day really. A lot too much work to do. It is worrying me terribly. I just can't see how I can get through it all. I phoned Norman up dinner time but he wasn't there. I am so disappointed. I do hope I can contact him tomorrow as he goes on holiday on Saturday. Keith phoned me this morning. We are going out tomorrow and I am quite glad. When I got home, I had a row with Daddy. Oh dear, he told me to get out. He has no idea just how much that hurt. I am so tired out and unhappy. Re-reading this diary, I don't think I have expressed the full depth of my unhappiness.'*

Friday 10th *'Not too bad a day today. A lot of work though. Phoned Norman up dinner time and he said he might be able to come out tomorrow evening for a short while and would phone me tomorrow morning to let me know. I do hope he can because I like him very much and would like to see him before he goes on holiday. Went out with Keith this evening. I did enjoy it. We went to a sweet little public house and had some ham sandwiches and a couple of drinks. Then we went into some woods and sat in the back of his car. He is so nice and yet, I don't believe a word he says.'*

Saturday 11th *'Wonderful day really. Norman phoned me this morning and said he could come out if I met him in Woodley. I was so pleased. Went round Edna's for tea this afternoon then we went to the Palomino where we saw Arnie from the band and his friend. Went with them to the White Hart and had a couple of drinks then went to Prospect Park. I do like him but he is going to Cyprus on Friday. He said he would write to me. Had an awful row with Mummy and Daddy when I got in. Ray had phoned to see if I was in and also two boys called to see if I was in. Daddy was furious.'*

Mary's parents are not speaking to her on Sunday morning and her father won't tell her who the other two boys were. By the afternoon though with Auntie V present, they seem to have forgotten all about it. Mary goes round to Edna's in the afternoon and Carol goes round as well. *'She is far too pretty for my liking but is very nice though. I do wish her and Edna wouldn't keep giggling. It makes me furious when I have got so many worries to hear them giggling away. I suppose I am envious because they are completely heart free with nothing to worry about at all. We all went for a walk then ended up in the Palomino where I met Ray. He isn't bad. I went off with him for a walk in the Forbury and then had to dash home.'*

Monday 13th *'An awfully busy day today. Worked until nine o'clock. Graham phoned me up today and he said he was definitely going to marry me one day. He was so serious and scared me rather. I do hope he won't do anything silly because I definitely don't love him anywhere near enough to marry him even if I was free to do so. Phoned LH up this evening after finishing work at nine o'clock. Oh, he is just as boring and yet just as sweet really. I do wish I could fall in love with him as it would solve all my problems in a flash, but he is so utterly boring and stupid. I know I can never marry him.'*

Tuesday 14th *'Not too bad a day today really. Still had an awful lot of work to do. LH came up this evening. He had bought Daddy a box of toffees, Mummy a letter rack, Auntie V a spectacle cleaner and me a condiment set with salt, mustard and pepper pots. I was so surprised. I didn't expect anything like that at all. I do wish I could fall in love with him but he is just not my type at all. I do wish I could give him up but Mummy and Daddy like him so much. It is such a problem and I just don't know what to do.'*

Wednesday 15th *'Another busy day today. I just don't know how to get through all my work. I'm sure I will be ill before much longer through over work. Went to the pictures with LH this evening. Oh, he is so boring. I hate him to be near me at all. I don't even let him hold my hand now at all. I really will have to try and pluck up courage to give him up. I just can't go on like this. I am losing weight rapidly, what with worrying about all my work and LH and all the others. I am so looking forward to our holiday. I certainly need it and do wish it would hurry up.'*

Thursday 16<sup>th</sup> '*Phew, what a day today has been. We have had such a lot of work. Went out with Keith this evening. We went to our usual spot and sat in the back of his car. Oh, he is so nice, I like him very much indeed although I still don't like him as much as I did before Christmas. After saying goodbye to him, I cycled up to see Graham. It was absolutely pouring with rain and I got drenched. Met Graham and we went into a pub and had a drink. Then we walked back to his place (in the rain) and he gave me a letter—19 full pages of slosh. Phew! I was absolutely drenched when I got back in and had to wring the water out of my frock.*'

Friday 17<sup>th</sup> '*Still awfully busy at work. The manager had me in his office today. He asked me if I was happy in my work etc. I think it was all to do with that trouble last week. I thought I was going to get the sack. Had my hair done this evening as I managed to get out of work at four thirty. Then met LH at six fifteen and we went off to the pictures. Oh, how I wish I had the heart to give him up. I find fault with everything he says or does and I feel so awful about it.*'

Saturday 18<sup>th</sup> '*Wonderful, heavenly evening. Saw Ray this afternoon and he did a bit of shopping with me. Went to the town hall with him, Mike, Edna and Carol in the evening to see Humphrey Lyttelton. Boy was that wizzo! After that we all went off to a party. I had a wonderful time and had bags of drinks. I got off with the same chap I did at the other party. Ray was jiving and I was sitting on this other fellow's lap. All the lights were out most of the evening. I did enjoy myself. Going to another party next Saturday. Got home 1:50 and am writing this at exactly three twenty.*'

Mary gets up on Sunday and travels to LH's for the weekend where she comments that it's so boring and they couldn't even watch television because it had gone wrong. '*I don't know whether it is just the excitement of last night which made it seem worse than usual or whether it really was more so than usual. I could have cried when I thought about what I could have been doing.*' After having such a lovely evening yesterday, she just wishes she could give LH up and hang out with Mike and his crowd all the time.

Monday 20<sup>th</sup> '*Phew, I'm tired. Got up at six o'clock this morning and came back from Basingstoke. I am so glad the weekend is over. I can't stand any more* like that one. An awfully busy day at work today and I have been worn out. I stayed in all evening thank goodness and sewed a strap on the dress I have made. I am quite pleased with it. I was awfully annoyed this evening as Daddy told me that Mike had come round for me four times yesterday to see if I could go out with them. I do wish I could have gone; they are so nice.'

Tuesday is another terribly busy day work wise and she mentions how very tired she is today. 'Sarah has told me she will come and do my hair for me tomorrow. I want it cut in some ways but in others I am dreading it. I wonder what it will turn out like. I should hate to look a mess as I am going to the Grosvenor on Saturday with Mike, John, Edna and all the others. I am looking forward to it. I rather like John. He is very nice and I certainly like him a lot better than LH. Went out with LH this evening. I can't even bare him near me now.'

Wednesday 22nd 'Another terribly busy day. I am quite worried about how to cope with it all. Sarah came round this evening and cut all my hair off. Oh, she has taken such a lot off. I am absolutely dreading it tomorrow. I wonder what it will turn out like, not too short hopefully. She tried on all my holiday clothes and did look so nice in them. I do wish I was as pretty as her. She really is beautiful although I would never tell her that I am very envious of her. She hasn't got any worries at all.'

Thursday 23rd 'Well my hair has turned out wonderfully. I don't think it has ever turned out so nice before and I know I have never been quite so please with it. I am thrilled and feel very posh. It is awfully short but I have a lovely little fringe. John Kean phoned me up yesterday to see if I could go to the pictures with him so I went tonight. Oh, I had such an enjoyable evening. He is such fun and I like him such a lot. He really made me feel glad to be alive which is something I had forgotten existed. He is going to take me to tea on Saturday.'

Friday 24th 'A day of ups and downs really. Everyone at work has been moaning as there has been an awful lot of work. John came to meet me from work and LH was only round the corner. John just wouldn't go. I think he knows about LH really because he keeps giving little hints away. He wanted me to go home with him but I had to go with LH. Oh, I was so disappointed as I would *love to have gone with John. I really will have to give LH up. He said he was going to buy a dining room table. I will have to stop him as it's not fair to him.'*

Saturday 25th '*An absolutely wonderful evening. I think at last I have found someone I really love—John. He is the most wonderful person I have ever met. We went to the Grosvenor with his twin brother Richard and his girlfriend Stella. Well, I have fallen hook, line and sinker. I have put him through my mental test and he has passed with flying colours. The test is…would I mind <u>anyone</u> knowing I went out with him and the answer is definitely NO! I have decided once and for all to give LH up. John came home with me this afternoon. There was no one in so he stayed for about two and a half hours and then we went to Heelas for tea. I really do love him already.'*

Sunday 26th '*An awful day really. LH came up this morning and we went round to Mike's to give him a birthday present but he wasn't in so I had a long talk to Auntie S about John and LH and she was so nice about it. Found Mike round Rob's, then went back home for dinner. We were sitting around doing absolutely nothing when Stella came round with her dog "Scruffy". She stayed all the afternoon and I was so thankful as I was bored to tears beforehand. She really came to see if I could go to John's party this evening. It's his and his brothers 21st birthdays, but of course Mum said I couldn't and LH said he wanted to go and see Ted Heath. So, we walked back with Stella, then LH and I had a row about it and I nearly managed to give him up but thought I hadn't better send him home, so off we went to Ted Heath. He was very good but I couldn't enjoy it as I was so disappointed at not being able to go to the party. Anyway, when I didn't speak to LH at all, he said he would go for a walk while I went to the party for a quarter of an hour. I was thrilled and so was John. I was nervous as I met all his people. They are all very nice. His father caught him kissing me. He was thanking me for my present. He knows all about LH thank goodness. I have told him I will have given LH up by next weekend and I know I will. Kept LH waiting for about an hour. I introduced John to him afterwards and they shook hands. Oh, I am so much in love with John.'*

Monday 27th '*Oh what a day today has been. I don't think, in fact I know I have never longed for anyone in the world so much as I have longed for John today. I don't know what's happened to me. I am just head over heels in love with him. I just can't put it into words, the way I feel about him. I went to the pictures with him this evening and with Richard and Stella. Mummy came along and saw me waiting for him (she thought I was waiting for Edna) and John came up so I introduced him. I think Mummy guessed I was going out with him. I have told John I will finish with LH tomorrow. I am scared stiff but I will try to do it. I love John enough to do absolutely anything for him.'*

Tuesday 28th *'Oh dear, never again do I want to go through a day like today. I have felt really ill all day. I have been planning what to say to LH this evening to give him up. I have been as nervous as anything. I have also been wondering whether I really want to give him up or not as I still like him but I like John more. Anyway, he met me from work and we had to take a doctors certificate round Grandma's for Daddy so we were round there all evening and I lost my nerve. I couldn't say a word so he did all the talking. He asked me if I was fed up with him and if I wanted to break it all off but I couldn't answer. I was dumb struck so I just got off the train and told him I would write to him.'*

Wednesday 29th *'I tried to tell Mummy this morning about my giving LH up but I just couldn't somehow. Oh, I am so nervy and mixed up. I have been thinking of John and LH all day and wondering if I am doing the right thing. I had an absolutely wonderful evening though as I went to the pictures with John. Oh, I love him so much. He has told me he will probably come to Jersey for one of the weeks I am there. I do hope he will. We will have such fun. I don't know what I will do if I can't see him for a whole fortnight. Just one day away from him seems a lifetime. I really am in love.'*

Thursday 30th *'I still haven't told Mummy about LH; I just can't bring myself to do it. I don't know what she would say. I'm sure I am scared stiff. I haven't seen either John or LH today but have thought about them both. I have felt so sorry for LH and am beginning to wonder if I do love him after all or whether it is just pity. I know I love John, but I am not so sure of him as I was LH. I know LH loves me and wouldn't change his mind but I don't know about John. I only hope and pray that he won't. Oh dear, I am in such a muddle. I went to London this evening with Edna and Carol. Bought a lovely short blue coat. I do wish our holiday would hurry up and come.'*

Friday 31<sup>st</sup> *'Well today was the day. I told Mummy about LH and John. Mummy, Daddy and myself were sitting down to tea and Daddy asked whether LH was coming here or I was going to LH's for the weekend, so I had to say neither and of course that started the questions flowing. They were both very nice about it and said they weren't really surprised. Of course, Daddy gave me a little talking to and I was embarrassed but not as much as I had expected to be. John met me from work this evening and we just walked home together; I am feeling so sorry for LH. I love John but can't trust him not to give me up the way that I could with LH, as I haven't been going out with him so long.'*

## SEPTEMBER

Finally, Mary ventures on her long-awaited holiday to Jersey even though she is sad to be leaving John behind. She finds it difficult to get back into work on her return and John has to limit his time spent with her causing some doubt as to his affections. Mary can't help seriously worrying about him when he becomes ill at the end of the month.

Saturday 1<sup>st</sup> *'Jolly good day really except for a row I had at work with Mr B because I went early yesterday being 1<sup>st</sup> of the month. John came round in the afternoon for me and met Daddy, then we went up town and had some tea in Heelas. We then went round the shops and John bought two shirts, a gramophone record and a pair of shoes. Walked home and John came in to play his new record. Grandma and Grandad were there so of course he had to be introduced to them. After that, we went to Barbara's house and sat and played records. John and CP were teasing her the whole time. I wish I didn't feel so jealous, but I love John so deeply that I don't want to lose him.'*

Sunday 2<sup>nd</sup> *'An absolutely wonderful day. I don't think I have had such an enjoyable weekend before. I am so madly in love with John, I have never felt like this before. I am going round in circles. He called for me about three and we went round to his place and phoned for Barbara. We waited for her and then the three of us went to Sonning and watched Barbara's boyfriend CP play cricket. The three of us then went to the White Hart and had some tea. Oh dear, Barbara did make me jealous and John kept teasing her. They kept talking of all the things they had done in the past. I had an awful job just to laugh with them but I really mustn't show how jealous I am as it might frighten John away and that would break my heart. Sat and watched television at John's house all evening, I did enjoy it. Sat on settee and I don't think we concentrated very hard on the TV. After Barbara and CP had gone, John and I made some tea and we had almost finished it when his parents came home. We sat and talked for a little while. His father asked me a lot of questions about my work. I am rather frightened of him. His mother is so very sweet.'*

Monday 3rd *'Not too bad a day really. I have felt in such a good mood today. I am so much in love I seem to like even my work, which is a change. Mr B told me off again today but I didn't listen to him fully as I was dreaming of John. Saw him dinner time. It was such a nice surprise as I didn't expect to see him until tomorrow. Oh, I'm sure this is love. I have never experienced a feeling like this before. I phoned him up this evening and we talked for absolutely ages. I feel sure he likes me but I wish he would tell me so. We are going out tomorrow. Went round Edna's this evening. Longing for our holiday.'*

Tuesday 4th *'Not really a very good day today but I suppose it could have been worse. I've had an awful amount of work to do. Saw Graham dinner time and we went and had a drink in The Peacock. Had my hair set after work then John met me from the hairdresser and we went to the pictures. John was very sad this evening. He said his father told him he has got to do some studying. He said that if he was to support a wife one day, he would have to get a better job. He said he may only be able to see me at weekends and that he didn't think he would be able to come to Jersey. I am so upset. I do wish he would tell me he loves me. I am dreading my holiday now. I love him so desperately. Oh God, how I love him.'*

Wednesday 5th *'Not too bad a day I suppose really. I don't know quite know how I have lived without seeing my darling John. If it is like this for a day, I certainly don't want to go away for a fortnight. I think I will go out of my mind. I have prayed so hard to let John come to Jersey even if it is only for a week. It would be absolute paradise. I am so desperately in love with him but I do wish I knew how he felt about me. I do hope he loves me, as it would kill me if he finished with me now. Stayed in tonight and packed my case. Keith phoned today but I love only John now.'*

Thursday 6th '*Phew, I'm tired. I just don't know how to keep awake. I've had an awful lot of work to do and I have been clearing up ready to go away tomorrow. Saw my darling John dinner time. I love him so much; I'm almost dreading my holiday. Went round the shops with him to buy lots of books for him to study. He has the chance to go to the Oxford University but that means he will have to study like mad so I won't see so much of him. He made me feel as though he really does love me. He said he would worry about me while I was away and that I was to write to him when I arrived to let him know I was safe. He is going to write to me. Oh, how will I live without him for a fortnight?*'

Friday 7th '*An exciting day today although a very tiring one. We started our journey to Jersey. After work, I met Edna and Carol in the Friars Tea Bar and then went to the station to catch our train. Mummy, Daddy and also John came to see us off. I'm afraid I didn't pay much attention to Mum and Dad as I was talking to John. Anyway, got to Southampton about 8:45 and got onto the boat— the Isle of Guernsey. We had to stay on it for two and a half hours before it sailed at 11:30. Edna and Carol went off with two fellows. I was so annoyed as I was left on my own while they snuggled up with these fellows. They also had rugs and I was frozen. I felt so sick and just wanted to drop dead.*'

Saturday 8th '*Managed to get some sleep during the night for about a couple of hours. A friend of the fellows who was also an Arab stopped with me and shared his blanket but even so, I didn't like him. We arrived in Jersey this morning about eight and managed to find our hotel. It is quite nice really. We have a lovely room. After a tremendous breakfast, we went all around the shops and got lost. We walked for ages and were an hour late for dinner. This afternoon we went down to the beach and again got lost and were fairly late for tea. I don't know how I got through dinner. I felt really ill as there was such a lot of it. This evening, we were going dancing although I felt more like dying but for the third time, we lost our way so just went to the café for a drink. I don't think I have ever been so worn out. I want to sleep for years.*'

Sunday 9th '*An absolutely wonderful day. I can't remember such a hot one before. The sun has been scorching down all day long. We are all sunburnt and so terribly sore. We got up at nine and were late down for breakfast but we all feel so much better today. After an awfully big breakfast of grapefruit, bacon and eggs and toast with marmalade we went down to the sea front and sat in a deckchair until dinner time. Oh, the sun was beautiful, but we got so red. After dinner, we put on our bathing costumes under our frocks and again went down to the sea front and sunbathed. We are all so red our faces look terrible. They are so red and shiny we feel like freaks and are so sore too that I can't bear anything on my arms. I do hope the weather will keep like this for the rest of our holiday. I want to get really brown. After tea, we went on a bus to Portelet Bay and went in the inn and had a glass of Champagne each. It made us quite happy and then two fellows brought us back to the hotel in their car. Oh, I am enjoying it here. I do wish it could go on forever, although I do wish John was here. We could have such fun. I wrote to him today and I am longing to hear from him.'*

Monday 10<sup>th</sup> *'The weather hasn't been quite so nice today so we went all around town and stopped in a little café for a blackcurrant milkshake. It is so wonderful here. I would like to stay for the rest of my life. This evening Edna and Carol wanted to go dancing but I wasn't at all keen as I was quite tired but I went. We went to the West Park Pavilion, a posh place. We had a page boy to show us to our table and waiters kept coming up to us to see what we wanted to drink. The fellows were there that we met on the boat. A horrible fellow brought me home. He asked me if I had ever had intercourse with a man. I was scared stiff.'*

Tuesday 11<sup>th</sup> *'I think today has been the most exciting one so far. We took picnic lunches with us to Devils Hole. It is supposed to be full of caves but we couldn't find them so we found an almost deserted beach and had our lunch there. About 3:30 we came back to St Hellier and went down on the beach to play with our beach ball but the wind was so strong it just blew the ball away from us. So, we went to Elizabeth Castle which can only be reached when the tide is right out. It was a wonderful castle, we thoroughly enjoyed it. This evening, we went to the Forum Picture House with some fellows we met.'*

Wednesday 12<sup>th</sup> *'Another absolutely boiling hot day. We took picnic lunches again and went with some fellows to St Brelades Bay. I was with a boy called Tom, who is nice but not so nice as John. Anyway, went in for a swim with all the fellows as Edna and Carol didn't want to. Then we took a boat out. It was glorious. The sea was bright blue. After we got out of the boat, we just lay and sunbathed. Boy, are we sore now. I don't know how I managed to get back to the hotel. My legs are covered in blisters. This evening, we were again, escorted by the same boys to a dance and cabaret. Oh, my poor legs. I do hope the blisters won't burst. I look just like a beetroot and feel so ill.'*

Thursday 13<sup>th</sup> Mary is still extremely sore. *'I could hardly walk and was in real agony. I never want to go through that again.'* They go into the town and she is scared stiff that someone will knock against her legs. They stop at Fortes where Edna and Carol both have knickerbocker glories and Mary has a banana split. In the afternoon they take a long walk to get some photos and manage to take some really funny ones. Afterwards Edna and Carol go to bed but Mary decides to go to the pictures with Tom. She is a bit upset that she has not heard from John yet but hopes he will write to her soon as she made sure he had the address.

Friday 14<sup>th</sup> *'We haven't done very much again today. Went up to town in the morning and I bought a musical box for Mummy, a box of cigars for Daddy and a necklace and earrings for Sarah. I do wish I had a lot more money. I think I will have to write and ask Daddy to send me some. I wonder if he would mind. In the afternoon, Carol went out with a friend of Tom's and Edna went off to the theatre by herself so I went for a short walk with Tom, then went back to the hotel.'*

In the morning on Saturday the girls go to the beach and laze around in the sunshine. After dinner Edna goes up town by herself to undertake an awful lot of shopping leaving Mary and Carol to just bimble about. After dinner they meet two Italians on the beach who sit with them all afternoon. *'This evening, we went to get some photos and we met three fellows whose names were A, H and J. They took us all over the place in their car. We went to the airport and looked all over it; I did enjoy that. Then later on we went into a little café for coffee.'*

Sunday 16<sup>th</sup> *'Beautiful day again today. Went for an awfully long walk this morning to St Aubin's Bay which is about two miles away. We took quite a few photos. It has such beautiful scenery. We ran most of the way back along the beach. It was wonderful. The beach was completely deserted and the sand was almost white and so soft, not a stone in sight. It made us feel so fit. I really did*

*enjoy it. After lunch, we felt a bit tired so laid down on our beds for a few moments and we all fell asleep and didn't wake up until five thirty. We were annoyed at wasting an afternoon. Still, I think the sleep did us all good as we have had so many late nights since we arrived. This evening, we went out with the fellows who brought us back from the Portelet Inn last Sunday. We went to about four different inns and I quite enjoyed myself. I was with J in one car and Edna and Carol were in another with the other fellows. Later on, we went to La Corbiere. Edna and Carol were scared stiff as these fellows turned out to be rotters. I can't say I was any too happy myself. I think J was a bit tipsy because I had to steer the car back home.'*

Mary has her hair done on Monday 17th and has some *'blondie pieces done. It looks lovely.'* They then have a lazy day and just sit on the beach as it is beautiful and sunny. Mary comments how she is now getting lovely and brown and is so hoping to go back to work with a lovely tan. In the evening, they frequent the Forum Picture House to watch "Forbidden Planet" which Mary says is *'jolly good but awfully scary. Oh, I am so enjoying this holiday, I don't want it to end.'*

Tuesday 18th they all go up to town again to do more shopping *'we are all nearly broke worst luck.'* Then go down to the beach in the afternoon and just lay in the hot sun. *'Oh, it is wonderful. I am dreading going back to work. I don't ever want to see the bank again. This evening, I went to the pictures with A to see Robert Mitcham at the Odeon. It was jolly good. After that, we drove to St Bouley Bay then Rozel Bay. Didn't get back until 2:00am. Phew, am I tired.'*

Wednesday 19th *'Beautifully hot day again today. We are all quite brown and I am peeling terribly. I do hope I won't peel completely before I go home. Went on the beach again all morning and again after lunch and I went in for a swim with one of the Italians we met the other day. The water was freezing to get into but once I was in, it was lovely and warm. I did enjoy it although I had a bit of a job getting dressed afterwards.'* Going out in the evening to a dance at the Ritz, Mary meets a tall, dark and handsome doctor but comments how he turned out to be *'a bad lot too.'*

She writes letters home on Thursday 20th and pops to the Post Office to send them. They then have a mooch around the town until lunch time. Edna then washes her hair while Mary and Carol go on to the beach. After dinner they all go off on a pub crawl visiting different inns with the fellows they had met. Unfortunately, Edna has a row with one of them cutting the tour short.

Friday 21ˢᵗ '*Another jolly good day today although feeling rather sad as we go back to Reading tomorrow. I am dreading going back although I am longing to see John again. We stayed in this morning to do all our packing. We had an awful job to do our cases up. We tried to get our big cases down to the docks ready for tomorrow but they were too heavy so we will have to get a taxi tomorrow. Went round town this afternoon for the last time then ordered the taxi for seven fifteen tomorrow. Edna went to bed after dinner so Carol and I went for a coffee at the Grimbles.*'

The girls are on the boat at seven twenty the next morning which sails at eight. They arrive back in Southampton around five fifteen having had a good crossing and are glad that none of them felt ill. The customs man makes Mary turn out her pockets which scares her a bit. They then catch a train from Southampton and arrive in Basingstoke at five past six where they wait until seven forty to catch the train to Reading. '*John came to meet me at the station and threw his arms around me and kissed me. Oh, I love him so much. I never knew I could love anyone so much.*'

Sunday 23ʳᵈ '*A wonderful day really although I am a little disappointed our wonderful holiday has come to an end. I can't remember when I have ever enjoyed anything more. We are hoping to go to Spain and if we do, I am hoping*

John will perhaps come with us (I hope John will still be going out with me then). It would also be nice if Mike and Rob could come as well. I expect we would have some fun. Went round to Grandmas and Grandad's this morning to give them their presents. Jean and her husband were round. I don't like them very much. I tried to go to Sarah's afterwards but couldn't get a bus. After lunch, John came round for me and we went to Sonning Golf Club to see some golf clubs for his birthday and then went for tea in the White Hart Hotel. I did enjoy it. I am so much in love with John but I do wish he would tell me how he feels about me. I know he likes me but I'm not at all sure how much. We came back to Florida Court and I tidied myself up then we went round to John's house and watched television for the rest of the evening. His parents are so nice. I need a new evening dress for John's birthday party and am hoping Daddy will lend me some money.'

Monday 24th sees Mary return to work commenting how she makes a lot of mistakes. 'An absolutely horrible day today. I just haven't known which way to turn. At least, I had thought all rows had been forgotten while I was on holiday, but just as I was leaving work, Mr B called me over to him and we had a proper row. He said I would have to leave the bank if I didn't pull my socks up, I nearly cried. I know myself and I am going faster now than I have ever done. There is so much more work in this section. It is all I can do to manage it all. Still, I will have to stick up for myself a bit more. Went to Friars Tea Bar after work with Edna and Carol. Saw Ray this evening too but I don't like him.'

Tuesday 25th 'A bit better day today thank goodness. Mr B has been so nice to me. I think perhaps he is frightened I might leave, because I told him yesterday, I didn't like my job now. I do really, I suppose although it is an awful worry. Oh dear, it does seem ages since I saw John last. I can't really see him during the week as he has so much studying to do. I wonder if our little love story will ever come to anything. I do hope it will as I am really in love this time. It is a wonderful feeling and I wouldn't care who knew I went out with him. Went out with Keith this evening but was thinking about John all the time.'

Wednesday 26th 'Not too bad a day today really, I suppose. I am missing my John terribly. It seems worse than the fortnight I was away. I think I will go crazy soon if I don't see him. I don't think I can wait until Saturday. Mr B has been so nice to me again today. It makes such a nice change. Auntie O, Grandma and Sandy came round this evening and Auntie O said she would send me an evening frock to see if would be alright to wear to John's party. I am going to try to get Daddy to lend me some money to get a new one as I do want to look nice.'

Thursday 27<sup>th</sup> 'Today has seemed so terribly long. Oh dear, I am missing John so much. I don't think I can have another week like this one. There hasn't been a minute gone past without me thinking about John. I think this must really be love at last. I have never felt quite like this before. I do wish he would tell me how he feels about me though, as I am not really sure. He has had so many other girlfriends; I am wondering just how long this is going to last. I had a letter from Tom today (the boy I met in Jersey). He is rather sweet, but not as nice as John. I went out with Keith for a short while this evening. I wish it had been John. I am absolutely longing for Saturday. I do hope he meets me from work.'

Friday 28<sup>th</sup> 'Another terribly long day. I am feeling so ill and fed up. I have such a horrible cold; it is making me feel like doing away with myself. I don't know when I have missed anyone quite so much as I have missed John this week, it has seemed an eternity. I do hope he meets me from work tomorrow. I don't think I can bear not seeing him much longer. I will have to try to get him to come out at least once a week with me. I just can't go on staying in every night because as the saying goes—all work and no play! I am looking forward to John's party on the ninth.'

Saturday 29<sup>th</sup> 'Not too bad a day today I suppose. Had an awful lot of work. I was expecting John to meet me from work at dinner time but he didn't turn up. I was so disappointed. Anyway, though perhaps he would call this evening. Went with Daddy up the Warren to pick blackberries and got quite a lot but we both got scratched and bitten, nonetheless I quite enjoyed it. After tea, I just sat and wondered why John hadn't come and thought he had finished with me. I was nearly in tears when Mike and Edna came round and told me that John was in bed with a temperature of 103 so we went round to Barbara's and watched television. I am awfully worried about John being ill but am thrilled that he hasn't finished with me.'

Sunday 30<sup>th</sup> *'Quite a good day really apart from the fact that I haven't seen my darling John. I wonder if he really does love me. I only hope and pray that he does. Got up early this morning and went riding with Doris. Phew, it was hard work. I had to do exercises on the back of the horse like standing up without reins or stirrups and then laying back on the horse without holding etc. At least, I am off the leading rein now. I love riding the horses so much but I am so stiff though. Phone Mrs Kean up afterwards to see how John was. He is a little better although he still has a high temperature. I do hope he'll be alright. Went round to Grandmas this afternoon to take her some of the blackberries and stayed all afternoon. I quite enjoyed myself. This evening after tea went to meet Mike, Rob and Edna and we all went to the Palomino for a coke. Then we went to the Twenty Club and listened to some jazz records, then back to Mike's place to watch TV. I love John!'*

## OCTOBER

Being invited to John's 21<sup>st</sup> Birthday party this month is a highlight for Mary, resulting in her investing in a new frock but sadly she has the biggest disappointment of her life on 8<sup>th</sup>. With work still incredibly busy and challenging Mary gets into trouble for being rude to one of her bosses. She also tries to come to terms with the depth of her feelings for her new love.

Monday 1<sup>st</sup> *'A terribly busy day today as it's the first of the month and we have had so much extra work. I have also been worrying about John all day. I do hope he will be alright; I just don't know what I would do if anything happened to him. I haven't liked to phone his mother again today so I will have to phone up tomorrow dinner time. Went to the Palomino with Edna and Carol this evening, but we bumped into Ray so I went for a walk with him round the Forbury for a short while. I didn't want to go really as I don't like him at all. I will have to tell John I saw him.'*

Tuesday 2<sup>nd</sup> *'An awful lot of work again today. I really don't know how to get through it all. I was going to phone John up dinner time but he phoned me first. He sounded quite worried as he said he thought I had forgotten him because I didn't phone him yesterday! Anyway, he told me to phone his mother this afternoon and ask if I could go and see him this evening. So, I did. I bought some grapes and went round about 8:15. Oh, it was heaven to see John again. I love him so desperately. We just sat and chatted until 11:45. I don't know what we found to talk about but I enjoyed every minute of it. John is so wonderful and I have never felt like this before.'*

Wednesday 3$^{rd}$ *'Another terribly busy day but I managed to get through it a lot easier today. It was seeing John yesterday. Went in to Sarah's today to book six appointments for Mummy to have her hair done as a birthday present. I couldn't afford a big present this time, I do feel awful. Went round John's again this evening and stayed for about an hour and a half. Oh, I do love him so very much and this is the very first time I have felt I would really like to get married. Daddy lent me five pounds today and Auntie V gave me two to help me get an evening frock for John 21$^{st}$ birthday party on Tuesday.'*

Having had another busy day at work Mary comments how happy she is lately *'I feel happier than I have for literally years now. I don't know why God bothers with me as I have really been so wicked in the past, although I am trying so hard now to be really good. I went to London this evening with Edna and Carol to C&A's to get an evening dress. I got a lovely long pink one and a lovely little fur cape to go on top of it. I am so thrilled and excited I just don't know whether I am on my head or my heels. Haven't seen John today worst luck but still, I am going to phone him tomorrow.'*

Friday 5$^{th}$ Mary acknowledges in her diary that she has seen a change in herself since her holiday. *'A terrific change has come over me since my holiday. I really must have been ill before as I was so miserable at the least little thing. I don't seem to mind the work now either. Phoned John up this evening and told him about my dress. Oh God how much I love him. I do wish he would tell me he loves me. It would make me the happiest girl in the world. Went out with Keith for a short while this evening. I do wish I could get rid of him as I do so want to be really good, I am praying to God to help me to be. I expect I will see John tomorrow thank goodness.'*

Saturday 6$^{th}$ *'Apart from the fact that I had an awful lot of work this morning, today has been very good. Went down to Grandma's after dinner to invite her to tea to see my frock but she couldn't come. After leaving her, I went round to Edna's and stayed there for ages. We are both terribly scared about the party on*

*Tuesday. Went round to John's this evening and sat and watched TV all evening. Oh, he is the most wonderful boy I have ever known. He is simply heavenly. I love him from the bottom of my heart. I only hope he won't ever finish with me. I don't know how I would carry on living if he ever did. Oh God, how I love him.'*

On Sunday Mary goes round to see her Grandparents in the morning to invite them to tea this afternoon to see her frock. *'Uncle T and G were round there and I did feel stupid. After leaving there, I went back home and had my dinner and then went down the road and phoned my John up. I was disappointed though as he couldn't come out this afternoon or this evening as he told me his father had told him he had to sew sequins on his mother's frock. I think that is a horrible excuse—if it was an excuse. I am so terribly muddled. I can't make out if he loves me or not. I won't be seeing him now until Tuesday. I am looking forward to it so much and am longing for John to see me in my new frock. Although I say it myself, I look quite good in it, anyway I feel good in it. Grandma came to tea and I put on my frock to show her, then I played Monopoly by myself for the rest of the evening as I was so bored.'*

Monday 8th *'I think I have had the biggest disappointment in my whole life today. Richard and Stella came round this evening to tell me John was in hospital so won't be coming to the party tomorrow which is still going ahead. He is quite ill and I feel so unhappy. I had a good cry but I still don't feel any better. I am hoping we can visit him on the way to the party tomorrow. I shall be so miserable all evening. I will be the only one without a partner. It just won't be the same without my darling John. Why did this happen just now. Oh, if this is love, I don't think much of it, I'm so unhappy.'* John was suffering with a blood clot in his left leg.

Tuesday 9th *'Well, went to the party this evening. We didn't manage to see John before going and I was so disappointed. The party was a lovely one really. Richard came to call for me. He did look nice but I wish with all my heart that it had been John. I had nearly all the dances but felt so unhappy all evening. Mr and Mrs Kean were so nice to me. Mr Kean kept telling me how pretty I was and that he thought I was the prettiest little girl there. I felt so pleased but so upset that John couldn't see me. I had to go out of the room after all the speeches and toasts as I know I would have burst out crying otherwise. I love John so desperately; I would have given the world for him to have been there. Mr Kean made the photographer take a photo of me especially for John, I was so pleased.'*

Wednesday 10th *'A terribly long day today. I have been thinking about my darling John all the time. I know definitely that he is THE ONE for me. I love him so desperately. Saw Mike dinnertime and I gave him a letter to give to John as he was going up to see him this afternoon. Saw Mike again this evening with Edna and he said John was feeling a bit better thank goodness. Apparently, Mr and Mrs Kean and Richard were there and Mike said Mr Kean had told him what*

*a nice girl I was. I seem to have made a hit with him thank goodness. I only hope I have with John too. I do wish I knew how he feels about me. I love him so much and I know I couldn't go on living if he ever gave me up. I am so upset and unhappy.'*

Thursday 11th is another terribly long day with Mary still thinking about John every five minutes and it is getting worse. It feels like an eternity since she saw him last and can't stand being without him much longer. Mike invites her to the pictures in the evening with Edna and Rob and she's glad of the distraction. She sees Keith after work and makes an excuse not to go out with him. She also sees Norman for a short while and comments how she doesn't like him at all now and only wants John. She loves him more than words can say.

Friday 12th *'I never ever want another day like today has been. I don't think I have ever been so miserable and worried before in my life. I don't think I have stopped thinking of my darling John for more than five minutes all day. Oh, I* love him more than words can say, I have definitely never felt like this before. I saw Edna this evening in the Friars Tea Bar and we arranged to go up to see John tomorrow, but when I got home, Mummy told me Richard had been round to see if I wanted to go with them, so I went round to tell them I would and they invited me to watch TV. I stayed the rest of the evening and Richard had his arm around me all evening.'

Saturday 13<sup>th</sup> 'Oh, I am so thrilled. Saw my darling John this afternoon. I nearly passed out though as we had to put masks on to go in and see him. He did look ill. I longed to take him in my arms and kiss him. Went to a party with Richard and Stella this evening. It was a smashing party. I got awfully tight. I was learning to jive; it was jolly good although could hardly stand up. I do wish John could have come. It would have been wonderful. PB was teaching me to jive, he kissed me quite a few times too. He is nice, I do like him but it is John who I love and couldn't live without now.'

Sunday 14<sup>th</sup> 'Richard came round this morning and I had only just got up (11:35). He asked me if I would like to go up to see John again this afternoon. Of course, I said yes. So, I went round after dinner and Richard took me to the hospital picking Stella up on the way. He and Stella went in first to see John, it seemed an eternity waiting for them to come out. Then Richard came out and went off home to pick his parents up and I went in to see my darling John. I was so pleased as he seemed a lot better today. He was a lot more cheerful thank goodness. He really looked ill yesterday. We didn't have to wear the masks today so I think he must be getting better. I am looking forward so much to him coming out. Richard told me John had said he wants to marry me. Oh, I only hope that is true. I would marry him tomorrow if he wanted me to. I love him so very, very much. This evening Stella and I went into the Palomino by ourselves as Richard has gone to Worthing with his parents. PB was in there. He walked us back to Stella's bus stop then walked all the way home with me. He asked me to go out with him and kissed me hundreds of times. He is nice but I am in love with John.'

9, Florida Court,
Bath Road,
Reading,
Berks

Saturday

My Dearest John,

I felt I just had to write to let you know how sorry I am about your leg, and also how disappointed I am at the thought of you staying in hospital for another month.

I'm afraid I was absolutely dumbstruck in hospital this afternoon. I don't think I even asked you how you were feeling. You must think I am terrible. I am not usually so quiet as that. I just don't know what was the matter

with me.

I do hope you are well and able to come out of hospital long before the month is up, it is quite lonely without you, although by the look of all your fan mail and the day and night nurses, I don't think you are doing too badly at all. I think I will have to get something wrong with me so that I can come in and keep an eye on you.

Did you like the photographs? I thought they were all very good especially some of the

Back at work on Monday 15ᵗʰ '*Quite a good day really, I suppose except for the fact that I have been missing my darling John so very much. I love him so deeply and every minute away from him seems like a year. I just don't know how I can last out until Saturday. Went round Stella's this evening. Ann came too and we watched television most of the evening. Then, Stella and Ann wrote a letter to my John on Stella's typewriter, it was a funny letter, but somehow, I felt so jealous. I would love to have stopped them from posting it. Oh, why do I have to be so jealous? I suppose it is because I love John so passionately. I only hope he loves me too.'*

Tuesday 16ᵗʰ '*Another terribly long day again today. I don't think five minutes have gone by without me thinking of my darling John. I have his photo in front of me now and can hardly take my eyes off it long enough to write this. Oh, I love him so very much, I just can't put the full depth of my love for him into words. I know this is the real thing at last. John is the only one for me. I had a letter from LH yesterday. I feel sorry for him but I just can't do anything about it. I am so deeply in love with John that even if he gave me up, I could never really love anyone else now. I am praying to God to make John love me as much as I love him.'*

324

Wednesday 17<sup>th</sup> *'Oh dear, I just don't know how to carry on living. I have never felt so desperately lonely and unhappy. I am missing John more than words can say. Saw Stella and Richard in the Palomino this evening and they say that John is very cheerful. Apparently, the nurses are all pretty and keep giving him little things. Stella says he is quite enjoying himself. That makes me even more unhappy as he can't be missing me at all. I am longing for him to come out of hospital. I love him with every ounce of love I have.'*

Thursday 18<sup>th</sup> *'I've had too much work today to notice the time thank goodness. Oh, I do wish Saturday would hurry up and come. I am longing to see my John again. I do hope he hasn't forgotten me. I think it would kill me if he gave me up now. I love him so desperately. I wonder if he really does love me. I am praying so hard to God to make him. I don't want anything else at all, but to marry John. I really am in love with him. Went to the Palomino with PB this evening, then he walked me home. He kept kissing me. I have told him I will go to the pictures with him tomorrow. He is nice but I love only John. I am wondering how to back out of going.'*

Friday 19<sup>th</sup> *'A terrible day today really. I had an awful row with Mr B at work today and I was horribly rude to him. I just couldn't help myself. I do wish I could control my temper. Went to the pictures this evening with PB. Now I am so worried in case John gets to hear of it. It would break my heart if John gave me up now as I love him so desperately. PB is awfully nice. I love the way he calls me 'darling' and 'pet' it makes me go all queer. I do wish John would call me that. I told Mum and Dad I was going to the pictures with Edna and just my luck they happened to see her. They asked me so many questions. Boy! Did I have to think quick. Going to see John tomorrow thank goodness. I do love him so.'*

Saturday 20<sup>th</sup> *'Awfully busy morning this morning. I just don't know how I got through all my work. It really is too much. I went to see my darling John this afternoon. He is much better, thank goodness and is a lot more cheerful. I am so jealous of the lovely nurses though. He seems to be enjoying himself and I don't think has missed me at all really, even though I miss him terribly. Ann came round this evening and we sat and looked at loads of photographs and read all my old love letters. Then I showed her some of my diary. I think I just felt like showing someone. She is the first person ever to see my diary. I am worried about PB as I was supposed to meet him this evening. He is nice.'*

Sunday 21st *'A day of ups and downs today really. I had to cook the dinner this morning as Mummy has a horrible cold and stayed in bed. It didn't turn out too badly. Richard came round for about five minutes to let me know about going to the hospital this afternoon. Anyway, we went to the hospital and I'm glad to say, John is a lot better. I think he will only be in hospital for about another fortnight but if this fortnight is as long as the last one has been, I just don't know how I will last out. I do wish I knew if he loves me or not. He just doesn't give me any indication at all. Stella was flirting with him a lot, much to my annoyance and Edna had written to him and sent him some peaches. I do wish she hadn't. After all, it's not quite the thing to do really as he isn't anything to her. Oh dear, I do wish I wasn't so jealous. I will have to try to get out of it. Had a bit of a row with Mummy and Daddy when I got back as Daddy moved my bedroom furniture about and I didn't like it, so I went down to the Palomino by myself. I didn't have the nerve to go in so I walked backwards and forwards outside for ages and was just about to go home when I saw Edna and we went in together and had a cup of coffee. Sat next to a Sam and Alec from the bank. They are very nice but I love my John best.'*

Monday 22nd *'Awful day today really. I had such a lot of work and it is wearing me out completely. Had to go to Mr I this afternoon. I was in his office with Mr B and the other Mr B for about twenty minutes. Phew, did I get told off. It was to do with the row I had with Mr B on Friday. He had told Mr I how rude I was, oh dear. I have been working harder than I have ever done before. It is Mr B that upsets me. He is such a stupid little man who wants too much waiting on. I have been thinking of my darling John all day and wondering if he really loves me or not. I do so hope and pray that he does. Saw Keith after work. I wish I could finish with him.'*

Tuesday 23rd *'Quite a good day all around really. Mr B, Mr I and Mr B have all been so very nice to me today. I just couldn't do anything wrong today. Mr B, bless him, has given me tomorrow afternoon off instead of Saturday morning so that I can go and see my darling John. I am so thrilled as it seems such a long time until Saturday. I nearly kissed him when he said I could have it off. I went into Friars Tea Bar with Graham this evening. I knew nearly all the fellows in there. PB was in there and he talked to me for quite a while. I do like him. Sarah came round this evening and I showed her my evening dress. She did like it.'*

Wednesday 24<sup>th</sup> *'Quite a good day I suppose. Had an awful lot of work to do this morning as I had the afternoon off. I went to see my darling John. Oh God how I love him. I have never felt like this before. I have the feeling that he doesn't love me though. Oh, how I hope and pray to God to make him. It would break my heart if he gave me up now. I just don't know what I would do. I went to the pictures this evening by myself and saw Alan Ladd in "The Black Knight". It was a jolly good film but I did feel lonely in there. I was longing for my John to be with me. Mum said LH came round this evening.'*

Thursday 25<sup>th</sup> *'A terribly busy day again today. I just don't know how I have got through all my work. I will have a nervous breakdown if I don't have less work before long. I have been thinking about my John today and wondering if I can really be in love with him. I don't really know him at all. Most of the time I have known him, he has been ill or else I have been away. I do wish he would hurry up out of hospital so that I can really find out if he is the one for me. At the moment I am almost sure that he is. I hope he loves me too. Saw PB this evening and said I would go to the pictures with him tomorrow.'*

Friday 26<sup>th</sup> *'A fairly good day today really, although I've still had an awful lot of work to do. Had a letter from LH today and it was quite a horrible one too. I just don't know how I am going to answer it. I will definitely have to finish it completely. I can't keep him in suspense any longer. I saw Richard dinner time and told him I wouldn't be going to the hospital in the afternoon but will be going in the evening. I am longing for it to come as it will be the first time I have seen my darling John alone for quite three weeks. I have almost forgotten what he kisses like. I went to the pictures with PB this evening. He is sweet but I love only John.'*

Saturday 27<sup>th</sup> *'Jolly good day today all around. I left work at 12:30 and went up to London with Mummy, Daddy and Grandma to see Cinerama but we couldn't get in, so just went for some tea and then came back to Reading. Went to Grandma's for about an hour, then Mummy and Daddy went off to the pictures and I went up to the hospital to see my darling John. Oh, it was heaven. It was the first time I have seen him alone for three weeks. It was all I could do to stop myself from throwing my arms around him and kissing him. I do so hope and pray that he loves me. He is the only one for me I know. Thank goodness I will see him again tomorrow. I do love him.'*

Sunday 28th *'Jolly good day again today really. I didn't get up until ten thirty. When I eventually did get myself up, I made a sponge cake and some buns and then wrote a letter to LH telling him I definitely wanted to finish our engagement. I know I have done the right thing, as I could never have married him because I love John so desperately. Went to see John in hospital this afternoon. Richard came round for me at two thirty and I went in his parents' car with his mother, father, himself and two of his friends. While we were waiting to go in, Mike and Rob came up so I was in the car with five boys. All six of us went into the ward but three of them got turned out. Later on, Barbara, Stella and Colin came in so in the end there were seven of us in the ward all at once. My darling John was in bright spirits thank goodness. It is so wonderful to see him looking so well again. He kissed Barbara goodbye as she is going to Cyprus on Thursday and then he kissed me. It was the first time for three weeks. Oh, it was paradise. I have never felt this way before. Went to the Palomino with Stella and Ann this evening. Richard came in and had a row with Stella and told her he had finished with her. PB took me home. Saw Sam and Alec in there. They are both so nice.'*

Monday 29th *'Another jolly good day really. Met Stella dinner time as she was going to get me some roses for John, but she couldn't get any till tomorrow. Went into Friars with Sam and Alec this evening, they are both fun. After they had gone, I stood and talked to Rob and Carol who were in there. Then Ray came in and we stood and talked for a while, then PB came in. Rob and Carol went and left me with the two of them. Anyway, I got rid of Ray and arranged to go to PB's for the evening. After P had gone, Ray was waiting for me and silly me, I arranged to go to the pictures with him. Saw Ray later this evening and told him I couldn't go. Met PB and went back with him to his house. A friend of his was there and we sat and watched TV. I still love only my darling John though. He is the only one for me. I simply know it.'*

Tuesday 30th *'An awfully busy day at work today. The inspectors have torn up half my statements. I had such a hard job to keep my temper but thank goodness it didn't get too much out of hand. Bought my John some red roses today and wrote a little verse to go with them. After tea, I took them up to the hospital but they wouldn't let me see him. It does seem ages till next weekend when I will see him again. After I had been to the hospital, I waited for PB and we went into the Palomino, then back to his place where he turned off all the lights as we were alone. He is very nice but what I feel for him isn't as strong as the way I feel for John. I love John with all my heart.'*

Wednesday 31st *'I feel so unhappy today. I've had so much work to do and am worried about it all the time now as it is just too much. I don't think I can keep up with it much longer. PB came round for me this evening and we went to the Palomino to meet Stella and Ann. Stella made me so jealous as she said John held her hand this afternoon and kissed her and she said she is going on Friday evening to see him again. I am so upset. Just the thought of her in with John alone makes me seethe. I am almost mad with jealousy because I know Stella inside out and I know all her thoughts and can imagine what she will say to him. If anything, or anyone made him finish with me I would seriously end my life. I am so worried and do wish I knew how John felt about me. I feel so terribly ill.'*

## NOVEMBER

A great month for Mary when she attends an enjoyable Ball on 2nd and John finally coming out of hospital. She changes sections at the bank relieving the pressure of too much work and has the most perfect 19th birthday on 27th. Mary also tentatively allows John to read some of her diary.

Thursday 1st *'Wonderful evening, in fact jolly good day all around I suppose. Had an awful lot of work but managed to get through it somehow. I went with Stella, Ann and Shirley to a dance at the police station this evening. It was jolly good. They had a small sort of show before the dancing. It was good and then we had the dance. A fellow tacked himself onto me, he wasn't bad I suppose but I kept thinking of John and wishing he was there with me. There was a cabaret after the dance which was good, and then Stella and Shirley found some fellows with a car so they could give us a lift home. This fellow that was with me came and kissed me goodnight. He said he was going to write to me.'*

Friday 2<sup>nd</sup> *'Never before in my whole life have I had such a perfect evening. It is one I will remember for the rest of my days. Went to the Olympia to the SLY Ball with Jeff, Sam, Alec and about nine other fellows. I was paid so much attention and flattered so much I just couldn't believe it was really happening. I got really tipsy and had so many drinks which were all mixed too. At one point in the evening, I had three sitting on my lap at one time and at the same time two others were pulling at my hands. 'Oh, it was heavenly. They were absolutely all over me. Jeff was definitely the best. I had so many dances with him including the last waltz in which we just stood in the middle of the floor with our arms all around each other. They quarrelled as to who should take me home and I chose Jeff as he is wonderful. I don't know when I have ever had so much male attention at one time. Stewart was shocking and I thought that he was such a quiet boy but apparently, I was mistaken. He was quite tipsy too and was sitting on my lap trying to balance a glass of ale on my head. They all wanted to take me home and I had a job to keep their hands off me. I went to the cloakroom to do my hair after they had all been mauling me about but just couldn't see in the mirror properly so just had to leave it. Jeff on the way home kept kissing me. He kisses so wonderfully. He is quite a bad lad too. The dance ended at 2 and I didn't get home until about 3 o'clock. I don't think I thought of my John all evening.'*

Saturday 3<sup>rd</sup> *'I say, my poor head this morning, it is splitting, but even so I wouldn't have missed last night for all the world. Jeff and the rest have told nearly everyone in the bank about it and I am quite the centre of attraction at the moment. Went with Mr and Mrs Kean to see John this afternoon. He really is the one I love. He had just thanked me for my roses and was just getting so nice and close when an ex-girlfriend came to see him—Susan. He spent the rest of the time talking to her. I do wish I knew how much he liked me. Went down the town afterwards to get Sarah a birthday card and saw Sam, Alec and three of the fellows from last night. They were all over me again and want me to go with them to the Police Ball next Friday. I will certainly go, as they are such fun.'*

Sunday 4<sup>th</sup> *'Not too bad a day today. I didn't get up until eleven forty-five. I went to see my darling John this afternoon. Oh, he really is wonderful. I love him so much. I do wish he would hurry up out of hospital, I am missing him so much. I am sure he really does like me but I do wish he would tell me so. I would love to hear him tell me he loves me. When I got home, Sarah was there. We both had a terrible row with Auntie V. She just got up and went off home. Poor Mummy was so upset. Went down to the Palomino this evening to meet PB. He was having some friends up at his house so he couldn't stay out long. He took me home; he is so nice. Going to the Police Ball on Thursday.'*

Monday 5th *'A terribly busy day today. Don't know how I have managed to get through it all. I didn't leave off until six forty-five. Phew, am I tired. Didn't do anything this evening, but sat in front of the fire with Mummy and Daddy and read a book, then at nine o'clock I got myself ready for bed and listened to Radio Luxembourg. I have thought such a lot about my darling John today. I feel sure I love him, and yet in the back of my mind I feel I am much too young to realise just what real love is. I feel so strongly towards all the other fellows I go out with too, like Sam, Jeff, Alec and PB. I like them all so much. I wonder who I will really end up with in the end.'*

Tuesday 6th *'Another terribly busy day again today. I have so much to do. I think it is absolutely impossible for me to get through it all. They really ought to let someone take one of my ledgers off me. Jeff hasn't been at work for the last two days. I am longing for him to come back. I like him so much although I still love only my John. I haven't found anyone to beat him yet. I have thought such a lot about him again today, I do wish he would write to me. I would so love to hear from him. Went to the FTB after work. Colin was in there. He is pining for Barbara. He walked to my bus with me and we consoled each other. He is nice. I went to the Palomino with Edna this evening. After that, we bought ourselves 4d chips and had a good feed.'*

Wednesday 7th *'Jolly good day really. Had an awful lot of work to do though, but I managed to get partly through it thank goodness. Jeff phoned me up this morning as he is on holiday. He asked me if I would go to the Olympia with him tomorrow. I agreed. Stewart phoned me up just afterwards to ask the same question. I told him I would see him in there. Met him dinner time as I wasn't sure if I could get a ticket or not. He told me how much he liked me. He's not bad but I like Jeff best. Richard came round this evening to tell me John is coming* out of hospital tomorrow. I am so thrilled. I really do love him so much. I know he is definitely the only one for me. I am wondering how to put PB off now.'

Thursday 8th *'Not too bad a day. Quite a jolly good evening. Went to the Olympia and wore my long frock. Stella and Richard met me and I sat with them at a table. Then Jeff, Alec, Sam, Stewart and JB came and I was with them part of the time. Freddie and Graham were also there and I danced with them. It was a bit of a muddle really as Mr and Mrs Kean were there as well. I do wish John had been. I still like him best and have never doubted that I love him. I went outside with Jeff in the interval, he is nice. I did the rumba for the first time this evening. I didn't quite know what I was doing but nobody seemed to notice. Jeff walked me home about 2:45. I am tired.'*

On Friday 9th Mary is so tired she has a job to keep herself awake. *'I phoned my John up yesterday before going to the dance. I have a horrible feeling that he doesn't really like me at all really. I don't think he cares for me at all and it hurts terribly. I love him so desperately and it would kill me if he ever gave me up. He is the only boyfriend I have had that I have ever wanted to marry. I wonder if my dream will ever come true. I do so hope so. Went to the Palomino this evening with Ann. Saw Freddie and Graham this evening. They took us home and arranged to take us tomorrow to the party.'*

Saturday 10th *'I have been so disappointed today as John hasn't got in touch with me. I can't stand being without him much longer and think I will have to give him up before he finishes with me. I just can't go on wondering whether he loves me or not any longer. Went to a party this evening with Ann, Stella and Shirley. John was supposed to have gone but was too tired. PB was there and he got quite annoyed because I was mucking around with Freddie and Graham. Went for a drive with Graham during the evening. He wasn't bad. Later on, I did a bit of jiving with PB, then sat in a room holding both PB's and Freddie's hands at the same time. PB took me home afterwards. He forgave me. At least I know, he likes me which is something I can't say about John. I got quite drunk this evening.'*

Sunday 11th *'Wonderful day today. John came round this morning and I was still in bed. Never got ready so quickly before. He stayed for about two and a half hours. Oh, it was wonderful and I felt so happy. I had my dinner then prepared myself for another long wait before seeing him again. I had just sat down trying to mend my work overall when Stella came round. She was on her way round to see Richard and stopped for about fifteen minutes then went. I thought how lucky she was to be able to see John as well. Anyway, I settled back to my overall when the bell rang again. This time it was John, Richard and Stella who had come to take me out. I was thrilled. We went back to John's house and sat and played records all afternoon and evening. John had his arm round me most of the time but he does flirt with Stella terribly and she with him. It makes me furious and so jealous. He kept putting his arm around her too. And stuck up for her every time Richard said anything against her. I think he at least likes me now but I have that horrible feeling at the back of my mind that he doesn't really want me. I feel sure he likes Stella a lot better than me. I do wish he would tell me he loves me. I love him so much.'*

Mary feels a bit miserable on Monday as she hasn't seen anything of John today. *'Went into the Friars after work this evening and saw Stella and Ann in there. Also, Freddie and Graham. Ann invited me round to her lodgings this evening, so at about eight o'clock, I went. It is a lovely house; she has such a sweet little bedroom. Stayed there about an hour and then we went to the Palomino. We stayed in there about one and a half hours and talked to two fellows Ann knows and they took us home in their car. I do wish it had been John.'*

Tuesday 13<sup>th</sup> *'Another fairly busy day today. We are changing sections tomorrow thank goodness, so perhaps I won't have quite so much work to do. Went into Friars again this evening after work and once again, saw Stella and Ann. They said they were going to the Palomino about eight o'clock, so I went down and waited in the Butts for about half an hour for them but they didn't turn up, so I walked up Broad Street and met Sam and Alec. They asked me to go and have a drink with them in the Boar's Head so I went. It was quite good but I would rather have been with my darling John. Stewart was in there and he took me home afterwards. I don't like him at all as he is so silly. I only love my darling John.'*

Wednesday 14<sup>th</sup> *'Wonderful day or should I say wonderful evening. Changed sections today thank goodness. What a relief! I have hardly any work to do at all. Went to Friars after work with Edna, Carol and Rob, and made arrangements with Edna to go to the Palomino later. Anyway, after tea I went round to Edna's for her and off, we went. We were sitting there talking when in walked my darling John. Oh, it was wonderful to see him. Richard had the car and John made him take the other girls home first. While Richard was saying goodbye to Stella, John and I had the car to ourselves. He has convinced me that he likes me!'*

Thursday 15<sup>th</sup> Mary goes into the Friars with Edna after work and sees Richard in there *'he is going to ask John to come and see me tomorrow to arrange about the dance. I promised to meet Edna at 8:15 so that I wouldn't be alone with Graham. Oh, it was so awkward. Graham came to meet me about eight and he took me down to meet Edna. Anyway, Edna wanted to go to the Palomino and Graham didn't, I felt terribly mean as I had told her I would go with her. Anyway, while Edna was walking on slowly to the Palomino, Graham and I went off to the Swan in Pangbourne to have a couple of drinks. He is awfully nice but I have such a guilty conscience about Edna. I don't deserve John at all. I am so horrible.'*

Friday 16<sup>th</sup> *'A perfectly wonderful evening. I went to the Olympia with my darling John. Wore my long frock. It was the first time he'd seen it and he did like it. We did three of the dances and then John's leg begun to hurt so Mr Kean took us back to his house and then went back to the dance leaving us alone. It was wonderful. We made ourselves some coffee, then sat on the settee and cuddled each other. Stella was awfully jealous at us going back to the house alone. She wanted to come but Richard didn't want to. I am so glad as I loved being with my John so much. At least I know, he really likes me. Mrs Kean was so nice to me. She told me how lovely I looked.'*

Saturday 17<sup>th</sup> *'Wonderful evening, wonderful day altogether. My John met me from work and we went round all the shops looking for a coat for me. We got one in the end and it was John's choice. I like it but it wouldn't have been the one I would have chosen. Anyway, it had to be altered a bit so we went and did a bit more shopping, and then went home for dinner around 2:50. After dinner,*

*John came round for me and we went back down to the town, collected my coat then went to the pictures. It was wonderful and the first time for quite some months. I am so very much in love with John, I can't think of anything else. John came home with me afterwards and Mum and Dad went off to bed and left us alone. At least, I feel that John at least likes me. I am so thrilled.'*

Sunday 18th *'A most wonderful heavenly day. I am so happy I could cry. John came round for me this morning and we went to church. It was nice. Afterwards John came back home with me until it was time for lunch, then off he went home. In the afternoon, Stella came round for me to go to the John's house. When we got there, we sat and watched television for a while, then had tea. It was a jolly good tea. After that, we played a few records and then watched a play on TV. Stella and Richard grabbed the settee much to my annoyance, so John and I had to sit in separate chairs. Thank goodness the play was a good one, I was quite engrossed in it. After that, we had to go home so Richard went off with Stella and John came home with me. Mum and Dad went off to bed again and left us alone. John begged me to show him my diary. I was terrified. I didn't really want to show him, but the way he looked at me just melted me so I held my breath and showed him (even such days as 27 October and 25 August). I don't know how I managed to look him in the face afterwards. He said he was satisfied and seemed pleased but I had made up my mind not to let him know my feelings until he had told me his but I just couldn't say no to him. He is in London all week taking exams but said he would write to me. I am looking forward to it.'*

Mary comes out with a nasty cold on Monday and coughs her way through much of the day. *'I have done such a lot of thinking about my darling John today. I have been wondering what he thought about my diary yesterday. I do so hope it hasn't frightened him off. I love him so desperately; it would break my heart if he finished with me now. I stayed in this evening and went to bed at nine o'clock, I had my radio on Luxemburg and there were some wonderful love songs on. I just lay and dreamed of Johnny. Oh, I know he is the one and only one for me.'*

Tuesday 20th *'Another shocking day for me again today. I have done nothing but cough all the time. I have such a sore throat and my head is absolutely spinning. I had a letter from LH today. He asked me if he could see me next Monday. I don't want to go at all and just don't know what to do. I was disappointed at not receiving a letter from my darling John today, but perhaps I will get one tomorrow. I do hope so. I had to phone Stan up today from 'The A's Band' to ask if he could play at the bank dance next March. He is going to ask the rest of the boys. Had some fun with Jeff at work today. He is nice but I love only my John.'*

The letter from LH is one she always kept and was tucked in her diary.

*'Dear Mary, I am sorry that I have not written before, but with my homework from Southampton Technical College and the lectures at Reading and Oxford that I have been going to, there has not been much time. I am sorry to hear that you feel that it would be better to terminate our engagement, although I am not really surprised. Could you meet me on the evening of Monday 26th? If I do not hear from you before then, I shall wait outside the Gaumont cinema at 5:30pm. Will you remember me to your parents and also my parents? Would like to be remembered to all of yours. Hoping that you are still enjoying good health. Yours sincerely, LH.'*

Wednesday 21st *'Another busy day, although I am managing to keep up to date thank goodness. I had a wonderful surprise today. My darling John phoned up. He said he will be coming home tomorrow instead of Friday and wants me to meet him from the train at dinner time. I am thrilled because every single minute away from him seems a life time. Never before have I experienced this feeling of true love. I know he is the only one for me. I feel it in every way. Stayed in this evening and had a bath and went to bed nice and early. I can hardly wait until tomorrow to see John. I love him so much.'*

Thursday 22nd *'A terribly long morning and I could hardly wait until dinner time to see my darling John. I went to meet John and his father was there waiting for him too. We all went into Friars for coffee then John met me from work this evening and we went to the Pavilion. Oh, it was wonderful going to the pictures with him again. Went back home afterwards and Mum and Dad had gone to bed so we just sat and talked and held hands. I did enjoy it. I wonder if anything will ever come of our romance, I do hope so. Jeff at work asked me to go out with him today.'*

Friday 23rd *'Well, I think today has been one of the most perfect yet. I am thanking God so very much for giving me my John. It is the most wonderful thing that has ever happened to me. John came round this evening and brought his gramophone and some records and we sat and played them. Then about eleven o'clock we took them back to his house. His parents had gone to a dance so we were all alone for about two hours. Oh, it was heavenly. We lay on the couch together. The one and only thing I would like different in John is I wish he would tell me how he feels about me. I long to tell him how much I love him but naturally can't until he has let me know his feelings.'*

Saturday 24th *'Another perfectly wonderful day. I just can't put into words my feelings of late. They are absolutely crammed full of love for my John. This really is THE THING. John came round this afternoon and we went round to Auntie S's and Uncle R's to take some photos, then onto David's and from there to Auntie A and Uncle N and Rob's. We then went back home for some tea. Daddy bought a heavenly radiogram today so we played a few records then listened to the radio. Sarah came up with Mitzig. John and I went back to fetch the photos of his 21st party for Sarah. Sat and listened to radio for the rest of the evening. Oh, how I love John, I only hope he never ever finishes with me.'*

Sunday 25th *'A wonderful day again today. Oh, I am so happy these last few days. I only hope and pray that it will last. I am so desperately in love with my John, I just wouldn't want to carry on living if he ever finished with me. Went to church with him this morning, I did enjoy it. After dinner, I went round to his house. His parents had gone to Worthing for the day so we were all alone. Oh, words cannot describe how much I enjoyed being with him. I just feel so completely happy and contented when he is with me. I do so wish he would tell me how he feels about me though. Still, I will have to have patience. We had a game of Monopoly on the floor. I won. After that, we sat on the settee together and to put it crudely, we had a "snogging session". I could have carried on till the end of time. Anyway, we got some tea about six. I toasted some crumpets while John made the tea. It was such fun. Played a few card games after tea and then watched TV for the rest of the evening. John is really the only one for me. If I can't have him, I just don't want anyone else.'*

Mary meets LH on Monday after work '*he had been expecting me to go out with him but I had arranged to meet John at six thirty so we went and had a cup of tea in the Friars. I did feel embarrassed. Anyway, he tried to get me to go out with him again. I told him I was meeting John. I gave him his ring back. I was quite disappointed as it was a beautiful ring. I do wish John had given it to me. Met him after saying goodbye to LH and we went home and arranged about going to London tomorrow. I am looking forward to it. I love my Johnny so very much.'*

Tuesday 27th '*An absolutely perfect 19th birthday today. Never have I enjoyed myself more. Went to London with my darling John. Arrived in London about six and went to the Chicken Inn in Leicester Square and had a wonderful dinner and with Barsac wine. It was beautiful. After that, we had a banana split with masses of cream. Then we went to the Palladium to see "Rocking the Town". It was a perfectly wonderful show. Caught the 12:05 train back and when we got back John came in and we made some tea then sat on the settee together. John gave me a whopping big box of chocolates with red roses on the front of the box. Never before, have I felt this way about anyone. I love him with all my heart and will never again love anyone so much. I am so happy I could cry. Got into bed at 2:30am.'*

This is a photograph of the front cover of the programme she kept for this show.

Wednesday is a terribly long day and Mary feels so tired after her late night last night but explains how it was worth it. She receives some lovely birthday cards from work, with one from Jeff having a sweetheart on it and being perfumed and everything. *'I had some fun with the new fellow at work—he is a John too. Saw Fred dinner time and he asked me out and also saw JB (another John) who also wanted me to go out with him. I am just not interested in anyone but my own darling John. He is the only one for me. This really is love, this time. I just seem to know it.'*

Thursday 29<sup>th</sup> *'Not too bad a day I suppose but I have been missing my darling John so very much. I love him so very much I just can't bear to be away from him for a few seconds. Met Freddie and Graham after work and they asked me to go to the pictures this evening so I went, but I had to go home first. Sat in the middle of them holding both of their hands at the same time. Graham took me home afterwards. When I got back, Mummy said my John had been there all evening. I have never kicked myself harder. If only I had known he was coming to see me, I wouldn't have dreamed of going out.'*

Friday 30<sup>th</sup> *'A terribly busy day at work today but I managed to get through it. Jeff at work kept asking me to go out with him today but I made some excuse. Went to the pictures with my John this evening. It was the same one I saw yesterday. After coming out, John came home and we had some coffee. He kept asking to see my diary again, so like a fool, I let him. I think it has scared him off. He made fun of it which made me feel awful. I do wish he hadn't but still it really is something to laugh about to outsiders but to me, it is something so serious. I do hope nothing in there has frightened him away. I don't think I could bare it as I love him so much.'*

### DECEMBER

Quite a happy month for Mary but all the late nights are starting to catch up with her. She spends more time with John trying hard to control her jealousy when it comes to him and other girls. And has good reason to forget her words singing with the band one evening. Finding out Johns true feelings on 22<sup>nd</sup> ends the month and subsequent year on a joyful and contented note.

Saturday 1st '*A horrible day today. I have been so busy at work this morning. My John came to meet me dinner time and he told me he was playing golf this afternoon with Alan and that he couldn't come out this evening. I was so disappointed. I am sure my diary has scared him. I do wish I hadn't shown him. I did some shopping this afternoon and saw Alan and he said he hadn't seen John. I am so desperately worried. I do hope he hasn't taken another girl out. I had a good cry but didn't feel any better. Went to the Palomino this evening with Edna and saw Stella and Ann in there. Stella has bought a coat like mine, damn her. I dislike her so much. I wonder what my John did today.*'

Sunday 2nd '*Lovely day today thank goodness. My darling Johnny came round this morning about ten forty-five and off we went to church. I do like going with him so much. It makes me feel so happy and contented when I am there with him. He came back home afterwards to listen to the record I bought yesterday— Lonnie Donegan "Rock Island Line". He stayed for quite a long time. It was nice. He told me he was playing golf with Alan this afternoon and played golf by himself yesterday. I was disappointed but tried not to show it because I don't want to interfere with any of his hobbies. Anyway, I did a lot of washing this afternoon and turned out my wardrobe and at about five fifteen John came round and we took a bus to Sonning. We went to the church there and it was jolly good but I enjoyed the service this morning better. John came back with me for coffee after and we talked about my diary. I am sure John has had a jolly good laugh at it and I don't really blame him. He at least told me he likes me but I am not sure now whether he said it because he meant it or because he thought I would just like to hear it. It was wonderful to hear, but I certainly don't want him to say it if he really doesn't mean it. I love him so much.*'

Mary doesn't see anything of John on Monday '*he has been up in Oxford and wasn't getting back until about eleven. Oh, I do love him so much. It seems an eternity when I am away from him. This really is THE THING this time. Never before, have I felt this way. I wonder if I will always feel this way. I do hope so. I wish John would tell me he loves me though. I just long for him to. It would make me the happiest person alive. Still, perhaps he will one day. Stan from 'The A's Band' rang up today to see if I would sing at the town hall on the 20th.*'

Tuesday 4th '*A bit better day today thank goodness but not so nice an evening. My darling John came to meet me dinner time and we walked all around the town looking for paints for John to work with. I was quite disappointed though as he said he had to do some studying this evening. I would love to have gone out with him. Anyway, I went home after work and then Mum and Dad came in and said they had just seen my John with a girl. Daddy kept on about it. I laughed about it at first but Daddy kept on so long I felt like murdering everybody. I am quite worried really and do wonder who she is. I will ask him tomorrow.*'

Wednesday 5th '*Wonderful day today and even more wonderful evening. Went round to my darling John's house. We went up to his study and John did some painting. I did enjoy watching him and just being with him. John said he had never been more contented in his life. I did feel so thrilled and I love him so much. We did have fun. I kept running to the bathroom to change his water for him. I think I would do absolutely anything for him. His parents were out so we had the whole house to ourselves. It was wonderful. He still hasn't told me if he loves me or not. I would so love him to.*'

Thursday 6th '*An absolutely perfectly wonderful evening. My darling John met me from work and we went to see a horror film at the Central. I was scared but didn't mind so much as John was there. Afterwards, we went back to his house. His parents had gone away for a couple of days so once again we had the house to ourselves. We looked at his paintings for about ten minutes then we went into his bedroom to look at his new golf bag. John sat down on his bed so I did likewise, then we kissed and slid down until we were laying completely on the bed. It was wonderful to be so close to him. I do wish we were married. How lovely it would be to do that every night. I would have loved to have stayed the night but of course that was out of the question.*'

Friday 7th '*Lovely evening again this evening. My darling John came round and we went down to the Agricultural Hall to see Stan and Ted from "The A's Band". They want me to sing at the town hall on the 20th of this month. We stayed until the interval and then came back home. John had to hurry off worst luck as he wanted to finish his painting off before tomorrow. He is coming to meet me from work tomorrow thank goodness. It was nice to see the band again but I am* worried in case John gives me up because of it. I love him so deeply. I just couldn't live without him now. He is all my life. I never think of anything else. I really do love him.'

Saturday 8th '*Wonderful day today. My darling John came to meet me from work today and we went round to his house to see some of his drawings. Then I went home for dinner. He came round later on and we met Pete and Ann in town to give them some photos. We all went to the High for coffee. Pete said he would get his car and take us all to St Ann's Hall this evening to the dance with "The A's Band", so that's what we did. Ann and her friend were supposed to come but didn't, so I went with Pete, Colin and John. Went to the Palomino first, then onto the Grosvenor, then on to St Ann's. We had a lovely time. I danced the Charleston with Colin with everyone watching then did some jiving. I really was thrilled with it. I do wish I could have done it with my darling John though.*'

Sunday 9th '*Phew, I do feel tired this morning. I haven't got over last night yet. I keep thinking of my John and then about doing the Charleston with Colin and then about Pete and then back to John's again. Oh, my head is so full of thoughts again. My darling John came round this morning about ten forty-five and we went to church. After that, John came back home for a short while, then off he went home to have some dinner. He had some studying to do this afternoon so I got down to some washing. I did absolutely piles and piles of it. I was dead beat by the time I had finished. Had some tea and then got myself ready to go to yet another dance. Mummy and Daddy went round Grandma and Grandad's so I was alone when my John called for me. I would have liked to have stayed in with him all evening but we had arranged to meet Ted from the band so out we went and Ted took us to Woodley. I was supposed to have sung but the microphone wouldn't go, so we just danced instead. I was pleased. John seemed so affectionate this evening. I don't know why. Several of the things he said— only small things—but oh, they meant such a lot. He really made me feel he cared for me. I think he does in a way, but I do so wish he would tell me so. He came home after the dance. We got back at 10:30 and he didn't go home until 1:0 am. Oh, I do love him with all my heart.*'

Mary feels worn out on Monday '*I haven't felt at all well today. I just feel so absolutely worn out which is not really surprising after all the late nights I have been having. Jeff at work gave me a letter of thirteen pages today telling me how much he loves me. I was so surprised. I had no idea he felt that way. He is very nice but I certainly have no love for him; I'm afraid John has every scrap of my love. Stayed in this evening and went to bed fairly early. All I do is dream of John. This really is true love.'*

Tuesday 11<sup>th</sup> *'Wonderful day today. My darling John came to meet me from work today, and we went to the library to get John a book and then went to a medical exhibition at the town hall. We were in there for about two hours. It was very interesting but my poor feet were killing me. John came home afterwards and we had some coffee. He was in a funny mood today—laughing and joking. Oh, I love him so deeply. I do so wish he would tell me how he feels about me. I am almost frantic, worrying as to whether he really does love me or not. I really do love him so much; I couldn't exist without him now. I am so jealous when he talks of other girls. I do wish I wasn't. I hope I don't show it. Oh, how I'd love to hear him say he loves me.'*

Mary with her John at a dance

Wednesday 12<sup>th</sup> *'Not too good a day at all today. I have felt so tired and worn out today and just don't know how I have done my work. I have felt like*

343

*sleeping all the time. I haven't seen my darling John at all today. It seems absolutely ages since I saw him last. I think this really must be the real thing. I have had "crushes" on people before, but they were nothing like this. I just love John with all my heart. I wonder if my hopes and dreams will ever come true. I do hope so. I am wondering what to do about Jeff. He is very nice and I don't want to hurt him but I just can't be unfaithful to John. I had an awful row with Daddy this evening. He did tell me off.'*

Thursday 13th *'Jolly good day really, I suppose. Still feel awfully tired though, I don't know what the matter is with me lately. Jeff has kept on at me all day to go out with him. I do wish he wouldn't as I only love my John—no one else. Anyway, my darling John came to meet me dinner time and we went and had coffee in the High, then did some of my shopping. He said he couldn't come out this evening. I know I ought not to expect him to come out every evening but I love him so desperately. I was on my way round to the Friars after work, when Jeff and Sam caught me up, so I went in with them and who should be in there with Stella, my John. It gave me quite a shock. I thought all sorts of things but John paid me so much attention, bless him, that I just couldn't be jealous anymore.'*

Friday 14th *'Wonderful day or should I say, wonderful evening. Had an awful lot of work again today. Jeff keeps asking me to go out with him, I do wish he wouldn't as I only love my John. I just don't want anyone else. I went round town with my darling John dinner time, he is so wonderful. Never before have I felt like this. I just can't hide my feelings from him and I do wish I could, at least until I know his. He met me from work again this evening and we went to the pictures. I had quite a strong feeling that we would meet Stella and that John would ask her to come with us but we didn't so it was alright. He came home afterwards and was in quite a serious mood. Oh, I do love him. I really do.'*

Saturday 15th is another perfect day. Mary mentions how happy she's been these last few weeks and thanks God so much as she really doesn't think she deserves this much happiness.

*'My darling John came to meet me from work dinner time and came home for about half an hour. Then, went off to have his dinner. As he had some work*

*to do this afternoon, I went down the town to do some shopping. I got back about five and had my tea. Then at six thirty my Johnny came round for me and we went back to his house. His parents were just going to a dinner and dance, so we were alone for the rest of the evening. Oh, it was heaven. John asked me if there was anything I wanted to ask him. He said he would answer any question at all. I think he knew I was trying to pluck up courage to ask him if he loves me but I just couldn't.'*

Sunday 16<sup>th</sup> *'Quite a good day really, at least the morning was. I got up early and had a bath and then my darling John came round for me and off we went to church. I enjoy going with him. It makes me feel so happy and contented. After church he came back home with me and we sat in the dining room for about half an hour. Oh, I love him with all my heart. I still didn't pluck up enough courage to ask him if he does love me or not. I do wish he would tell me. I have waited so long for him to tell me. I think I will burst before long if he doesn't. He couldn't come out this afternoon or evening and I was so disappointed, but I really mustn't try to make him come out too much. He would perhaps get tired of me and that would just about kill me. I do wish he would tell me how he feels about me but I will just have to be patient that's all. Stayed in this afternoon and decorated our Christmas tree. It does look nice and took me the whole afternoon. This evening, I wrote out a few of my Christmas cards then played a few card games by myself, listening to the radio. I have been thinking of John all the time though. I just can't seem to get him out of my mind. It really must be love, this time.'*

Monday 17<sup>th</sup> *'Wonderful day today. My darling John came to meet me from work dinner time and we went into the High and had some coffee. He came to meet me from work again this evening and we went home first and had our tea. Then John came round for me and off we went down to the Palomino. We saw Edna and Carol in there. After a while, John and I went back to his house. His parents were out so we sat on the settee and watched TV. We were still talking about certain questions which I wanted to ask him. How I wish I had the nerve to ask him if he loves me. I think the reason I don't is because I'm afraid he might say no and that would break my heart. I love him so much.'*

Mary is expecting John to meet her dinner time on Tuesday but he doesn't so just goes off round town on her own. '*I was just going back to work when I bumped in to John with Ann and another girl. Oh, did my poor heart miss a beat! I don't think I have ever spent such a miserable afternoon. My jealousy was terrible. I started to imagine all sorts of things and I made so many mistakes at work that I have loads of statements to do again. Anyway, John came to meet me from work and explained it all to me (thank goodness) so I am not jealous anymore. I love him so much. I do hope he doesn't ever find out how jealous I really am. Sarah came round this evening. I sat and drew some pictures and thought about John all evening. This really must be love.*'

Wednesday 19th '*Not too bad a day at all really. My darling John came to meet me from work dinner time and we went and had a coffee in the High Café and then did a bit of shopping. I wasn't expecting to see him this evening at all, but he came to meet me from work, bless him. I was thrilled. I am so happy when I am near to him. He came home with me and said he might be in the Palomino later on this evening. Anyway, I went down and met Edna and we were sitting in the Palomino when Mike came in. He invited us up to his Auntie P's, so up we went. We had quite an enjoyable evening but I was thinking about my darling John all the time.*'

Thursday 20th '*I think this evening has been one of the most perfect ones for a very long time. I went singing at the town hall. John came with me. I was so scared but I managed to sing alright although I completely forgot the words every time, I looked at John. I sang the song "More" and I happened to glance at my John and I just melted. I forgot every single word but still managed to cover it up alright. After that was over, we were going to the Olympia but decided to come home instead, so grabbed a taxi home. We made some coffee and sat on our couch. John said he had never been so jealous in his life. I felt sorry for him having no one to dance with while I was singing but I was thrilled he was jealous as that means he must think something of me. Oh, I love him so much.*'

Friday 21st '*Not too bad a day at all today. I was standing waiting for the bus this morning when it went sailing by full up and there on the platform was my John. I was flabbergasted. He was supposed to have met me dinner time but didn't turn up. Thankfully, he met me after work and said he had been working* all day and I thought perhaps that was what had happened. We went in to the Friars Tea Bar and met Stella and Richard, and all went to the pictures. Oh dear, John does flirt with Stella and Stella (damn her) flirts back. I do feel so hurt and jealous as John keeps on touching her and holding her hand. I just can't bear to see him do it. I wonder if John does love me.'

Saturday 22nd 'Well at last my patience has been rewarded. Went to the Grosvenor with my daring John. He had a small birthday party seeing as he had missed his and there were 12 of us. It was wonderful. Dear John paid me quite a lot of attention although naturally he had to dance with all the other girls. I was a weenie bit jealous but I knew he had to. He came home with me afterwards. Mr Kean brought us home in his car. John came in for a few moments and then was just on the point of going when I suddenly felt I just had to know whether he loved me or not. So, I asked him and I'm happy to say, he said yes. I asked him to tell me so...he did! It was wonderful and I know I could never have asked him if I hadn't had something to drink. I do love him.'

Sunday 23rd 'Quite a good day today. Got up fairly early (phew am I tired) and went to church with my darling John. Oh, I did enjoy going with him so much. After that, he came back home for a while and then went off to have his dinner. After dinner I sat and waited for John to come and fetch me. I expected him around three and he didn't come until about four thirty. Oh, I was so worried about him. I wondered all sorts of things, but still none of them were true so that was alright. We went back to his house and Stella hadn't arrived so we watched television until she came. When she did come, she had had her tea so she just sat and watched while we all had ours. After tea, we watched TV again for the rest of the evening. Oh, I love John so much. He came home with me afterwards and we sat down and had some coffee. Then my John suddenly became quite serious and asked me to ask him the same question that I asked him yesterday, so I asked him if he still loved me. He said yes and said I could have twenty questions. Well, I asked him about seven or eight and he answered them all bless him. At last, I really feel that he loves me. I do hope he does anyway as I love him with all my heart.'

Christmas Eve 'Not too good a day today as I've had an awful lot of work to do and I have felt so tired all day. Went to the Great Western Hotel for lunch *today with Stella, Richard, Angela, Rudi and my John. I was quite disappointed as I had to leave half of my lunch as I had to get back to work. John walked back to work with me then ran back to have his Christmas pudding. This evening, I went to the pictures with Richard, Stella and John. Before we went, I met John from work and then met Richard and they both came back to my house and met Grandma, Granddad and Auntie O. Anyway, Richard apparently has had a row with Stella and he asked me how he could get her back. I did feel sorry for him. When we picked her up, my darling John flirted with her so much. He kept holding her hand and putting his arm round her. I was so upset and jealous as I love him so much.'*

Tuesday 25th Christmas Day *'A perfect day today. At least, I should say perfect evening. We got up fairly early and opened all our presents. I then went round to my darling Johns to tell him I couldn't go for dinner but would go afterwards. They were all still in their dressing gowns. Richard kissed me under the mistletoe. It was nice but not so nice as John, who I think was a bit jealous. After dinner, I had to cycle down to Rob's and Mike's and then to Edna's, and Grandmas and Granddads to give them their Christmas presents. I then dashed back home and waited for John to call. Oh, it was ages. I had expected him about 3:30 and by 5:00 he still hadn't come. I was so worried. In the end, Stella came round and back we went to 48. It was wonderful. We watched some TV, had a bit of a snow fight as it had started to snow and then had the most wonderful tea possible. We were sitting down to tea at midnight and had it by candlelight. It was heaven. I do love my John so much. After tea, we had a few games. I got home about 2:15. My darling John was so good; he didn't make me jealous at all. I think he must have realised how much he hurt me yesterday. Oh, I do love him with all my heart.'*

Boxing Day *'Another perfect day. I keep writing that but I have had so many perfect days since I have known my darling John. Didn't get up until 11:30 this morning. Just finished dinner when John came round to invite me round to his again this afternoon. I went round about 3:45 and we sat and watched television again. It was wonderful just sitting there with John. Had another lovely tea then we had a game of draughts (I won). After that Stella, Richard, John and I went down to the station with Richard's cases as he had to go back today. Then we watched TV for the rest of the evening. Before Richard went, he kissed me under the mistletoe again with his mother, Stella and John watching. I think John was jealous. John took me home and came in for coffee. I sat on his lap for about an hour. He told me he loved me again and I told him (for the first time) that I love him, which I do with all my heart.'*

Thursday 27th Mary is back at work and sees John briefly on the bus in the morning. *'It seems to give me such high spirits and I worked a lot harder than I have for a long time. I arranged to see him this evening at 6:00 but by 5:55 I still hadn't finished my work and Mr B told us we had to finish before we went and because we all wanted to get out, we had a bit of a row, but anyway, I got out about 6:10 and met my darling John. We had a coffee in the Palomino then caught the same bus home as Mummy and Daddy. I feel so wonderfully happy when I am with John. He said he was jealous when Richard kissed me yesterday. At least, it means he must like me anyway. I love him so much. This really is love, this time. I just seem to know. I have never felt like this before.'*

Friday 28th *'A terribly busy day. I didn't finish work until nine o'clock. I am so tired and yet I feel so happy. I have missed my darling John today as I haven't seen him at all. It is the first day I haven't seen him for weeks. It seems an eternity since I saw him last. I do hope I see him tomorrow. I love him so deeply. I wonder how much he loves me. I know he can't possibly love me as much as I love him, but even so, I still try to pretend to myself that he does. I also wonder if anything will ever come of our perfect friendship. I know what I would like to happen, but I will just have to have patience. Since I have known John, I have been so happy. This really must be true love; I love him so much.'*

Saturday 29th *'I think today I have discovered that I love John even more (if that is possible) than I did before. I saw him this morning in the High at coffee time. He told me he was meeting Jackie for coffee and funnily, I wasn't jealous, I don't know why. We arranged to meet at 3:00 but he turned up at 4:40 and said he'd arranged for us to go to the pictures with Stella, Ann and Joan. Well, I was flabbergasted! Never before have I experienced such a deep feeling of jealousy. Anyway, I tried so hard not to show it and we waited for them for about two minutes when John said he didn't want them to come and that he wanted to please me. Well, he certainly did but now I feel so selfish. I ought not to stop him seeing his friends. He came home afterwards and Mum and Dad were out so we just lay on my bed and played a record. It wasn't necessary for words, we just looked into each other's eyes. Oh, I love him so deeply.'*

Getting up late on Sunday at 10:25 Mary has an awful rush to get ready before John comes for her. '*I made it somehow and off we went to church. John came home for a while afterwards then went off to have his dinner. He came round for the afternoon and evening. Mum and Dad went off to church so we were alone in the house. I do love being with my John so much. We played chess, draughts and a few other games. Oh, I love him so much. I don't think I could possibly live without him now. I am going round his house tomorrow and we will be alone as his parents are going out. I have a horrible feeling he will invite Stella and a few others. I do hope he doesn't. I am so selfish; I want him all to myself. I love him so much.'*

Monday 31st New Years Eve '*A terribly busy day today, but another perfect evening made me forget all about it. I certainly had a perfect evening. I finished work about 9:10 and got round to John's about 9:35. He is the most wonderful*

*person I have ever met. I just don't know what I would do without him now. We sat and watched TV. His parents were out so we were alone and my fears of yesterday were unnecessary. It was heavenly. At midnight, we had a glass of sherry and toasted each other. Oh, I love him so desperately. I only hope and pray that in the New Year some of my hope and dreams come true. This is the real thing this time. I just know it. We had a game of draughts (the first of the year) and I won. Well, this is the finish of this year. I only hope next year will be just as happy.'*

Well, that's where we leave Mary for now. I do hope you enjoyed the first instalment as much as I did. There are another five years' worth of diaries that she has written, divulging her antics in detail leading up to the beginning of 1962.

These I hope to transcribe in the near future. They are every bit as intriguing, with Mary writing about her courting days with John, her coming of age party, life at the bank, her marriage and honeymoon, in amongst every day events, pressures and general daily life.

Thank you so much for reading this book. Until next time…

## THE END

Printed in Great Britain
by Amazon